This is Not a Remix

This is Not a Remix

Piracy, Authenticity and Popular Music

MARGIE BORSCHKE

Bloomsbury Academic
An imprint of Bloomsbury Publishing Inc

B L O O M S B U R Y

NEW YORK · LONDON · OXFORD · NEW DELHI · SYDNEY

Bloomsbury Academic

An imprint of Bloomsbury Publishing Inc

1385 Broadway	50 Bedford Square
New York	London
NY 10018	WC1B 3DP
USA	UK

www.bloomsbury.com

BLOOMSBURY and the Diana logo are trademarks of Bloomsbury Publishing Plc

First published 2017

© Margie Borschke, 2017

Library of Congress Cataloging-in-Publication Data

Names: Borschke, Margie.
Title: This is not a remix : piracy, authenticity and popular music / Margie Borschke.
Description: New York : Bloomsbury Academic, 2017.
Identifiers: LCCN 2017003346 (print) | LCCN 2017013333 (ebook) | ISBN 9781501318931 (ePDF) | ISBN 9781501318948 (ePUB) | ISBN 9781501318924 (pbk. : alk. paper)
Subjects: LCSH: Remixes--History and criticism. | Sound recordings--Social aspects. | Popular music--Social aspects. | Music and the Internet.
Classification: LCC ML3918.P67 (ebook) | LCC ML3918.P67 B69 2017 (print) | DDC 781.64--dc23
LC record available at https://lccn.loc.gov/2017003346

ISBN:	HB:	978-1-5013-1891-7
	PB:	978-1-5013-1892-4
	ePub:	978-1-5013-1894-8
	ePDF:	978-1-5013-1893-1

Cover design by Clare Turner
Cover image © iStock

Typeset by Fakenham Prepress Solutions, Fakenham, Norfolk NR21 8NN

CONTENTS

CHAPTER ONE

This is not a remix

1.1 Introduction

Kim Dotcom's arrest in 2012 was just like a movie: helicopters swooped in; hounds were unleashed; and semi-automatic weapons were waved in the air, wielded by the New Zealand police who stormed into the rural mansion where the Megaupload billionaire, his wife, three children, and house guests were sleeping. On the day before his thirty-eighth birthday, Dotcom was charged with numerous offences including copyright infringement, racketeering, money laundering, and piracy.

A few hours before the raid, the American Federal Bureau of Investigation, who orchestrated the police operation, seized MegaUpload's servers at a data center in Europe. Precisely what was on these servers is unknown—at the time the cloud-based file hosting service had approximately 180,000,000 registered members—but in the aftermath, there were anecdotal reports from users claiming that several significant and admired American MP3 bloggers, aficionados of the obscure and forgotten, were among those who lost access to their data. Just like that, their collections were wiped clean.

Internet outrage ensued. Fans held up the bloggers as latter day Alan Lomaxes, people who collected and harvested songs in the name of posterity and cultural knowledge, in some cases working in tandem with the overlooked and rediscovered artistic geniuses that they loved. Posting on WFMU's Beware the Blog that week, Jason Sigal (2012) wrote, "The best music blogs aren't pirates. They are libraries, sound archivists and music preservationists sharing recordings that would not otherwise be available. And now sites like Global Groove, Mutant Sounds and Holy Warbles have lost large swaths of the material they'd salvaged from obscurity." After tweets of outrage and posts of fury, listeners from around the world swiftly began the work of reassembling the collections, relying on the very action that made them exist in the first place: they posted their copies to the Internet and the copying began anew.

Same as it ever was.

Even so, the influence of the MP3 blog on popular music culture began to fade and the enthusiasm of its most enthusiastic participants waned. The chilling effect of the Dotcom raids and other antipiracy efforts took its toll. Simultaneously, streaming sites like Spotify and Apple Music produced yet another change in listening habits, away from the downloading, collecting, and the virtual hoarding that characterized the first decade of the twenty-first century, towards on-demand streaming and "social" listening; vinyl made its notorious comeback in the mainstream media; and even the most ardent free culture evangelists began to wonder about the human cost of the so-called "sharing economy." And yet, while more industry-friendly practices and technologies may seem to shift priorities away from the copy, copying remains functionally essential, one of the central practices of digital culture. Likewise, recordings (*qua* copies) are still the animating artifact in popular music cultures. The sea of big data is fed by a river of copies and, to paraphrase Heraclitus's ancient paradox, you still cannot step twice into the same stream.

Again and again, we see culture transformed and sustained by repro-duction and repetition. This book considers the relationship between media and culture, by focusing on the social and material histories of copies and their circulation. As Jussi Parikka (2008: 73) has noted, "The material processes of copy routines have often been neglected in cultural analysis, but the juridical issue of copyright has had its fair share of attention." In this monograph, I offer an argument not about the regulation of copies and copying, but about their poetics, highlighting the material, rhetorical, social, and cultural dimen-sions of copies and aesthetic dimension of distribution and circulation, both now and in the past. Copy is concept that requires critical investigation. We must simultaneously consider "copy" as a relational property of objects, but also as a concept and practice that has a history, one that is intermingled with the particular histories of different technologies of representation, reproduction, and exchange. Particular cultural histories offer answers to questions about the role of media technology in cultural change, and in this book I recount and resurrect neglected material histories to consider what a study of copies can tell us about the relatively recent transition from analog to digital reproduction in music culture and the intersection of this shift with the rise of network culture and the ability to distribute, discuss, and connect musical artifacts, knowledge, and communities of listeners. I argue that we can better understand this transition if we focus not only on regulatory questions pertaining to copyright, but also on aesthetic questions related to the status of sound recordings as copies and the materiality of media technologies and formats as well as their rhetorical weight.

To ask questions about the present, I look to media's recent past and ask, in turn:

- Why copies now?
- Why remix now?

- Why vinyl now?
- Why redistribution now?

Some of my answers to these questions, I hope, will help carve out a space for talking about the aesthetics of circulation within media studies and in our wider history of ideas.

1.2 Critical approach

This study approaches questions about media technology and cultural change through a focus on media artifacts as copies, and thus takes an interest in similarities and continuities as well as difference. I believe a focus on copies can do two things: It can help us understand media artifacts as objects that have material, social, and cultural histories, and it can help expand how we use them to understand our world and express our place within it. I begin with the assumption that since the twentieth century, cultures of popular music were also *recorded* music cultures (Hennion 2001, 2008; Toynbee 2000), and that, within these popular cultures, copying practices were often more common than they were controversial. Yet, we also know that in discussions about copyright and use, digital replication, sampling, and the distribution of sound files via peer-to-peer technologies or websites are flash points for debate. Many critiques of copyright raise concerns about the policy's possible overreach in an era of digital technologies. These concerns are well documented and discussed across disciplines (e.g., Berry 2008; Berry and Moss 2008; Coombe 1998; Lessig 2002, 2004, 2008; McLeod 2007; McLeod and DiCola 2011; Vaidhyanathan 2003), and such scholarship often cites the history and importance of musical borrowings and reuse in many of the twentieth century's most cherished innovations in popular music, and uses these histories in the service of arguments about the possible effects that the expansion of copyright can have on free expression and competition. Stories about the collaborative origins of blues and folk music, as well as potted histories about the origins of Jamaican dub and New York hip-hop, are now on heavy rotation in scholarship that aims to defend digital copying practices and remix culture.

This repetition of a canon of birth narratives serves a rhetorical function as well as an explanatory, or descriptive, one. My concern is that our discussions about what one ought to do with copies and reproduction technologies may be overshadowing our understanding of what people are actually doing now, or what they have done in the past. "Remix," a term borrowed from audio production and dance music, is now used rhetorically to describe and defend digital practices of copying and recombination. This metaphorical usage, however, in its zeal to defend current networked media use, overshadows the form's own history and overlooks the material dimensions of that history and the agency of the media users who participated in that history.

In my own experience, and among my peers, the use and "misuse" of technologies of reproduction didn't start with digital technologies and networks. Rather, digital practices were linked to earlier reproduction practices, such as my own crude efforts to tape songs off the radio (an experience so common that it is now used to evoke 1970s and 1980s nostalgia in television ads) or those of my more sophisticated friends who made masterful mix tapes filled with tracks that radio stations never played, carefully chosen from their beloved collections of records, tapes, and (eventually) CDs. To many music lovers of a certain age, the cries from music-industry associations about peer-to-peer technologies were familiar, sounding an awful lot like the "home taping is killing music" campaigns we ignored and snickered at in the 1980s. Our own experiences with small-scale replications in our bedrooms and living rooms, and their use in social and cultural situations, were pleasurable—perceived as innocent, even— and no doubt shaped how we approached and used new technologies of replication, and, in turn, how we felt about them. The mass domestication of computers and high-speed digital networks changed the scale and reach of these practices and disrupted business models and industrial hierarchies. Yet, industry actions to prevent consumers from using the technologies at their fingertips in the 2000s seemed to only inflame existing antagonisms toward the corporate music industry, and debates over the replication of copyrighted material became increasingly polarized as both "sides" claimed the moral high ground. The question became: Who was killing music, and who was supporting it?

The dichotomy is a false one, but as I looked closer, in between the rhetoric about stealing versus sharing, producers' rights versus consumers' rights, and original artists versus parasitic pirates, I began to observe two intriguing undercurrents in arguments about copies and digital networks:

1　The arguments that vilified copying practices and those that valorized them appealed to the same romantic ideals of creativity and self-expression when demonizing or defending downloading and file-sharing practices.

2　In addition to appeals to ethical principles and arguments about the intentions of copyright as a policy, media users were also presenting aesthetic and social justifications for copies and copying as well as for their control.

These aesthetic and social justifications struck me as a rich area of inquiry, one that would potentially illuminate the conceptual questions I had about the historical relationships between copies and cultures. If we want to understand the cultural consequences of technologies whose functioning is dependent on replication, as digital and network technologies are, we need to be able to account for digital copies as material artifacts and copying as a social practice, while simultaneously accounting for their histories and how they do and don't shape their current use. That is to say, the material and social dimensions of reproduction is shaped both by copies as an historical phenomenon and copies as an abstraction or transhistorical possibility. To do this, we need a cultural poetics of copies, one that can help us make sense of the recursive relationship between media and culture and decipher some of the contradictions and tensions that characterize the human experience. A poetics of copies and networks would have to grapple not only with legal and political issues, but also with how copies have functioned historically, rhetorically, and materially. It would have to grapple with use as a generator of meaning, as something that was shaped, but not determined by, its history and material makeup, and the rhetorical, as well as the aesthetic, uses to which it is put. It would have to acknowledge the place of the media object and its material dimensions, as well as the place of the media practice, in understanding cultural change.

The central problem then is how do media objects as copies shape media practice, and vice versa? This problem prompts a number of related, big-picture questions including

- How can something that is just the same bring something new into being?

- How do some things become the background for other forms? (Acland 2007: xx)

To approach these questions, this study necessarily operates on several levels: material, formal, rhetorical, and historical. It takes an interest in questions about the relationship between form and format as they relate to the materiality of media and its use. It is also concerned with how we talk about these forms and formats, what we think they mean, and what we believe they can and cannot do. Issues of form and rhetoric are clarified by a consideration of the histories of each, and a focus on copies and copying in popular music practice highlights material, social, and cultural continuities and changes. Throughout this study, I recover lesser-known historical narratives, the analog antecedents to digital phenomena as well as persistent forms and formats, and use them to illuminate contemporary problems and issues and to highlight the (often overlooked) material contours of particular innovations in form and function.

Digitization and networking are issues for all cultural artifacts and systems of communication, not just for musical ones. I chose to focus on popular music not only because it has been at the forefront of battles over copyright (which brings questions about copies to the fore), but also because it has historically proved itself to be an important source of innovation with regard to copying technologies, artifacts, and practices. Music provides an ideal field in which to test questions about copies and replication because repetition and reproduction operate on so many different levels in musical culture. Repetition is a feature of all music (Middleton 1999), and sound recordings as reproductions are the central focus of nearly all music cultures since the early twentieth century (Hennion 2001, 2008; Toynbee 2000). Copies and copying feature in the crystallization of popular music genres (Toynbee 2000). They are listened to and collected by individuals and used to facilitate the formation of identity (DeNora 2000; Thornton and Gelder 1997) and communal experience (Frith 1981a, 1981b; Thornton 1995; Thornton and Gelder 1997). Musicians make recordings, and the recording industry is in the business of selling them (as well as licensing the right to copy or use them). Music is also a cultural arena in which unauthorized recording and replication has a long and colorful history (Heylin 2003; Johns 2002, 2010; Marshall 2005), with the earliest unauthorized recordings, bootlegs of operatic performances, predating the idea of copyright in those recordings (Heylin 2003: 22).

Another key theme in my research is the persistence of analog technologies and practices in the networked era. The shift from analog to digital technologies in music has been as hotly contested as it has been embraced with enthusiasm. The shift has had consequences for producers, distributors, and consumers, for issues of sound and composition, circulation, and access. The shift has also had repercussions for the uses and meanings of systems of representation and media formats themselves; that is, for their rhetorical use. A vinyl record today has different meanings and cultural possibilities than a vinyl record in 1975 (sometimes even the very same record). Even in the course of writing this book, vinyl's status and meaning has radically changed, from object of obsolescence and ridicule to a revered object ripe for revival and affection. What was once an underground preoccupation, the purview of the DJ and the obsessed collector, is a now a mainstream fashion, still small but significant enough to be used to signify authenticity and good taste—banks, car companies, and condom manufacturers have all used crate digging and vinyl in advertising campaigns in recent years (Spice 2013). No doubt its meaning will have shifted again by the time these words reach you. I want to make a case for not dismissing fashions and fads as cultural phenomena, and instead acknowledging these cultural formations as significant forms of situated knowledge however fleeting they may be. It strikes me that in doing so we might be able to better account for both individual agency and collective meaning when we account for cultural change.

When choosing and framing research objects for this study, I was careful to select forms of musical composition and discourse that offered something to say about the transition period and presented an opportunity to think about copies that were functionally equivalent but materially different. These choices were intended to prompt questions related to the specific expressive form that would, in turn, help to answer the following key questions:

- Is remix an apt metaphor for digital culture?
- What does remix reveal about contemporary cultural practice, and what does it obscure?
- Why do analog formats persist in an era of digital networks?
- How do disco edits made with digital technologies in the early twenty-first century differ from those that were made with analog technologies in the mid-1970s?
- What are the consequences of networking private collections of music and rendering visible ways of knowing?
- What do new forms of musical discourse, such as MP3 blogs, reveal about our perceptions of creativity and expression, as well as our understanding of musical works?
- How can we explain the simultaneous persistence of romantic ideals of expression and the valuing of authenticity and participation in online discourse?
- What lessons do these artifacts and practices offer about the relationship between circulation and meaning?

Rather than ask the very worthy question of what these tensions between users and industry say about the success or failure of copyright as a policy mechanism (e.g., Berry 2008; Berry and Moss 2008; Coombe 1998; Lessig 2002, 2004, 2008; McLeod 2007; McLeod and DiCola 2011; Vaidhyanathan 2003), I ask what the tensions surrounding these regulations and the rhetoric that frames them suggest or imply about the relationship between users and artifacts, media and culture. As Marcus Boon reminds us "Copying ... is real enough and we do not have the luxury of describing whether we like it or not. The question—in the words of Buddhist poet John Giorno—is how we handle it" (2010: 234). This book is about how we handle it.

Like Boon, I am not interested in questions of copyright *per se*, and I agree that popular practices of copying "are not reducible to the legal-political constructions that dominate thinking about copying today" (2010: 8). This is not to say that I intend to ignore the importance of copyright to the music industry—it is its main structural feature (Frith and Marshall 2004)—or the roar of the copyright wars, but that I want to look at the cultural and social ramifications of copying that have occurred, despite such regulatory frameworks, and while the battle rages. The regulation of copies lends a certain power or character to "copy" as an attribute or property of media objects but copy as a relative property that describes an object itself lends that object and related practices particular dispositions and possibilities. As I will argue, copy is both an historical idea, one that changes over time and is dependent on particular cultural formations and values, and it is transhistorical, a metaphysical universal. Because copies weren't invented yesterday, a study of copying as a cultural practice and concern sharpens big-picture questions about cultural change and continuity and their relationship with media technologies. Different technological methods of representation, reproduction, circulation, and exchange make use of copy as a property and as a situated ideal. In this book, I focus on the relatively recent transition from analog to digital reproduction in musical sound recording and argue that this transition is better understood if we focus on the status of sound recordings as copies, on how we account for them, on why we do or do not value them, and on what we have done with them.

My approach to these questions is motivated by the belief that a sustained focus on artifacts as things that simultaneously possess material properties, cultural histories, and rhetorical functions can enrich our understanding of cultural practices and change. We cannot study one at the expense of the other. Another driving theme in this research is the assumption that a focus on similarity offers insight into the phenomenon of cultural change. My approach draws upon and combines theories and critical approaches from media studies, philosophy, literary theory, cultural studies, musicology, and the sociology of popular music as they pertain to questions about copies and their use. My aim in designing this study was to find an approach that would be flexible enough to allow me to combine an analysis of artifacts, forms, and formats, with a critical reading of practices, histories, and rhetoric, and to allow each case study to drill down on a different aspect of media use. I assume that, while we can treat questions about production, distribution, and consumption separately, these traditional categories of economic exchange don't always adequately capture the fluidity of cultural practices and the circulation of knowledge. One of the aims of this research was to highlight how consumption practices—which I often describe more simply as "use"—shaped production and distribution practices, as well as cultural forms of expression and meaning. I frame my investigations into copies around cases studies related to compositional forms: remixes, edits, MP3 blogs, anthologies, collections and playlists. My aim in each chapter is to use a focus on copies as a conceptual tool to interrogate the form's relationship with other cultural artifacts, practices, and forms, as well as their uses and histories. As an analytical approach, this was flexible enough to allow me to draw on a number of different methods and approaches to cultural phenomenon and media, including archival research, textual analysis, discourse analysis, formal and informal interviews,[1] and participant observation. In each case study, I use a different combination of critical methods and analytical approaches, and I outline my approach in each chapter.

On the one hand, I'm using copies as a conceptual tool to help me understand media and culture; on the other hand, I look to examples in media and culture as a way to understand the affordances of copies. As I will explain in greater detail in Chapter 2, copy is a relational property of an object—a copy is always striving to be the same as something else, a repetition—and yet, while participating in this multiplicity, copies are also instances, only ever similar and never one in the same. My focus in this study is on the interrelation between use, form, and materiality; thus, I assume that media artifacts are social and cultural artifacts *of* communication and also *for* communication. They are, as Lisa Gitelman notes, both material and semiotic (2006: 20), and must be studied as such. By doing so, I am also able to home in on questions about remediation and convergence, and to consider how the relatively recent mass adoption of network technologies has and has not shaped social and cultural expression.

This study is not a history, but a critical comparative reading of contemporary media forms and their relationship with use. Throughout, I use historical narratives about popular music and sound recording in combination with material analysis to shed light on the rhetorical contours of new material practices and media artifacts. My approach to this research draws on Lisa Gitelman's approach to media history in *Always Already New* (Gitelman 2006), in which she offers a comparative study of early sound recordings and network technologies. Like Gitelman, I aim to present case studies from different moments in media history, and to get them to "talk" to one another and reveal something about change and newness. By comparing the analog history of disco edits with contemporary practice, for example, I intend to illuminate each as historically situated practices connected by form. A study of innovations in musical form, then, should take interest in the recording formats and technologies that were used in their development, and in how they interact. But any history of a form or format is tricky business because, as media artifacts, their history is complicated by their own participation in the production of history.

My approach to each case study, then, is to offer a comparative critical reading. I read the analog antecedent of various digital and networked media phenomenon into their contemporary use, and the rhetoric that surrounds them, as a way to critique their status as "new" media. By revealing obscured histories of use and participation in relationship to copy, I reveal that romantic and modern tendencies persist in networked culture

---

[1] All interviews were conducted in confidentiality, and the names of interviewees are withheld by mutual agreement.

and ask why that might be. In Chapter 3, I read the history of remix into its current rhetorical use and ask what this disjuncture might reveal about our hopes and fears about network technologies. In Chapter 4, I turn to a precursor of the remix—the disco edit—and read its own history into the recent proliferation of unauthorized edits distributed digitally and on vinyl and ask what this reveals about the materiality of media, the history of use, and, to revive Harold Innis' question, to consider the possible "biases" of networked media. In Chapter 5, I look at MP3 blogs in the 2000s to consider the persistence of romantic ideals of creativity, authenticity, and authorship in forms that seem to disregard them. I do so as a way to glimpse how it is that new authenticities build around networked expression and how the meaning of networked forms of expression, formats, practices, and artifacts can change overtime. I also look back at the *Anthology of American Folk Music* as an analog antecedent to MP3 blogs as a form of expression and knowledge, drawing parallels between these artifacts in order to excavate and highlight patterns of use and possibility that relate to the social, material, and rhetorical dimensions of media formats and their status as copies. In each case study, I highlight the status of media objects as copies to investigate utopian and dystopian claims about networked culture and raise questions about network biases and the social, cultural, and economic uses to which they are put.

CHAPTER TWO

Copy, a brief history

2.1 The ghost in the digital machine

It is now common to celebrate digital empowerment: the idea that digital technologies and broadband networks put the tools of production firmly in the hands of many (Benkler 2006; Bruns 2008; Lessig 2008; Shirky 2008). Less common is a consideration of the special role that copy, as a relative property, plays in everyday life in network culture. Although the property is not unique to digital technologies—analog technologies also produced copies and developed cultures around their existence—but "copy" as a concept plays a special role in the functioning of digital technologies and networks. In digital networks the creation and movement of copies is ubiquitous, practically effortless, and, as David Berry (2008) and others (Vaidhyanathan 2003) have pointed out, even unconscious or unintentional. Digital technologies depend on replication to perform everyday activities such as browsing the Web, checking Facebook, or listening to music. Explains Berry,

> [The web browser is] continually downloading web-pages and displaying them for the user to read and view, held locally as a "copy" of the web files located on the website ... To place a file on the web server or computer hard disk is to make a copy, to send via email is to make multiple copies, even to play a file as an MP3 or edit it as a document is to work on copies downloaded and opened temporarily in to memory. (Berry 2008: 12)

Copying is ubiquitous, necessary and commonplace, yet, despite its pervasiveness, outside of debates about copyright, we remain indifferent to the prominence of the concept and the role it plays in our everyday lives. We make veiled references to the 0s and 1s that are the symbolic atoms of the digital world, but pay scant attention to copying as a force within that system of representation and computation. Cultural scholarship about digital culture often downplays or ignores the ubiquity of copies and copying—as is evidenced by the dominance of remix and other ideas about transformative use to describe and analyse digital culture. Shining a spotlight on copy as a property and copying as a practice, however, highlights and illuminates the intersecting relationship between this abstract relationship, technology, and culture. This chapter offers a brief overview of the history of copy as an idea, by examining key debates in philosophy and demonstrating how the etymology of the English word is intertwined with the history of media technologies (or, more modestly, can be read alongside that history).

Copy as a property—and why it matters

Digital technologies depend on copies and their replication to function but they are not the first media artifacts that can be characterized by the relational property "copy." Properties are attributes of objects, and relational properties are those attributes that describe objects in relation to other objects. Copies, replication, and repetition predate the introduction of digital technologies, and they are familiar concepts in modern media culture: Printed books and periodicals, vinyl records, and films all can be described by various properties—that is, they have various attributes— yet "copy" is a property that they all share. Throughout history we find evidence of copies in various guises, artifacts, and actions that contributed to new ways of thinking about the world: For example, the practice of writing objectified knowledge and freed up memory and time, and printing enabled new kinds of discussion by fixing and stabilizing texts (Eisenstein 2005). Whereas to study was once to copy, the advent of print separated the processes of writing and reading, making more room for reflection and synthesis. The fixity of texts facilitated discussion as well as correction as all readers found themselves "on the same page" and thus could "compare notes" (cf. Eisenstein 2005). Copies, copying, and repetition have been essential to the development and circulation of ideas and debates so a focus on copy as a property of media inscriptions serves to highlight material and rhetorical differences related to media, and that this, in turn, will illuminate cultural changes and continuities that digital and network technologies have brought about.

Sameness, difference, and the problem of universals

Does it matter if something is a copy? What might it mean to emphasize that artifacts such as a book, a DVD, or an MP3, are copies—to highlight that they share a relational property, "copy"? In everyday speech, it seems that, when we talk about a copy, we sometimes mean that it is the

same as something else, in the sense that it is identical to it—if we both
have the same edition of a book, for instance, we say that they are copies to
indicate that they contain *identical* content; that they are, in a sense, one—
and sometimes we mean that a copy is the same as something else, in the
sense that it is *similar*—my copy of *What Bird Is That?* and your copy of
What Bird Is That? are still two different books, even though they share the
same content. We use the word *copy* to highlight that they are independent
instances. In many situations, we treat the fact that there is more than one
of any media artifact as trivial or incidental. When you are faced with a
stack of books at the bookstore, whether you purchase the one on the top of
the pile or any of the copies beneath is considered inconsequential (leaving
aside any dog-eared corners, scuffs, or other imperfections of the book as a
physical object). You and I may jump in the car and find that we both have
copies of Chet Baker's "Let's Get Lost" on our phones—whether we listen
to your copy or mine over the sound system really makes no difference. So,
too, when it comes to listening, assuming that they are stored at the same
bit rate, the fact that yours was purchased from the iTunes store and mine
was downloaded from an MP3 blog is irrelevant—because, as copies, they
are functionally equivalent. Press play, hear "Let's Get Lost." (Of course,
there are also other functional descriptions and groupings by which they
may be equivalent—say, how much space they take up on a hard drive.)
This is not to say that all of the copies in the stack of books are the same
book—clearly, there are many distinct copies—or that your MP3 and mine
are the same digital file—they may be identical code, but they exist in
different locations, have unique identifiers, and have different points and
stories of origin—yet, what we care about, the quality that makes us call
them copies, is that their *content* is in some way identical, and, a lot of the
time, it is this sense of being a copy that makes these two similar artifacts
functionally equivalent.

   One of the reasons that it is difficult to talk about copies is that, in
everyday speech, we treat these two senses of sameness—being one and
the same, that is, identity, and similarity, the sharing of many properties,
but not all—as synonymous, thereby muddying our meaning. As well, the
word *copy* has other meanings that complicate the discussion: Copy can
also mean that something is imitative, in a sense that can have normative
connotations as well as descriptive ones; it can be used to mean "without
reference to an original," or to mean "that which is copied" ("copy, v.1,"
2011). As a verb, its most recent sense comes to us from the discipline
of computer science, and it refers to the reading and replication of data:
"To read (data stored in one location), or the data in (a disc, etc.), and
reproduce it in another. (Const. *from* the first location *to* (or *into*, etc.) the
second)" ("copy, v.1," 2011). Copy is a description of automation in a
digital environment—it describes the movement produced by reading data
and reproducing it. Copy is the ghost in the digital machine.

Although difference has preoccupied post-structural thinking, I would like to suggest that, when we talk about copies in media studies, we would do well to also consider debates in analytic philosophy that teach us to pay close attention to differences between similarity and identity when considering sameness (cf. Armstrong 1989; Kripke 1980; Noonan 2009). In the following analysis, I highlight distinctions between similarity and identity as a way to tease out what the property of being a copy might tell us about historically situated mediated experience (where experience includes expression, distribution, and reception), as well as about changes and continuities in these cultural experiences. I think about copies both as independent instances and as things that share something in common with other things. To do so, I draw on philosophical debates and responses to the ancient problem of universals and suggest that we need to take care to distinguish between those things or relationships that are identical and those that are merely similar—and to be aware that these are different relationships; that is, they are different properties. It is all too easy to conflate the various meanings of copy.

Simultaneously, although we can take care with the definitions we invoke, it is also important to remember that our sense of what it means to be a copy today is shaped by media and cultural history and that there exists another set of debates about aesthetics and the relationship among copies, originals, and authors that, like copyright, stems from romantic period aesthetics but that we also tend to read into metaphysical and ontological questions. What it means to be a copy then, becomes tied up with both ancient and modern ideas about mimesis, transcription, repetition, and multiplicity, and these related ideas shape our opinions about the value of copies and their use. I make a case for changing tack in media studies, away from the post-structural preoccupation with difference and toward a renewed interest in that which is the same, a move that I hope can benefit from this rich history of ideas.

The problem of universals

The ancient problem of universals asks how we might account for the sense that distinct instances can be said to be similar or the same. It poses two questions: First, what makes something what it is (e.g., what makes the teacup on my desk a teacup and not, say, an elephant), and, second, what makes us say that two individual instances are the same (e.g., why we say that the two rainbow lorikeets outside my window are the same, when they are clearly two different birds). The problem of universals attempts to tackle such questions by asking if universal properties actually exist, or are just a way we talk about things.

Plato's theory of universals posits that there is a common entity—a "form" (sometimes translated as "idea")—that accounts for (1) why something is what it is (e.g., the object on my desk is a teacup because it participates in the universal form of "teacup"; the elephants at Taronga Zoo participate in the universal form of "elephantness"), and (2) why it is the same as something else (e.g., why the teacup on my desk and those that are in the cupboard all instantiate the same thing; the universal is what these unique objects have in common and what makes them the same). Forms for Plato are *transcendent*—that is, they are not of this world, inhabiting instead a separate realm of being. The things of this world are lesser imitations, or representations, of the transcendent forms, or, as some translations have it, "copies." Aristotle, on the other hand, believes forms are *immanent*—that is, they exist only in their instantiations, which is to say they are of this world. We don't need to use two levels of being to account for universals in Aristotle's theory, only one.

Contemporary philosophy continues to debate the problem of one over many, but analytic philosophy has all but abandoned transcendent theories of universals focusing instead on either immanence or nominalism.[1] Platonic dualism, however, has had a lasting influence on other areas of philosophy. Plato's ideas about *mimesis* and, as Plato scholar Elizabeth Asmis argues, his use of the mirror simile in *The Republic* "has had an overwhelming influence on the interpretation of his aesthetic and on aesthetic theory in general" (Asmis 1992: 352). These theories of aesthetics and representation often come into play when we talk about copies. Western anxieties about copies can be traced back to Plato's writings on mimesis (Boon 2010: 18), and romantic ideals about authenticity and originality have proven remarkably resilient. However, it is important to recognize that, though these debates about mimesis and universals intersect, they should not be conflated. Quite simply, multiple copies of books or MP3s present us with a different set of problems than a flock of birds or a herd of elephants do.

Plato's theory of the forms, however, also shapes his opinions on the proper role of mimesis in his ideal city-state, a place ruled by philosopher-kings and all that is good. Plato believed such a society should be cautious with regard to poetry and art because of its reliance on *mimesis*—an ancient Greek word that means something like imitation or impersonation, although, in his translation, Francis Cornford advises that "the nearest English word is representation" (Plato 1941: 323). The problem with mimesis is that it can only represent appearance, not essence; hence, it is two steps removed from the world of forms (which is the realm where "the good" resides). Plato invokes the simile of the mirror to argue that the artist is a kind of charlatan, someone who has no real knowledge of truth, but who tricks the viewer or listener into thinking he does by merely representing the world of appearances. This trickery is conveyed by Socrates in

---

[1] For a good introduction to these debates in analytic philosophy, see Armstrong (1989).

The Republic when he suggests that an artist is akin to a craftsman who produces all things by holding a mirror up to the world, but who has no knowledge of the things he produces (e.g., Van Gogh might be able to paint a nice pair of boots, but put him in a cobbler's workshop, and the chances are high that he'll go barefoot). One of the problems with representation in Plato's thought stems from a representation's distance from the world of forms—the realm where beauty, truth, goodness, and other ideals reside. Representations are two steps removed from the good; they are distortions of imperfections. Says Socrates, "What he makes is not the reality, but only something that resembles it."

Poststructuralism continues to take an interest in Platonic dualism and these ideas about representation—if only to "overthrow" such notions, as Deleuze suggests (Deleuze 1983: 45). Where many theories of universals seek to find the source of sameness, Deleuze's "reverse Platonism" seeks to shift the focus away from questions about the relationship between "essence" and "appearance," to focus instead on "difference as a primary power" (Deleuze 1983: 53). This position is different from saying that universals are produced by their instantiations: Instead, he argues against their existence altogether. Sameness, for Deleuze, is just how we talk about things—this is a kind of nominalism. In doing so, Deleuze locates simulacra, representation, as the source of the real and repetition as an effect of that power (Williams 2004: 244). Deleuze writes, "The simulacrum is not degraded copy, rather it contains a positive power which negates both original and copy, both model and reproduction" (Deleuze 1983: 53). The simulacrum defines modernity for Deleuze, a position that, Robert Williams (2004: 244) argues, "excavates the conceptual depths beneath Benjamin's insights about mechanical reproduction" and that contrasts with Jean Baudrillard's (1994) disdain for the pervasiveness of the "simulacra" of the postmodern world, a world of copies without originals.

Deleuze's reading of Plato is a thoroughly modern one, dependent upon distinctions between originals and copies that arise with romantic period aesthetics rather than upon ancient accounts. The use of the mirror as a doubling technology is the likely source of our sense that Plato's theory of the forms can be (and is) read as a theory that has something to say about copies and originals, yet it seems clear that modern conceptual distinctions are not made between originals and copies until after the advent of print technologies (Boon 2010: 48). As I have noted, key translators and commentators highlight that the ancient meaning of the term *mimesis* is not equivalent to its use today, and they caution that Plato deployed it in very specific ways. For example, Cornford warns that the distinction Socrates draws between things as they are and things as they appear "is needed to exclude another possible sense of mimesis, the production of a complete replica" (Plato 1941: 328). Perfect copies in the sense that we understand them today didn't figure in the discussion. I point this out not to dismiss Deleuze's critique, but, instead, to historicize his reading and to highlight the idea that what counts as a copy, and the meaning of that property, also has a history. To begin to glimpse these changes, I now offer a brief overview of the word's etymology and its various usages and meanings. I take special notice of the role that media technologies play in the word's history and connect these senses with other significant contributions to our ideas about copies in aesthetics.

The etymology of copy: A secret media history

In English, copy is used as a noun, adjective, and verb. The Oxford English Dictionary (OED) dates the word to the fourteenth century and outlines four branches of the noun: copy as abundance, or multiple; copy as transcription; "without reference to an original;" and "that which is copied." I will discuss each in turn.

Copia: Copy as abundance

The English word copy is borrowed from Old French (copie) and has Latin roots: cōpia, meaning "abundance, plenty, multitude" ("copy, n. and adj.," 2011). This sense of the word is mostly obsolete; however, multiplicity continues to be part of our understanding of what it means to be a copy. To call an object a copy is to imply that there are others that are either identical or similar. In Marcus Boon's groundbreaking work on copies (Boon 2010) he sought to account for the cultural pervasiveness of copies and imitation, without relying on legal-political constructions. Drawing on both Western thinking about copies and Eastern traditions, with an emphasis on Buddhist philosophy, Boon presents an "affirmation of copying" (Boon 2010: 6), arguing that copying is a fundamental to humanity and the nature of the universe. Boon draws our attention to this older sense of copy as an abundance for this purpose, reading the word's semantic history into its present usage. He writes,

> When we talk about copying today, when controversy around copying occurs, these meanings of "copia"—coming to us from before the age of print, the age of mechanical reproduction, or the age of the computer—reassert themselves. Although we no longer associate copying with abundance, but link it rather with the theft or deterioration of an original, and thus a decrease, the phenomena we label "copies" and the activities we call "copying" still manifest this abundance and this increase. Copia as abundance continues to speak to us as a trace

reverberating through the shifting historical meanings of the word "copy," and various practices of copying that are prevalent today still evoke the [Roman] goddess [Copia], even if the practitioners no longer know the meaning of her name. (Boon 2010: 41–2)

Boon draws attention to this older meaning to argue that this sense of copy as abundance is antithetical to notions of private property—that, instead, it is evident in collective cultural forms and styles (Boon 2010: 76). Replication is often aligned with participatory practices in contemporary thinking about copies and I will draw attention to and examine the strengths and weaknesses of this pairing in the chapters to come. For now, I want to highlight that copies are seen to lead a double life: They are both one and one of many. Writes Boon,

The copy [is seen] as an object that is inherently multiple, that is more than one, that is a copy of something, and thus part of an excess or abundance, of a more. And at the same time, the copy is part of a storehouse, an object created or appropriated in order to be an object of use, made part of a store that is available; and as a part of a store, something that is counted or measured, named and/or labeled, owned, and no longer freely existing for itself. (Boon 2010: 45)

This double life of media artifacts, this inherent multiplicity and independence, creates possibilities. Identifying and understanding these possibilities and how they intersect with the material dimensions of media motivates my work on popular music in the chapters to come.

Copy as transcription

The most common contemporary usages of copy stem from the second branch, which groups together definitions that stem from the sense of copy as "a transcript or reproduction of an original." This branch stems from medieval Latin, and the OED cites the phrases *dare vel habere copiam legendi* ("to give, or have, the power of reading") and *facere copiam describendi* ("to give the power of transcription," or "to allow a transcript to be made") as the likely source of this denotation ("copy, n. and adj.," 2011). One of the earliest uses in English, with examples found as early as 1330 CE (110 years before Gutenberg's first press was completed), indicate the results of a transcription; that is, "the writing transcribed from and reproducing the contents of another transcript." This suggests that an assumption that writing and reading are related practices seems to be embedded in the oldest usage of copy. These practices are linked by "copy" (of course, the sense of words on the page as "copy" is another meaning of the word, although this stems from another branch). It is worth recalling that, prior to the advent of print, reading and writing would have been more closely aligned than they are today: In medieval scribal culture, if you wanted to read or study a text, you also needed to copy it (Eisenstein 2005; McLuhan 2006; Greenblatt 2011: 24–9). That said, "writing" in the thirteenth century should not be conflated with our conception of original authorship.[2] Still, it is worth reminding ourselves that it was handwriting as a technology, rather than print, that shaped the earliest instances of copying, and, as Eisenstein warns, we must remember that handwriting and print are not the same technology, that they have different cultural implications and effects. That said, whether handwritten or printed, copying preserved texts and facilitated reading and scholarship, although each technology enabled and shaped these practices in different manners.

Transcription carries with it a sense of movement from one form of communication to another: We transcribe speeches and dialogues so they can be read rather than heard. It shifts information from one space and time to another; or in McLuhan's terms copies may remediate. Copy as a representation, imitation, or specimen also stems from this sense of copy as transcription or reproduction. Today, when we call something a copy, we often mean that it is an *imitation* or reproduction of some *more authentic* original. For instance, I can order a copy of Vincent Van Gogh's 1888 painting *Shoes* from an artist-copyist in Shenzhen, China (Tinari 2007), and while the resulting painting will be very similar to the original that hangs at the Metropolitan Museum of Art in New York City (depending on the talent of the artist), the hand-painted replica cannot be a perfect copy; it cannot be said to be identical in any way, only similar. (Two prints of the same photographic negative, by comparison, are said to have identical content, as the printed representations are seen as identical, not as imitations of one another.) Mass-produced consumer goods make this question of imitation even trickier. If I buy a high-quality knockoff of a mass-produced chair, it may be that the only way in which the knockoff differs from the original design is with regard to price and to authorization, or legal legitimacy (cf. Coslovich 2011). In this case, we use the notion that the chair is a copy both to indicate that it is the same as the "authorized" design and to indicate that it is somehow fake or inauthentic, despite being physically identical. Moral valuations begin to creep into the question, suggesting that some copies are good (the mass-produced chairs by the company who owns the license to the name), while others (the knockoffs produced by some other company, or even the same manufacturer) are somehow transgressive and wrong, or less authentic—even if they are exact replicas and a couple of hundred dollars cheaper. This sense of copying as imitation—the question

---

[2]Print historian Elizabeth Eisenstein (2005: 95) explains, "A writer is a man who 'makes books' with a pen just as a cobbler is a man who makes shoes with a last."

of mimesis—motivates Boon's (2010: 3) study of copies, but it is not a primary concern of my investigation but it does intersect with my interest in the persistence of ideas and ideals of authenticity.

In practice, it seems that leaving aside questions of mimesis and representation is almost impossible, as is suggested by the influence of Plato's ideas about mimesis on aesthetic theory and, in popular discourse, by the intermingling of current debates about intellectual property regarding the unauthorized reproduction of cultural goods such as music, film, and literature and the counterfeiting of branded consumer goods (think "fake" Louis Vuitton handbags and the like). We can trace contemporary notions about authenticity, copies, and originals to the development of romantic aesthetics in the eighteenth century. A distinct movement in art and literature, romanticism is understood to be a reaction to the rationalism of the Enlightenment, one that produced a set of principles about creativity. These include:

> 1) Placing emotion and intuition before (or at least on an equal footing with) reason; 2) a belief that there are crucial areas of experience neglected by the rational mind; and 3) a belief in the general importance of the individual, the personal and the subjective. In fact it embodies a critique of that faith in progress and rationality that had characterized the main trend of Western thought and action since the Renaissance. This resulted in an opposition to the dominant contemporary values and social structures. (Vaughan)

Although the artistic movement passed, romantic ideals about creativity persist and have had a particularly strong influence on our notions of subjectivity, originality, and literary property (Taylor 1989; Marshall 2005). This is particularly evident in understandings of originality as a source of authenticity. Writes Boon,

> The notion of the "Copye," in the sixteenth and seventeenth centuries, had an ambiguous meaning when used by publishers, since it referred both to the text which the publisher had the right to publish (the "original"), and to those copies of the original "copy" that were made by authorized publishers as well as by unauthorized parties. It appears that the concept of the original or authentic text, as something separate from the copies made from this original, was absent at this time, and only emerged in the eighteenth century with the evolution of Romantic aesthetics. (Boon 2010: 48–9)

Questions of authenticity, then, seem to be related to questions about imitation. Drawing on Deleuze's work, art critic Rosalind Krauss (1985) challenged and deconstructed the preoccupation with originality in *The Originality of the Avant-Garde and Other Modernist Myths.* Postmodernism, she suggests, is dominated by the discourse of the copy, a cultural conversation that knocks authors off their romantic pedestals and dismisses the heroic posturing of the avant-garde. "Originality," she writes, "is a working assumption that itself emerges from a ground of repetition and recurrence" (1985: 7). The pictorial plane is itself a doubling, and "the grid condemns these artists not to originality but to repetition" (1985: 9). The idea that the copy is prior to the original, also arises in sound studies when Sterne (2003: 221) argues that "reproduction precedes originality," or when Thornton (1995: 42–3) argues that our notion of "live" music comes about with the advent of recorded music. I will return to these claims later in the book, for now I would like to note that these reversals of common-sense notions of originals and copies takes us back to the question of universals—in particular, to its second question: What makes us say that two individual instances are the same? Rather than ask how originals and copies are related, we might focus our attention on how they are used, and how these terms function.

This sense that copies are prior to originals can also be found in the third branch of the word's usage: "Without reference to an original." Chiefly, this means "one of the various (written or printed specimens of the same writing or work; an individual example of a manuscript of print)." According to the *OED*, "Originally, the idea of 'transcript' or 'reproduction' was of course present; but in later use an original edition itself consists of so many 'copies.' In *fair copy, clean copy* of a writing, the idea of 'transcript' is distinctly present; but it disappears when the original draft is called the rough or foul copy." Later copies are seen as an improvement upon prior ones, a shift in meaning that coincides with the rise of print.

That the words on this page can also be called copy is a meaning that arises with the shift from the manuscript culture of the medieval period to the early modern days of print and these usages are grouped under the word's fourth major branch: "that which is copied" ("copy, v.1," 2011). This sense of "copy"—what we might now call "content"—comes about with the advent of the printing press in the fifteenth century, when *copy* became a technical word in the printing process and began to indicate "manuscript (or printed) matter prepared for printing" ("copy, v.1," 2011)—that is, the words that would be copied with the aid of this new media technology: print. This sense still abounds in publishing: Journalists file copy, and a copy editor at a copy desk edits it. This sense of copy as content also now refers to the content of your recordings and the images that fill your screens. It is the sense of copy as the master or original or the work; it is the sense that copyright seeks to protect and regulate.

You can't step twice in the same stream

Music-streaming services like Spotify and Apple Music are often thought to have solved the contemporary problem of unauthorized copying (i.e., piracy). Yet, streaming technologies, like all digital technologies, are still dependent on copying and the affordances of copy as a property—for a digital machine to read and to write is to copy—yet most on-demand platforms are able to obscure their debt to both the noun and the verb, leaving users unaware that fragments of files are uploaded, downloaded, and erased as we listen. To better understand the social, cultural, and aesthetic dimensions of contemporary listening practices, we need to excavate the copy from the stream and consider the material dimensions of seemingly immaterial recording and storage formats. We also need to consider how these platforms and practices were shaped by their antecedents: As a peer-to-peer platform for listening, Spotify was designed to respond both to the new expectations that music should be accessible by anyone, at any time and as an attempt to monetize these behaviors and expectations.

Listening practices also have histories that are illuminated by a close study of copies as objects and replication as a cultural practice. Or, in other words, to treat copies as part of a larger material history of media. To excavate the copy from the stream we must return to these philosophical questions related to the ontology of the copy and its role in epistemology as well as its many media histories.

In the coming chapters I will consider how media has shaped the way we think about and value copies and copying using forms, formats, micro-trends, and fashions in music culture as key sites for understanding media change and network aesthetics. As my brief examination of the etymology of copy has shown, a secret media history lurks behind the different usages. These histories of media technologies and inscriptions have shaped our contemporary ideas and ideals about copies and copying as artifacts and practices; becoming aware of them alerts us to the tensions and possibilities that arise around the copy and its use. In the chapters that follow, I consider copy as an historical concept in tandem with the ancient problem of universals; I claim that sustained attention to the distinction between instance and identity, will reveal something about how copies and copying can create new meaning out of something that is just the same. In doing so, my method of inquiry echoes another ancient quandary: the problem of identity over time. "One can not step twice into the same river" is a paradox that is usually attributed to Heraclitus. Fittingly, we only have fragments of Heraclitus' work and it remains unclear as to whether he ever uttered these precise words (Robinson 1987: 83–4), and yet, its inscription and repetition over time have ensured that this ancient philosophical problem continues to open up new possibilities for understanding existence and meaning. "We step and do not step into the same rivers; we are and are not" (Heraclitus, fragment 49a in Robinson 1987: 35).

2.2 The trouble with media history

Reproduction changed music. It changed how music was produced and how we listened to it. Recording also altered the meaning of performance, promoted the development of genres, influenced the proliferation of new styles, and facilitated the development of repertoires and histories. Walter Benjamin was among the first scholars of the modern era to take seriously the aesthetic ramifications and possibilities of reproduction. For Jonathan Sterne, the very *possibility* of reproduction reconfigured ideas about originality and authenticity. "The possibility of sound reproduction reorients the practices of sound production; insofar as it is a possibility at all, reproduction precedes originality" (Sterne 2003: 221). In Sterne's contemporary reading of Benjamin (2007b), the concept of an art object's *aura*, is a retroactive quality, that is, a characteristic that Benjamin could recognize and conceive of only in the context of the new mechanical mode of composition such as cinema and recorded music. Sterne (2003: 220–1) uses Benjamin to make a strong argument for understanding the social construction of sound recording and to demonstrate how their material histories can be best understood via a social lens. Media have human histories.

Yet, media are difficult historical subjects because, as Lisa Gitelman (2006: 5) explains, they "are historical at several levels." Media artifacts are from the past and at the same time represent and index the past in the present. Recordings exist as situated instances that have a relationship with other, similarly situated instances; they participate in a shared history at the same time as their history is particular and specific. They are, at once, same but different.

In the chapters to come, I focus on the material dimension of the media used in the creation, circulation, and consumption of remixes, disco edits, MP3 blogs and other forms of playlist and compilation with the hope that it will foreground and help us make sense of what Gitelman refers to as the "unsettled assumptions" of new forms of media, and the "bibliographic questions and entanglements" (2006: 95) raised by digital networks. Any investigation into form is also an investigation into its mediations and remediation. Every disco edit carries with it a history of storage formats and playback technologies as well as the variety of social rituals and uses that were associated with them. Remix may have been born analog but it has become the dominant descriptive and explanatory metaphor for the artifacts of networked new media, an all-purpose compositional pattern, or, to borrow Andres Fagerjord's (2010: 197) astute metaphor, a "template" for digital creativity. By untangling this template's specific histories from its present use, I hope to illuminate both continuities and changes associated with the shift to digital networked media. I share Sterne and Gitelman's concern with the social histories of media, but I am not convinced that theories of social construction alone can explain their histories. My broader aim is to begin to reconcile these social histories with the possibility that media objects are also independent and autonomous in some significant way and to consider how this duality relates to their materiality and their status as copies.

Networked music makes music audible by first making it visible—and that visibility has ramifications for discovery and encounter. Networked music seems to be both ephemeral—it is in "the cloud"—and object oriented—that is, every digital file is a copy that is also capable of being copied; as a recording that can be replicated. Simultaneously, the sampling practices that are often said to be the building blocks of digital networked expression are grounded in the history and materiality of analog sound-recording technologies and embodied listening. In the forthcoming chapters I highlight how users discovered that particular kinds of recording formats had particular affordances and acted upon these qualities to create new forms. These forms continue to shape digital expression, yet their material histories are overlooked and format is often seen as an irrelevant aspect of creative expression.

Before turning to the case studies, I would like to outline what I mean by "materiality." Like philosophical materialists, I assume that matter matters. That media, like mind, is material in the sense that it is of the physical world, and like all matter, is subject to the laws of nature. Given this assumption, I challenge theories of media that assume that the physical properties of a particular storage format or delivery system are irrelevant, that they are "simply and only technologies," as Henry Jenkins (2006a: 14) has claimed. Such theories appear to be committed to a functionalist theory of media—the idea that the content is functionally equivalent. However, just because materiality might not matter in one functional description does not mean it does not matter in another one. Writing "Love Is the Message" on a piece of paper and in the sand is functionally equivalent, when it comes to content—in both cases, the message is the same—but if I need to stuff that message into a fortune cookie, the material differences between sand and paper then matter quite a lot.

Popular music provides us with particularly good examples to probe because its status is so tricky. For example, does a pop song exist in some pure sense outside of its performance, whether it is recorded or not? Once recorded, can the sonic content be separated from the format on which it is delivered? I argue that it remains an unsettled question as to whether "Let It Be" on tape is equivalent to the musical notation and lyrics to "Let It Be" in print, or to "Let It Be" encoded in an MP3 file. (If we include differences in playback technologies, this quandary compounds.) A question persists about the relationship between "Let It Be" as a recording and the performance of "Let It Be," as seen in the 1970 documentary film of the same name. This is a question about copies, one that precedes any questions about copyright, and has relevance for questions regarding the production, consumption, and circulation of knowledge. Common sense tells us that all the versions of "Let It Be" are copies of the same thing; their equivalency stems from the musical event they can produce in conjunction with a playback system. The music is the thing that matters here—not the format—just as we might say that a paperback, a hardcover, and an e-book contain the same textual information. We might say these formats share a "functional equivalency," but they are only functionally equivalent if you also have a system on which to play each one. If I bring my vinyl copy to your house, and you have a computer rather than a turntable, "Let it Be" on vinyl is no longer functionally equivalent to the copy I downloaded from the Internet.

Looking back to the work of Harold Innis (1995), I assume that the study of cultural systems is enriched by studying the material properties and structure of a culture's communications and delivery systems, their relation with time and space as well as bodies and minds. If you want to understand the popular music of the last hundred years, for instance, you need to think about how the material characteristics of recording and playback technologies shaped musical forms, sonic content, and cultural use. Similarly, though digital technologies may seem to produce immaterial texts, the electronic technologies needed to produce them are undeniably physical and dependent on material forces.

By positing that media and texts are always material, I am not assuming that materiality is causal or deterministic. I want to avoid a theory of media and culture that posits technological determinism or naively assumes technological progress. As I have highlighted above, to say that a media's material dimension and structure doesn't always matter is not to say that it never matters, nor does this imply that it can be ignored or bracketed out. I argue that media can neither be reduced to its physical properties nor fully understood without recognizing when these material properties matter, and why. To understand why this is, I return to the tradition of cultural materialism and the work of Raymond Williams. Williams set forth both explanatory and methodological reasons to pay attention to the materiality of culture. Building on the Marxist theory of historical materialism, with its explanatory emphasis on how our physical needs shape our social and economic lives, Williams extended this material outlook to claim that culture was also material and subject to material forces. In doing so, he turns his back on the Marxist notion of superstructure and its implication that culture can be divorced from economic life. As Terry Eagleton (2008: 198–9) explains,

[Cultural Materialism] was a way of bringing an unashamedly materialist analysis to bear on that realm of social existence—"culture"—which
was thought by conventional criticism to be the very antithesis of the
material; and its ambition was less to relate "culture" to "society," in
Williams's own earlier style, than to examine culture as always-already
social and material in its roots. It could be seen either as an enrichment
or a dilution of classical Marxism: enrichment, because it carried materialism boldly through to the "spiritual" itself; dilution, because in doing
so it blurred the distinction, vital to orthodox Marxism, between the
economic and the cultural.

To say that some thing or phenomenon is a social or cultural construction is
not to deny its materiality, but, rather, to highlight how a host of material
interactions produce complex phenomena.

Though my approach is not strictly a cultural materialist one (or, at least,
not in the literary-theory sense), I share a deep interest in the historical specificity of media as material artifacts, and phenomena as a site of reading. By
studying the specificity of media production—that a recording is produced
in a particular place, over a particular period of time, by a set of players,
who, in turn, bring particular histories and experiences with particular
technologies that also have cultural and social histories (in tandem with the
specificity of media consumption; for instance, that the particular artifact
was, or was not, played at a particular time)—and media distribution, I
am able to highlight changes and continuities and recover unspoken values
and submerged ideologies. Culture is material both in the sense that it
has some kind of existence in space and time—it can be made of paint on
canvas, words in print, bums on bar stools, or hands in the air—and that,
as Eagleton says, it is "always-already social and material in its roots," that
countless material interactions produce complex social phenomena.

The complexity of material influence is the focus of recent work in
literary and archival studies, where questions about the material nature
of digital texts (and, as Gitelman [2006: 96] has noted, ontological
questions about the nature of a text itself) are posed in order to facilitate
their preservation and future scholarship. Digital media, in particular, that
which is "born digital" (this book, for instance) should not be understood as "less" material than the texts that preceded them: "Writing is a
material act: textual production in any medium has always been a part
and product of particular technologies of inscription and duplications"
(Kirschenbaum et al. 2009: 105). If you start with the assumption that
all cultural production is somehow material, whether you are recording a
song or reenacting an Alan Kaprow happening (Ihlein et al. 2009), then the
question you need to ask about digital objects and texts involves why (and
when) does their particular material configuration matter, how does it help
us understand the social and cultural construction of media, and in what

way does a focus on cultural materiality help us to understand cultural forms. These are the questions that motivate the analysis in these chapters.

2.3 "Again, back": Repetition and music's materiality

In the history of cultural criticism, repetition as a property of musical recordings has been perceived as both a feature and a bug. Modernist and industrial mass production, with its steady output of identical consumer goods, sparked interest in the aesthetics of repetition in the early and mid-twentieth century. In his influential essay "The Work of Art in the Age of Mechanical Reproduction," Walter Benjamin (2007b) lamented that mechanical reproduction resulted in the loss of an artwork's "aura," that elusive quality that had something to do with an artwork's status as a unique object and the time, care, and attention that it represented, but he was also optimistic that repetition and reproduction might become important sources of renewal. He wrote,

> The technique of reproduction detaches the reproduced object from the domain of tradition. By making many reproductions it substitutes a plurality of copies for a unique existence. And in permitting the reproduction to meet the beholder or listener in his own particular situation, it reactivates the object reproduced. These two processes lead to a tremendous shattering of tradition which is the obverse of the contemporary crisis and renewal of mankind. (Benjamin 2007b: 221)

Repetition could shift art in time and space to places where unique art objects could never travel or, indeed, bear witness.[3] These properties of reproducibility and repetition, he hoped, would have revolutionary potential.

Theodore Adorno (1990), on the other hand, looked upon the quality of repetition with disdain and viewed what he perceived as the highly repetitive nature of popular music, its use of standard song structures and familiar details, as cause for concern. Popular music, as music, was "wholly antagonistic to the ideal of individuality in a free, liberal society" (1990: 306). For Adorno, the culture industries facilitated a world of standardized choices, pseudo-individualism, and escape rather than edification. Although many music collectors would bristle at Adorno's stance, echoes of Adorno

---

[3]Writing of photography, Benjamin (2007b: 220). notes that it "can capture images which escape natural vision" and can "put the copy of the original into situations which be out of reach for the original itself."

can be heard in many of our most cherished rants against the music industries. Also echoing Adorno (although marginally more optimistic) is Jacques Attali's (1985: 90) notion that, while recording and repetition have led to an era where "nothing happens, except for the artificially created pseudo events," this era might also contain the seeds of its own emancipation. Attali saw promise in the growing number of unauthorized uses of music in the late 1960s and 1970s, and cited "the proliferating circulation of pirated recordings, the multiplication of illegal radio stations" as "herald[ing] a radical subversion, a new mode of social structuring, communication that is not restricted to the elite of discourse" (1985: 131–2). These subversions of the technologies of recording might herald a new era, he speculated, one of pure composition (1985: 20). While Attali did not write specifically about remix (his book was written in the 1970s during the dawn of the practice) he sees certain copying practices as potentially liberating and revolutionary; in particular, he pins his hopes on the unauthorized use of the culture industry's technologies (i.e., pirate radio and bootlegs.) After Attali, the question that many scholars of popular culture ask is whether remix as a creative approach represents the beginning of this utopian era of pure composition.[4]

Deleuze's embrace of copies and repetition returns us to Benjamin's more hopeful position. For Deleuze, repetition was an effect of the copy and a source of power; repetition generates difference. This notion that something that is just the same can bring something new into being seems more familiar in a musical context, where repetition is part of what makes sounds, well, musical. "There's a stubborn repeatability to music at every turn," writes Elizabeth Margulis (2014: 4). Indeed, repetition is an element of formal composition (Middleton 1999: 146)—the repetition of riffs or phrases in musical works, for example—and, according to current research in cognitive neuroscience, repetition appears to be a property or characteristic that is a source of aesthetic pleasure. Neuroscientist (and former record producer) Daniel Levitin (2007: 167) explains that repetition is "emotionally satisfying to our brains, and makes the listening experience as pleasurable as it is." Repetition also facilitates reception practices; the nature of our recordings is that they allow us to capture sound and also to play it again. We usually obtain recordings not only because we would like to hear a song, but because we would like to hear that song again. And again. Radio stations aim to pique our interest in recordings by playing them frequently, to breed familiarity (and, if all goes well, not contempt).

---

[4]English readers seized on this glimmer of hope in *Noise* (Attali 1985) when, in 1985, at the start of the era of digital sampling, an English translation was first published. Today, *Noise* continues to be read with digital technologies in mind. It is worth recalling, however, that *Noise* was first published in French, in 1977, and, thus, Attali's book can also be read as a predigital meditation on repetition. Read as such, it offers probing questions about the influence of recording, playback, and collection on distribution and reception in an analog era.

We attend concerts and go out to nightclubs as much to hear songs that we've heard before as to hear something new. When we listen to DJs, we hope they'll play our favorites but we want to hear them played as if we were hearing them the first time. We turn to the predictive algorithms that power streaming services such as Spotify for new discoveries alongside our personal classics. And again back. *De capo.*

It is then well accepted that music is an art form with a special affinity for repetition and, since the early twentieth century, it has also developed an intimate rapport with sound recordings (i.e., copies). Music is not the only cultural practice reliant on copies and repetition, and it is worth comparing recorded music with other media artifacts to think through this relationship between repetition and copies. The two properties seem to be interrelated, but we must consider whether there are copies that do not enable repetition or repetitions that are not copies? The answers to both questions seems to depend on where the line is drawn between what counts as a copy and what does not. Ditto for repetition. For example, every live performance of the song "I've Got to Be Me" can be said to be a repetition of Walter Marks's now well-known composition. But no one would ever say that Michael Jackson's rendition, or Ella Fitzgerald's, was *a copy* of Sammy Davis Jr.'s well-known recording, or of his subsequent performances. We would, however, call any recordings of these performances copies, and it seems that in common usage, "copy" has an affinity with the material storage of information, whereas repetition is related to enactment of that information. Similarly, those copies that are similar to each other, but are not precise repetitions, are deemed imperfect. Consider medieval manuscript culture, an era when scholarship depended on handcopying to preserve, disseminate, and study texts. Handwritten "copies" of manuscripts may have been similar to that which they copied, but they were never identical to them: They were copies in that they had a similar mimetic relationship with the original text (or with a copy of that text, as the case may have been), but each was ultimately unique, and, thus, an imperfect instantiation. Different handwriting is an obvious divergence from the original, and, as Elizabeth Eisenstein (2005) and other scholars of the book tell us, handwritten copies were subject to human error; hence, in this case, repetition produced textual drift. The printing press, on the other hand, facilitated an exact repetition of a text—a perfect copy—thereby stabilizing texts and warding off transcribing errors and textual drift. Rather than producing many differently corrupted copies of some original document (or, indeed, copying from an already imperfect copy of that document), the printing press enabled the production of multiple copies that were the same as the master copy. This element of multiplicity is a kind of repetition, as well as a quality that increases the likelihood that such a repetition will recur across time and space. Perfect copies, in turn, facilitated repetition; mechanical reproduction guaranteed that a diverse group of scholars, separated by space and time, could work on a text that contained identical content. Repetition enabled stable texts, and stable texts enable repetition. Repetition and copy, while not coextensive properties, are interdefined and interrelated ones. Technologies that improve repetition also seem to improve the accuracy of copies, and vice versa. Something that is a copy is both the realization of repetition—it is the thing repeated—and the artifact that enables future reenactments of the action or event that it contains. This circularity—that repetition begets copies beget repetition—rather than being problematic, seems apropos in a musical context. It is, after all, the perfect loop.

However, it is the ultimate irony that all copies are not created equal. In the pages to come, I will consider how and why various kinds of media and media formats are materially different, and how a focus on an artifact's status as a copy highlights that difference. If, as Anna Munster posits, "It is the clone that offers us the full promise of what digital code will offer—repetition" (2006: 26), then how does digital repetition differ from its analog antecedents? It is common to say it is easier, faster, and more resilient, and that networks tear down barriers to distribution, but we know that tapes and records also facilitated repetition. Do these technological and material differences matter? Do they matter sometimes, but not always? Does it introduce a scale to the cycle of repetition/copy that alters aesthetics in some new way?

Attali did not take an interest in the materiality of recorded sound. For Attali, music is an immaterial pleasure; he even seems to imply that the status of recorded sound as material objects is sullied, tied up as it is with its status as commodity. He writes, "Music, an immaterial pleasure turned commodity now heralds a society of the sign, of the immaterial up for sale, of the social relation unified in money" (Attali 1985: 3–4). I do not share Attali's assumption that music is properly immaterial. Music has always had a material dimension, existing in both time and space as sound, and embedded in the social, cultural, and historical moment and technological possibility as cultural expression. Its materiality seems more evident in the age of recorded music, as the materiality of the media shapes the experience of reception—which, in turn, feeds back into production. Listening to someone sing "My Way" in the shower, playing a vinyl record of Frank Sinatra crooning "My Way," or watching a YouTube video of Sid Vicious belting out "My Way" in 1978 are materially different experiences, but material ones nonetheless. Even if we leave aside the storage format, there is a materiality to sound that cannot be denied. Whether we listen to two hands clapping, or we synthesize a sound that can be perceived as two hands clapping, sound is physical—vibrations in air that we humans perceive via our natural capacities—both at the points of production and reception. Writes Levitin (2007: 24), "Soundwaves impinge on the eardrums and pinnae (the fleshy part of your ear), setting off a chain of mechanical and neurochemical events, the end product of which is an internal mental image we call pitch ... . Sound is a mental image created by the brain in response to vibrating molecules." As we play music, music plays us. Music's materiality, then, must include all the significant events and artifacts in the life of a sound—it's production, reception, and distribution—and consider how formats for storage and playback intertwine with embodied reception.

CHAPTER THREE

The rhetoric of remix[1]

3.1 Remix as trope

As a technical process and a compositional form, a verb and a noun, the word *remix* foregrounds the centrality of the studio and recording technologies. A remix is a new arrangement, an alternative mix of a composition. The prefix *re* (in Latin, "again, back") signifies remix's reflexive relationship with its source material. It signifies a return, or a repetition of sorts. It is recursive. Rather than suggest that studio recordings document an actual event, the word *remix* acknowledges, and even emphasizes, that most recordings are the end result of a process of recording multiple tracks that are then mixed into a coherent whole by an engineer or producer. "The word 'record' is misleading," wrote Evan Eisenberg (2005: 89) in *The Recording Angel*. "Only live recordings record an event; studio recordings, which are the great majority, record nothing. Pieced together from bits of actual events, they construct an ideal event. They are like the composite photograph of a minotaur."

The history of remixing as an extractive musical practice is notoriously imprecise and, although there exists some controversy over the origins of remixes and the 12-inch vinyl format (Straw 2002: 165–8), the nascent disco and hip-hop scenes in New York City in the 1970s are thought to have made key contributions to the form as we know it. Both popular and scholarly histories of remix also tend to trace the roots of the practice to the sound systems and productions of dub plates or versions in Jamaica in the 1960s.[2] Versions, like remixes, were tailor-made for the dance floor—they

---

[1] Some of the material in this chapter was previously published in an earlier version: Borschke, Margie (2015), "Extended Remix: Rhetoric and History" in Eduardo Navas, Owen Gallagher, and xtine burrough (eds), *The Routledge Companion to Remix Studies*, 104–15. New York: Routledge; and in Borschke, Margie (2011b), "Rethinking the Rhetoric of Remix", *Media International Australia* 141 (November): 17–25. This material appears with the permission of the publishers.

[2] For example, in a newspaper article about remixes, music journalist and DJ Bill Brewster reminds his readers that "the art of taking a track and retooling it for another market, began

made a song easier to use in a dance context and, with any luck, made the
crowd go wild. Remixes as a form of composition were instrumental in
the blossoming of disco as a dance culture and, indeed, a dance craze. Or,
as Simon Frith (1981: 246) wrote at the height of disco's reign, "Disco is
dance music in the abstract, its content determined by form." Later, in the
1980s and 1990s, remixes as a form came to be associated with a number
of global dance, club, and youth cultures (cf. Thornton 1995) from house
to trance to dubstep—and form is arguably all that the seemingly never-
ending multiplication of dance genres (McLeod 2001) and scenes have in
common. Remixes were—and still are—commissioned by recording labels,
but, in some dance genres, records were released with DJs in mind, offering
a cappellas, instrumentals, and bonus beats (percussion-only) on the flip
side to facilitate on-the-fly mixing and sampling, as well as the production
of new unauthorized remixes. In popular-music and cultural studies, this
culture of unauthorized and creative use meant that dance remixes were
seen to be undermining questions about authenticity, troubling notions
about authorship and originality, and upending our understanding of the
relationship between audiences and performers of both live and recorded
music (Marshall 2005: 58–68; Thornton 1995). Although many of the
creators of these unauthorized remixes and bootlegs saw their work differently, these are the qualities and quandaries that cultural scholarship would
extend to other nonmusical forms of digital expression and creativity.

Indeed, "Remix" is seen by many scholars of culture and media to be
the defining characteristic of digital culture (e.g., Deuze 2006; Fitzgerald
and O'Brien 2005; Jenkins 2006a; Lessig 2005, 2008; Manovich 2007a,
2007b; Schütze 2003). According to Lev Manovich "it is a truism today
that we live in a 'remix culture'" (2007a: 39; 2007b), and legal scholar
Lawrence Lessig proclaimed remix to be a new kind of speech (2007),
arguing that, today, the practice is essential to "participation in cultural
life" (2005: 6). Remix, once only a reference to a postproduction process
and product in popular music, has come to signify all that is new, digital,
and participatory. Writing in *Wired*, sci-fi novelist William Gibson (2005:
18) sums up a popular sentiment: "Today's audience isn't listening at all.
It's participating. Indeed, 'audience' is as antique a term as 'record,' the
one archaically passive, the other archaically physical. The record, not the
remix, is the anomaly today. The remix is the very nature of the digital."

In this chapter I challenge and critique these claims, first by analyzing
the etymology of the word and the ascendance of its current metaphorical
usage and second, by using selected cuts from vinyl's history, persistence,
and recent revival to show that what we refer to as remix is not a uniquely

---

with the Jamaican version, a rendering of a song done with the vocals stripped away so the
deejay (Jamaican term for MC) could use the track to add his own live patter at soundsystem
parties" (2009).

digital approach to composition and expression. This critique foregrounds the rhetorical dimensions of remix as a metaphor, highlights the materiality of both analog and digital artifacts and network technologies and offers an argument for understanding how these rhetorical and material dimensions are at once intertwined and independent. I use the shadowy history of remix in dance music to shed light on the metaphors we use to understand the networked present. Remix is such a common trope[3] in twenty-first-century cultural scholarship, that its etymology and changing rhetorical status tend to be glossed over, and the assumptions upon which the metaphor rests are left unexamined. A poetics of the copy can probe this secret history.

Today, the word *remix* has multiple meanings in both scholarly and popular discourse. It is used as a verb to describe a process in audio postproduction, and as a noun to describe the product of that process. Remix also has come to be used as shorthand for many modes of digital expression; it can be used to *describe* media that is made from existing media and it can also be offered to explain the influence of digital technologies on cultural practices and artifacts. Its usage, then, is literal—as in a remix of a piece of recorded music—and figurative, referring to the recombination of existing expressions. The metaphorical use of remix draws an analogy between the literal and the figurative, that is between a specific kind of musical expression—one that occurs after the initial recording, mixdown, and mastering is complete—and other kinds of expressions that are dependent on extant records, recordings, or documentation.

In the context of cultural scholarship, remix appears to be a trope that is no longer conceived as one.[4] By tracking and foregrounding the development of the metaphor over time, I hope to highlight overlooked differences between musical remix and remix as a generic description of a creative approach. A consideration of these differences will reveal that behind this conceptual metaphor lurks a rhetorical agenda, one that plays a prominent role in discussions and debates about copyright and fair use in the age of the Internet. Remix, I will argue, is less a description or explanation of a practice than it is a defense of one.

Today, remix is used to describe the vernacular use of copyrighted material in online discourse, as found in video parodies, Photoshopped images, homemade media, and other forms of expression (e.g., Burgess and Green 2009; Heffernan 2008; Lessig 2008). Online communication,

---

[3]Manovich (2007a) argues that "electronic music and software serve as the two key reservoirs of new metaphors for the rest of culture today, this expansion of the term is inevitable; one can only wonder why it did not happen earlier."

[4]Sebastian Faber (2004: 156) writes, "The slip into ideology occurs when one ceases to distrust the power of language; when simplifications, summaries or short cuts take the place of the complexities that inspired them. Ideology occurs when language, in a Frankensteinian way, 'takes over' from its producers and consumers—which is a way of describing what happens when a trope stops being conceived as one."

particularly in social-media environments, is often indirect, and makes use of copyrighted material to offer comment, to express taste, or to construct and maintain identity and networks. For instance, I might post a copyrighted image to my Twitter feed or to my Facebook profile in order to comment on the news of the day or let my friends know what I like. I might pin images to my boards on Pinterest to build my personal brand. Calling such practices "remix" might seem like a stretch, but these activities (no matter how complex or banal) have become associated with the term (e.g., Davis et al. 2010; Seneviratne and Monroy-Hernandez 2010) because of their reuse of found or extant media. When we talk about remix culture, gossiping on Facebook is as significant a phenomenon as a laptop DJ performance or a YouTube parody video. However, in all of these cases, a copyright holder can contest such uses because they, and they alone, have the exclusive right to *reproduce* their work. When we call such practices "remix," the word functions both as description of a copying practice and as a rhetorical defense of that practice: that said, it does so by downplaying the role of copies and copying in creative expression historically and in the contemporary era. Remix may be a persuasive argument under particular regulatory frameworks, but does it also ask us to avert our gaze from the status of replication in digital networks and in the production and circulation of knowledge? To answer this question, I first explain why metaphor matters, and then show how and why remix came to be used metaphorically.

Does metaphor matter?

Metaphors function by creating an analogy between a familiar source and an unfamiliar or difficult-to-understand target. Or, as linguists George Lakoff and Mark Johnson (1980: 5) theorized, "the essence of metaphor is understanding and experiencing one kind of thing in terms of another." Understanding is facilitated by highlighting some aspects of the source while obscuring other ones. A metaphor does not equate the target and the source, but, instead, highlights similarities and obscures differences (Herman 2008: 235).

If remix functions metaphorically, then remix as a metaphor draws attention to similarities between, for example, a dance-music remix and a video mashup, while ignoring both obvious and subtle differences between such media forms. We understand mashups and remixes as similar in some significant way. In this case, we highlight that both are compositional forms based on the recombination of extant media. When we call both of these things "remixes," we do not concern ourselves with the qualities and aesthetic affordances of different media (video versus audio), with how they are consumed, or with questions about access—all questions that are significant to an historical understanding of the political and economic status of such recordings. We render them similar, based on their reliance on fragmentation and repetition.

Lakoff's analysis of metaphor in everyday language is increasingly influential outside of cognitive linguistics, and his recent work on politics and metaphor is often cited by scholars interested in the legal, social, and cultural questions surrounding intellectual property (e.g., Hagen 2016; Herman 2008; Lessig 2008; Loughlan 2007). It should be noted that, for George Lakoff and Mark Johnson, metaphor is not just an influence on how we think: They claim that our conceptual system is, in essence, metaphorical (1980: 3). This claim is by no means a settled theory in the fields of cognitive linguistics and cognition, and some scholars (notably, Steven Pinker [2007: 235–78]) have raised concerns that such theories are based on faulty assumptions about cognition. So, too, if metaphor creates meaning, how is it that some are able to stand outside of it and see the light, while others are blinded and forced to take refuge in the shadows? But leaving aside questions related to cognition, Lakoff and Johnson's work collecting and analyzing metaphors can help illuminate the use of metaphor and the rhetorical choices made in contemporary discourse about the status of intellectual property.

The rhetorical effects of metaphor

The metaphors we rely upon in political discourse merit analysis because they set scenes, serve as catalysts, and frame debates with the hope of influencing outcomes. Legal scholar Patricia Loughlan (2006: 215–16) has argued that the communicative power of metaphor is often overlooked in the legal context. Using Lakoff and Johnson's (1980) work on metaphor, Loughlan's research identified and analysed the metaphor clusters that exist in the legal discourse about intellectual property. How we talk about intellectual property—that is to say, the metaphors we use—shapes and influences the political debate regarding the scope, duration, and limitations of legal protection. Metaphors can "yield to the interests of a limited class, if that limited class can dominate and manipulate the discourse by *inter alia* the use and misuse of metaphor," writes Loughlan (2006: 222); however, she believes that they can also be resisted and wielded to different ends, as long as metaphor is first recognized as such.

Loughlan is primarily interested in the use of what Lakoff and Johnson call "submerged" metaphors. These are metaphors of which we are not immediately conscious, and that, Loughlan (2006) argues, have a "potential rhetorical effect."[5] It is only by foregrounding the metaphor

---

[5]Frith and Marshall have also noted "the importance of rhetoric for copyright practice" (2004: 4). Their work highlights the rhetorical use of the artist in antidownloading campaigns

as a metaphor that we can start to unpack the assumptions or implied values upon which it was built (2006: 215). Loughlan's aim is to understand how the metaphors about intellectual property might prejudice fair judgment[6] in favor of certain groups, and not others when they are used in legal discourse. In particular, she is concerned that "The 'pirate-predator-parasite' and the 'agrarian' metaphor clusters are rhetorically beneficial for the producers and owners of intellectual property rights, damaging to unauthorized users of intellectual property and possibly damaging to the public interest, in that the metaphors seem to leave no rhetorical room for a public interest argument" (223). If we extend this concern to other metaphors used in digital culture—be it remix, the cloud or the sharing economy—we become alert to possible rhetorical effects.

By the middle of the 2000s, when debates surrounding file sharing and music copyright were polarized and stagnant, Kate Crawford (2005: 31) observed two key narratives: "thieves are downloading music and thereby exploiting struggling artists and the companies that foster their talent, or peer-to-peer services are beneficently taking profits from corrupt infotainment industries to give back to overcharged consumers." Rather than enrich our understanding of cultural practices, Crawford saw this rhetorical standoff as "masking the networked interrelations between the production and consumption of creative work" (2005: 30). The complex relationship between media production and media use was oversimplified and for scholars who were interested in understanding cultural change this impasse was problematic. Crawford (2005: 31–2) argued that "defining the debate as a war between two opposing sides stymies a deeper analysis of downloading practices and networked content, and obscures the legal, philosophical and technological intricacies of the file-sharing phenomenon."

It is under the shadow of this copyright culture war that remix comes to take on its new meaning. Following Loughlan's (2006: 217) approach, I take "academic notice" of the widespread use of "remix" as a general description of digital culture in popular and academic discourse, asking, what does the metaphorical use of remix illuminate, and what does it obscure? Does it benefit some, and not others? My aim is not to dispute the word's contemporary meaning, or to establish correct usage—clearly, many creators call their work "remix"—instead, I want to consider the rhetorical

---

and the attempts of academics such as Siva Vaidhyanathan (2003) to change the terms of the debate away from the metaphors of property and toward a renewed understanding of fair use (2004: 5).

[6]Loughlan (2006: 226–53) explains: "Metaphor functions within a language of moral and political persuasion in helping to portray where the 'right' lies ... metaphor in legal discourse can also help to lock us into the internal logic of an image or set of images, structure our thinking in a way that may weaken or distort our rational decision-making capacities."

work that remix is asked to perform as a way to probe the assumptions and aspirations that lurk behind it. My concern for cultural scholarship is that, as a submerged metaphor, our rhetorical use of "remix" might, as Crawford (2005: 31–2) suggested, also be hindering deeper analysis of "downloading practices and networked content," and obfuscating the long history of copies and copying.

Remix as an explanatory metaphor for digital culture

The current widespread use of remix as an explanatory metaphor for many types of creative expression is curious, given that the metaphor's source—remixes in contemporary pop music—are not particularly well understood as either cultural artifacts or a technological process of composition. The American DJ/Producer Diplo once told *GQ* (Fennessey 2011): "People don't know exactly what I do, they just know I'm 'cool.'" Many remixers complain that even some musicians and record labels who commission remixes are unaware of the process's limits and possibilities.[7] Dance remixes began as a behind-the-scenes technical process—the "magic" of the modern recording studio—and, as such, it is unsurprising that many remain unaware of the details of this process, as well as its possibilities and limitations. However, this also suggests that remix as a conceptual metaphor, one that compares a diverse range of activities of reuse and recombination with the specific activity of dance-music remix, can be seen to be a comparison with an *unfamiliar* source rather than a familiar one. It is this awareness of, but lack of familiarity with, and understanding of, the practice, product, and history of remix that, I argue, the current metaphorical use of remix relies upon. It depends upon the fuzziness of the source, its lack of clear definition, and its somewhat fluid borders. That is, the metaphor has rhetorical effects that are aimed at defending practices rather than probing and understanding them. By tracing the historical rise of remix as a descriptive and explanatory metaphor in the following section, I hope to contribute to a more nuanced understanding of media history and cultural change.

---

[7]One common misunderstanding is that any element of a song can be separated from the other elements. "At the time of writing there are no processors, hardware or software that can reliably remove a single instrument or vocal from a complete mix, so many dub remixes are constructed from a mixture of exposed parts (commonly at the intro and middle eight) and hard-line equalizing to home in [*sic*] and, hopefully, expose specific instruments" (Snoman 2004: 385).

3.2 The extended remix: In the press

When "remix" is evoked as a metaphor for digital culture and its creative techniques, popular music is often acknowledged as the source. What was a postproduction technique and compositional form has broadened since the late 1960s, when the word first began appearing in trade magazines ("remix, n.") for audio engineers and recording artists. In the following sections, I have charted this change in usage and meaning via a survey of mass-media reporting as well as through an examination of some common approaches to remix in cultural scholarship.[8] To examine the use of "remix" in popular discourse, I paid special attention to changes in its frequency and meaning and the context of its use over time. I focused on mainstream news outlets, rather than on niche-industry and cultural publications, because newspaper editorial policies encourage journalists to use standard English and to "avoid colloquialisms, neologisms and jargon," unless they are using them for effect (Corbett 2010). Hence, such publications tend to be conservative about word usage, aiming to communicate with as large an audience as possible by using "plain English." In addition, music coverage in major news outlets in the 1970s, 1980s, and 1990s was extremely limited and tended toward major-label recording artists and top-selling recordings. Hence, even though the market for dance music and remixes was a respectable niche in the 1980s (Lawrence 2003), and remixes were counted in industry certification of wholesale sales, these markets received little coverage outside of industry journals or niche newsletters and fanzines. Because of these factors, I would like to suggest that mentions

---

[8]Some notes on my archive: I examined the use of "remix" in popular discourse, paying special attention to changes in its frequency and meaning and the context of its use over time. In addition to the OED's entries on remix as noun and verb, as well as on their etymologies, I created an archive of almost 500 stories, published between 1969 and 2010 in major English-language newspapers, that contain the word *remix*. To do this, I used the Factiva database (and, in the case of the *New York Times*, I cross-checked results with the paper's online archive). As usage of the word *remix* increased, due to the proliferation of commercially released remixes in the 1990s, I narrowed my search by looking for stories that discussed remixes and samples, or sampling. For the 1990s and 2000s, I searched references to "remix culture." I also surveyed *Billboard* during the 1970s and 1980s, to gain insight into how remix and remixes circulated within the discussions of the mainstream recording industry. *Billboard* plays a special role in histories of disco. Writes William Straw (2002: 176 n.3), "Histories of disco rely heavily on *Billboard* magazine from this period. The magazine's role in pulling the various elements of disco's unfolding history into a relatively unitary chronology cannot be over-estimated. *Billboard* announced the formation of disc jockey pools (and the meetings to organize them) in different cities, organized symposia for disco industry personnel and, perhaps most importantly, published the charts which—until the fragmentation of dance music culture in the late 1970s—held some authority." And, finally, I conducted a Google Ngram to assess the change in use over time in books and selected magazines. I am indebted to lexicographer Jessie Shiedlower for his advice on creating a suitable corpus for my purposes.

and usage in large-circulation papers can be read as an indicator of how "remix" was understood by the average person, rather than of how it was used by specialists at various points in time. My analysis of the data suggests that the semantic change aligns with shifting critical positions on copyright and its expansion. This semantic shift, then, can be understood as a rhetorical phenomenon, and I show that these submerged rhetorical agendas and the emphasis on the mix over the copy, obscures our understanding of copies, fragmentation, and replication in a variety of networks and technologies of production, distribution, and reception. What are the consequences of privileging difference over being just the same?

Popular use: 1970s and 1980s

The first commercial remixes—new versions of songs commissioned by the record labels for the dance market—were released in 1974 (Lawrence 2003: 145–50; "Labels Mix Records for Club Scene" 1974). While the disco phenomenon received coverage in conjunction with the popularity of the 1977 film *Saturday Night Fever,* 12-inch remixed releases generally went without mention in general-interest publications—and were sometimes called "12" disco records" (e.g., "12-inch 45 r.p.m. disco disks A&M experiment," *Billboard,* 1976). The first mention of remix in a news publication indicated that it was interchangeable with "overdub" and was used in an article about direct-to-disc recording (DDR), a technology that, ironically, was capable of neither remixing or overdubbing (Leibovitch 1977). The reporter explains that, by "removing the master tape from the recording process, some of the capabilities afforded to the artist are lost. Taping allows musicians to overdub or remix less than perfect sessions and to delete or change the order of various cuts on the album." Here, remixing is used to refer to a kind of "correction," or a process intended to achieve an ideal representation of a performance (even if this ideal was unattainable). This notion of remix as a "fix" and a production technique is echoed in other articles published in the 1980s.[9] In a Robert Palmer (1980) review of a James (Blood) Ulmer record, the critic slights the U.K. release of the recording by suggesting that "the Rough Trade version of the LP does need a remix." Palmer goes on to explain that he believes that the U.K. mix is somewhat dishonest. He writes, "Mr. Ulmer isn't a domineering soloist like the late Jimi Hendrix, to whom he's often been compared. He voices his

---

[9]A film review in 1984 similarly suggests remix is a correction (Maslin 1984) and one could even view a business news story that suggested investors might want to "remix their portfolio" (Leibovitch 1984) as the first metaphorical use of the term in a major paper but I suspect that it was not a reference to the music production process, but a compound construction just like the salad dressing that readers were asked to "remix" in 1981.

guitar with the other instruments in his bands and has come up with some particularly interesting textures by combining guitar and various horns ... the album's English mix tends to bury [the horns] and to emphasize Mr. Ulmer's guitar in a manner that gives a somewhat misleading impression of what he's up to ... listeners who want to experience the full force of the guitarist's sound and style would do well to wait for the record's American release." Here, we have a critic who assumes his readers are not only interested in the content of the recording, but also in how well the recording represents the artist's style as a live performer. While the writer reveals his bias toward naturalistic and documentary representations, his perspective still stands as an example of how, among a general readership, there was an awareness of the studio process, and, indeed, that a discerning fan might prefer certain mixes over others.

In the 1980s, most mentions of remix in the general-interest press were not in association with illegal use, but with the mainstream music industry. The *New York Times*'s year-end review of pop music, for instance, noted the influence of black dance music on the year's offerings. It stated that "... white pop artists almost unanimously capitulated to the sway of black rhythms. Even Bruce Springsteen, the poet laureate of America's white working-class kids, hired an expert blender of black funk rhythms, Arthur Baker, to remix a 12-inch single for the dance-music market" (Palmer 1984). Notably, while the word *remix* appears just eleven times in the *New York Times* throughout the 1980s, two of these instances refer to Baker's remix of Springsteen's hit "Dancing in the Dark," which was "aimed at clubs and urban (or black) radio" (Pareles 1985), and it is clear that remixes are increasingly associated with the creation of a pop success story. They are presented to the public as a marketing, as well as a studio, technique (Stibal 1977).

The idea that remix was part of the creation of a pop hit is also evident in a 1984 *Financial Times* article about the U.S. debut of the U.K. pop group Frankie Goes to Hollywood (Rapoport 1984). The paper explained to its readers that the marketing and promotion campaign would include "remixing the product, which in other businesses would be called extension. It involves producing new versions of the same song to extend its commercial life. The song is 'remixed' in the studio without the musicians." In 1986, *Billboard*'s Stephanie Shepherd also argued that the major labels saw 12-inch singles as "a tool to broaden the base of an established artist or build the groundwork for pop and black crossover." Once thought of as a disco fad, "today, that fad is strong enough to support a larger number of releases than ever before in history." A *Washington Post* story about the release of "We Are the World" hints at another way remixes helped create hits for the majors when it revealed that "Yesterday CBS filled domestic and international orders for 800,000 copies of the seven-inch single, and with requests for 200,000 copies of John 'Jellybean' Benitez's 12-inch extended dance remix of the song ... the record has already turned gold" (Brown 1985). We know that dance remixes continued to proliferate in the 1980s (Straw 2002), yet these records and the various clubs where they were played received little to no coverage in the major media. But then, at the end of the decade, we begin to see mentions of "seasoned remix producers" (Sinclair 1989b), and remixers are referred to as "hitmakers" (Campbell 1988). In addition, some coverage of specific popular remixed releases can be found (e.g., Brown 1989a, 1989b, 1989c; Cramb 1989; Gliatto 1989; Harrington 1989; Jenkins 1989; MacInnis 1989; Nobles 1989; Potter 1989; Ruffin 1989; Sinclair 1988; 1989a, 1989b).

This coverage nods to the form's popularity and influence and creates the impression that these remixers aren't seen as outsiders, but as a crucial part of the star-making machinery in the industry's production process. (As Toynbee points out [2000: 1–34], this binary of insiders and outsiders fails to capture the dynamics of the music industry, in which figures like remixers are essential professionals—even when they remain marginal or aspirational.) In a 1989 *USA Today* story about the influence and popularity of remixes, remixers are portrayed as moving in on the producers' territory (Jones IV 1989); it is the remixer who can turn "struggling" songs into number-one hits (Jones IV 1989). This article also explains the process and product: "The remix, named for the way the instruments are 'mixed together on separate tracks in a recording studio, are praised as embellishments of the original by those involved in their creation'" (Jones IV 1989). It also offers a definition: "Dance remixes—songs made into different versions by extending them and/or altering the rhythms and instrumentation—are rocking radio airwaves and turning non-dance acts into disco raves" (Jones IV 1989). While this article does not shy away from some of the power plays that are going on behind the scenes, it certainly does not present remix as a shady underground or DIY phenomenon, and it discusses the remixing of major Top 40 acts by well-known DJ remixers, such as Steve "Silk" Hurley. Remixes may have been big in the underground, but they were also part of the system.

Popular use: 1990s

In the 1990s, there is a steady increase in the number of mentions of remix in the mainstream press, and this is also seen in books and magazines from that period. During the decade, remix also begins to become associated with sampling and, in turn, with copyright violation in major general-interest news outlets.[10] Kembrew McLeod (2007: 66) noted that Public

---

[10] A story by Jon Pareles (1989a) suggests that discussions about the artistic merit and legality of sampling were well under way in the late 1980s. Pareles suggest that remixing is one of

Enemy's Harry Allen "vividly remembers that in the late 1980s sampling was the new music-industry Boogey man." Allen believes that these controversies "look[ed] forward to the controversies that would bloom around Napster" (McLeod 2007: 66). Allen's comparison between sampling and Napster is notable in that he is not trying to distance sampling and mixing practices from replication and circulation practices, as some thinkers do (cf. Lessig 2008: 144). Regardless, these early discussions about the legality of sampling were not usually associated with "remix." (There are exceptions: In 1988, it was the remix of the sample-heavy MARRS track, "Pump Up the Volume," that led to a lawsuit from Stock Aitken Waterman [Dafoe 1988] rather than the original track itself.) While the landmark U.S. legal case against Biz Markie (McLeod 2007: 78–9) heightened awareness about the legality of sampling practices, most coverage of remix in the early 1990s continued to be presented as an industry practice, even if the remixers were beginning to receive more mainstream attention. Writing in the *New York Times,* journalist Rob Tannenbaum (1992) discussed the practice:

> Unfamiliar to most record buyers, [Frankie Knuckles] is considered an innovator by dance-music cognoscenti and a last hope by record moguls, who pay well for his expertise. Says a director of dance music at Elektra Records: "Remixers can salvage records." For just a few thousand dollars—pocket change, considering the half-million-dollar budget of a standard album—these audio wizards refashion records to match changing styles. Success has made the practice rampant; one executive estimates that half the singles on the US Top 100 chart are remixed. For instance, there are 24 incarnations of Michael Jackson's "Jam," created by seven remixers.

Remixers may have been known only by the cognoscenti, but remixes were clearly seen as a part of the music industry's production team and apparatus.

While most mainstream music coverage in the archive I compiled did not associate remix with sampling until the mid-1990s, I found one of the earliest metaphorical uses of remix to indicate pastiche or borrowing in the fashion pages. Fashion reporter Cathy Horyn (1991) wrote, "What it comes down to is one giant remix of tough and chic, old and new. Even most of the runway music these days is a remix of old tunes. Nothing is excluded from this cultural sampling." Here, Horyn plays with the fashionable status of the club scene and the prominence of the remix within it, to highlight

---

the many ways that the industry tries to guess what listeners will like, with "the advent of hip-hop's virtuoso disk jockeys and of sound sampling technology, listener-musicians now regularly remake borrowed noise into new material. Sooner or later, their efforts are hoping to force lawmakers to reconsider the notions of copyright and public domain."

a trend of borrowing and referencing among a new generation of fashion designers. Remix, it seems, was ready for its close-up.

Popular use: "Remix culture" in the 1990s

By the mid-1990s, there is a steep increase in mass-media mentions of remix in the mainstream press. Dance remixes were getting more press—and, particularly outside of American media, so was dance-music culture. The first use of the phrase "remix culture" to be found in my search of major news publications was in a 1996 article in the *Observer* about the "Richard Branson Interactive Experience." Jim McClellan (1996) (then a journalist, now an academic) wrote, "Certainly, people who have grown up with the remix culture that's flourished in the clubs have got used to the idea that art/entertainment can be open, unfinished and collaborative." This sentence was intended to contextualize an interactive multimedia experience for readers by drawing an analogy to something they already understood: going out to a dance club or rave. Also worth noting is the phrase "have grown up with the remix culture," which suggests that the cultural phenomenon McClellan was representing was established, something readers of the *Observer* could easily understand. With this early usage in a major publication, we also see how the values that were ascribed to 1990s dance-music cultures—"open, unfinished and collaborative"—began to be applied to what were then new digital-media experiences. The new was made understandable through association with the old.

This close association between "remix culture" and cultures associated with genres of dance music seems to dominate usage in this decade. For example, in each of the five instances of "remix culture" that showed up in a search of major English-language publications in the 1990s, the phrase is tied directly or indirectly to dance music or club culture. A 1997 article about U2 mentions "the hum of dance music's remix culture" (Gundersen 1997); an article about musicians and clubbers using video conferencing quoted multimedia artist and musician Derek Richards as saying that "club culture is the natural home for multimedia and new technology … . Modern digital technology enables fast communication and the ability, literally, to sample and remix culture" (Carter 1997); a profile of American musician Bill Laswell argues that remix culture had done away with the canonical masterpiece, "with some help from new playback formats and the availability of such a vast quantity of music that the notion of consensus seem futile" (Williams 1998); and, in a review of a Massive Attack singles compilation (one that included many remixes), the critic sniffed that "remix culture has its moments but not nearly so many as its practitioners imagine" (Spencer 1998). The key point I want to make here is that, throughout the 1990s, remix and remix culture are still very closely associated with music production and styles of music making. A Google Ngram for "remix culture" in the period similarly shows increased use of the phrase, beginning in the mid-1990s. The examples in question are predominantly in music publications, such as *CMJ, Billboard* and the *Wire*—and, notably, in Negativeland's 1995 publication *Fair Use: The Story of the Letter U and the Numeral 2*, which is about lawsuits against them.[11]

Popular use: 2000s

In the first decade of the twenty-first century, I found evidence in my archive to suggest that "remix" and "remix culture" underwent a shift in everyday usage. Though it is still used to refer to official reworkings of musical compositions (as in a remix of Britney Spears's latest offering), remix is now widely used in conjunction with a variety of other media forms made from extant media. For example, a 2006 story in the *Guardian* stated, "Remix culture now exists beyond music with dozens of remade trailers on YouTube (search for remix trailer)" (Dee 2006). As the decade progresses, "remix culture," synonymous with dance or rave culture in the 1990s, is now associated with digital and network technologies and, increasingly, with amateur, rather than professional, production. In particular, remix is often used to indicate *unauthorized* remixes; that is, copyright violations, and the circulation of those productions on the Internet.

A 2001 story about Bjork's Internet marketing strategy discusses a website that had functioned as a clearinghouse for fan-made remixes since 1997. It quotes the U.K. producer Matthew Herbert as saying, "Digitally remixing music 'is a new genre, and no one seems to have quite realized it yet … . It's like a recipe. You take the ingredients that they've already got and construct a different dish from it'" (Mirapaul 2001). In this story, remix cuts both ways: On the one hand, it is a mainstream exposure of an extant grassroots culture—people were recutting and trading Bjork songs, and what was notable was that the singer was embracing the practice instead of suing her fans—and, on the other hand, remix is presented as something new and, significantly, something digital.

The expansion of "remix culture," and the notion that it exists in opposition to corporate culture, is also evident in coverage of Creative Commons, an alternative licensing scheme launched in the U.S. by Lawrence Lessig and others in 2001. A 2004 article entitled "New UK Copyright License to Enable 'Remix Culture'" is exemplary of the new usage of "remix" and "remix culture":

---

[11]David Toop (1995) also used the phrase used to describe the increasingly hybrid flavor of Indian pop culture.

A new flexible form of copyright for creative material is set to launch in Britain next month, at a time when "remix culture" is gaining in popularity despite the fact that its often illegal ... . Creative Commons ... has created a copyright license that lets musicians and authors decide what limits to put on their creations—enabling DJs, for example, to remix legally ... . Inexpensive software has made it possible for anyone to remix songs or video, and distribute his or her creation on the Internet. But rights holders rarely approve of unauthorized mixes and in some cases have filed suits to enforce their rights. (Pasick 2004)

In this example, remix is no longer the purview of top-down music-marketing executives. Instead, it has become associated with bottom-up practices that are enabled by cheap digital technologies. Again, we see the increasingly common notion that remix is something done without permission, and also that permission is difficult to obtain. This new association between "remix culture" and Creative Commons was also evident in a 2005 *New York Times* story about unofficial podcast tours of MOMA, in which the writer refers to Lawrence Lessig as the "guru of so-called remix culture" (Kennedy 2005).

As the decade progressed, remix culture was increasingly used as a synonym for cultural production associated with the Internet and with digital production using extant media. A review of a show at the Cooper-Hewitt design museum sums up this new understanding of remix as commentary when it declares, "The most significant message the Triennial offers is that originality itself has been redefined. Living as we do in a cut-and-paste 'remix culture,' where nothing is devoid of commentary of context, what's new now isn't so much a look or style but a perspective" (Von Hahn 2007).

By 2008, "remix culture" can be found semi-regularly in the mainstream press with regard to discussions about a wide range of media production, consumption, and distribution activities (Freeman-Greene 2009; Fry 2008). One story claims that "our era's 'remix culture' is a vast exercise in intel-lectual-property modding, one that included everything from sampling to YouTube video parodies, from software 'mash-ups' to customized action figures for sale on eBay and the intricate web of blogs" (Fry 2008). Remix is the culture that challenges intellectual property (Nuttall 2008) and is associated with the "democratisation" of media and DIY cultural expression (Freeman-Greene 2009). In some articles, it does so while still nodding to the metaphor's musical roots: "'Certainly things like structure, flow, revelation, juxtaposition and other elements of DJing and mixing are considered an art,' said Mr. Plagenhoef [the editor in chief of *Pitchfork*] ... . 'Remix culture is a form of creative expression in its own right'" (Williams 2009). Remix culture is not only new, but a force to be reckoned with: a game changer, a force of resistance, and something that culture had suppressed for too long.

In just four decades we witnessed a shift in the usage and meaning of "remix," veering away from its associations with the music industry and towards vernacular digital culture. "Remix" is now commonly used as an all-purpose cultural term associated with a wide variety of creative, unauthorized reuse that flourished with the mass uptake of digital technologies and is facilitated by broadband Internet access. But does this shift matter? What assumptions about culture underpin this newer metaphorical usage? Does it obscure something about copies in its defense of usage that violates copyright? To begin to answer such questions, I turn to the use of this newer meaning of "remix culture" in the academic literature, where it has been enthusiastically adopted as a description of culture.

3.3 The extended remix: Scholarly use

In contemporary cultural scholarship, the ascendance of "remix" as a general descriptor of cultural production coincided with improvements in the speed, ease, and affordability of digital technologies and networks in the first decade of the twenty-first century. "Remix culture" began to be invoked as a description of cultural practices, artifacts, or phenomena that are made with digital technologies. In some circles, the mediated process of electronic postproduction is now generalized to refer to any kind of human creativity or communication (cf. Manovich 2005; Markham 2013; Navas 2009, 2010), and it has come to be associated with contemporary challenges to copyright and intellectual property (Lessig 2008), along with grassroots social and political empowerment (e.g., Edwards and Tryon 2009; Markham 2013).

Most scholars acknowledge that the meaning of "remix" has expanded (or, if we wish to continue to borrow from the language of dance music, extended) beyond its original scope (e.g., Manovich 2005; Markham 2013; Navas et al. 2015). Some acknowledge that the origins of the technique/form can be found in the analog era (e.g., Diakopoulos et al. 2007: 133), although the role of analog technologies in remix often tends to be glossed over, even as we recognize the influence of precursors such as 1960s Jamaican dub (Schütze 2003). The implication is that the digital phenomenon is qualitatively and quantitatively different (e.g., Davis et al. 2010; Lessig 2008).

This expanded understanding of remix is associated with cut/copy/paste technologies (Navas 2010: 157; Schütze 2003), social networking (Davis et al. 2010; Markham 2013), user-generated content (Lee 2008), "commons-based peer production" (Benkler 2006: 60), participatory media (Jenkins 2009), distributed authorship (Logie, in Navas et al. 2015: 296–309) and a variety of other concepts, descriptions, neologisms, and buzzwords associated with networked culture at the turn of the twenty-first century. Many thinkers conceptualize remix as a challenge to corporate production and the ownership of culture (Russell, in Navas et al. 2015: 217–23; Schütze 2003), which, in turn, either threatens late capitalism, or are just what capitalism needs to flourish in digital ecologies (Lessig 2004; Mason 2008). As I will elucidate, remix is all-encompassing: It is presented as new at the same time as it is proclaimed as old as the hills; it is a natural phenomenon that is simultaneously an electronic and a technological one. Or, as the title of a Web video series puts it, "Everything Is a Remix" (Ferguson 2010). It is precisely because *everything is not a remix* that we should think about how this metaphor works and what its rhetorical effects might be.

Critical assumptions and arguments

It is clear that the use and meaning of remix has changed in the last half century: Its early associations with dance music and the production of 12-inch disco records by both independent and major labels between the 1970s and 1980s overlapped with an understanding of remix as a studio technique that was first associated with the niche marketing of popular songs to music scenes or "genre cultures" (Toynbee 2000: 102–29), and, in the 1980s and 1990s, was aligned with unauthorized sampling (often by participants in the "genre cultures" that were identified, targeted, and perpetuated in the first place.) This association of remix with the music industry and with music culture (both broadly defined) persists, but it has also given way to the more metaphorical understanding of remix in circulation today. "Remix" has come to mean media made from parts of extant media—and, for some, it is used to describe creativity in general, offering a tacit critique of romantic notions of authorship and promoting an understanding of knowledge as collaborative. Similarly, the idea of a "remix culture" has broadened from references to music culture in the 1990s to digital or networked culture today. That is to say, we are soaking in it.

In the following sections, I attempt to tease out some of the assumptions about media, culture, and society that lurk behind this current usage of remix in cultural scholarship. Following Ted Friedman's interrogation of how techno-utopianism functions in discourse about digital technologies (Friedman 1999, 2005), and David Schulz's (2002) analysis of technological determinism as a rhetorical trope, I want to consider what sorts of assumptions the metaphor makes about past, present, and future technologies and cultures. What sorts of assumptions does it make about political and economic systems, individual agency and moral obligations? What does it critique, and who or what does it legitimize? While Friedman aims to evaluate the underlying political ideals and assumptions that are revealed by discourse about the future and the rhetoric of technological determinism, Schulz (2002: 6) asks, "What political and socio-economic processes do political and popular uses of technological determinism naturalize, obscure, and institutionalize?" With an eye toward understanding how remix functions as a rhetorical trope, I ask similar questions about how it is used to explain or describe technology and its relationship to cultural production, distribution, and consumption. What kind of story is being told about remix, and what is the meaning of that story? How does this current narrative compare and contrast with the particular history of remixes in the music industry and in dance culture? Remix, I will reveal, has a particular history, one that veers from current narratives about remix and its underlying values, and a consideration of this disjuncture, I hope, will prove productive in our understanding of the intersection of technology, culture, and cultural artifacts.

Remix is a common trope in twenty-first-century cultural scholarship, a metaphor that attempts to explain, understand, and often *defend* creative works (especially those produced with digital technologies) as analogous to dance remixes typical of the late twentieth century. In the following sections, I will highlight some common assumptions that seem to circulate in critical discourse. Can the assumptions behind this broad metaphorical usage of remix accommodate its namesake? If not, what does this disjuncture reveal about particular assumptions lurking beneath the metaphor?

Given that "remix culture" has come to be so closely associated with Lawrence Lessig and his argument for copyright reform in the face of its expansion, I will devote much of this analysis to untangling Lessig's particular understanding of remix from his rhetorical use of the term. It should be noted that while remix may now be associated with Lessig's work, it is a term he has come to use in recent years. His earlier books (Lessig 2002, 2004) explored and documented the tensions surrounding intellectual property, corporate control, and personal freedom, but they did not employ remix as a metaphor. My intention in this section is not to represent or critique Lessig's work as a whole but to interrogate the rise of remix within recent discourse. As legal scholar Steven Hetcher (2008: 1871) points out in his study of the social norms that regulate fan fiction and remix culture, Lessig never defines remix in his 2008 book *Remix: Making Art and Commerce Thrive in the Hybrid Economy*. Instead we are left to tease out his understanding of the term from the examples he gives, as well as from his discussions of those examples.

I have identified a number of themes or assumptions that are common to many uses of remix. Woven throughout Lessig's conceptualization of remix are four themes that prove problematic. First is the claim to newness— that remix is a *new* kind of speech, a *new* kind of writing, a *new* form of political expression, etc. Second, and related to the idea that remix is new, is the claim that remix is *digital*. Third is the idea that remixes represent a return to a flourishing culture of amateurs (by association, this idea also subscribes to a folk ideology of participation that is caught up with a gift economy). Finally is the claim that remix should be understood as a generational practice that is associated with the current generation of teenagers and young adults.[12]

3.4 Lawrence Lessig's "Remix Culture"

American legal scholar and copyright-reform activist Lawrence Lessig (2002, 2004, 2008) makes a persuasive argument about the overreach of U.S. copyright law in an era of digital and network technologies. He has made groundbreaking contributions to our understanding of how recent changes in these laws overreach their intentions, also launching important experiments by way of creating alternative licensing schemes with the introduction of Creative Commons. From the standpoint of social and cultural history, however, Lessig's use of remix as a general descriptor of cultural practice and output is problematic: This usage seems unable to accommodate its musical namesake and obscures a particular history of media use in recent music culture, one that offers important lessons about reception and distribution. For Lessig, remix is understood to be a digital-media practice and expression that is made by copying, editing, and recombining pre-existing digital media. It is used to describe a wide variety of sample-based and digitally manipulated music, video, text, and mixed media. As the preceding discussion showed, "remix" has expanded beyond its origins in the world of audio postproduction—most notably, in music production—where, since the 1970s, it has been used to describe the process of making an alternate version of a song (usually a dance version) by manipulating the tracks contained on the multi-track master.

Today, remixes are often considered a contested form of expression because many contemporary examples violate the copyright of the work they sample. The student who edits together snippets of Disney's *Winnie the Pooh* and replaces the soundtrack with audio from *Apocalypse Now*, for instance, is in violation of Disney's exclusive right to copy its work. (Unless, of course, the student has paid to license Disney's work. The example in question, an impressive analog cutup made by a Toronto art student in 1987, most certainly did not seek such permission [Mackenzie 2007].) Lessig, along with many other media scholars (notably, Vaidhyanathan 2003: 29), asserts that the regulation of expression was not the intention of copyright law.

---

[12] Writes Lessig, "I worry about the effect this [copyright] war is having upon our kids. What is this war doing to them? Who is it making them? How is it changing how they think about normal, right-thinking behavior? What does it mean to a society when a whole generation is raised as criminals" (Lessig 2008: xvii). Lessig's rhetorical use of "remix" gives way to the emotional plea that, at the very least, we think of the children.

His concern is that current copyright regimes criminalize artists like Gregg Gillis—a laptop DJ-producer, known as Girl Talk, who composes music using hundreds of recognizable samples from commercial pop songs. Lessig (2008) claims that Girl Talk's compositions, his "remixes," or mashups, should be recognized as a *new* form of expression, and that, moreover, they should be recognized as a kind of speech (Lessig 2007) worthy of protection under the Constitution of the United States, where freedom of expression is enshrined in the Bill of Rights. Lessig further wants to argue that remix is not only a form of individual expression, but should also be understood as a participatory mode of creativity and communication, one that marks a return to Jeffersonian ideals of democratic discourse. In *Remix,* twenty-five-year-old Girl Talk is Lessig's stand-in for the yeoman farmer, a figure poised to protect civil society from the corrupting interests of established business models (and, presumably, aging rock stars).

But how did remix—a production technique whose origins are intertwined with the marketing and promotion of popular songs, and a form whose greatest ambition is to ensure that we can get our groove on—come to represent such heady aims? How did it come to describe so much more?

The following analysis is based on a close reading of Lessig's argument in *Remix.* I compare and contrast his understanding of remix with scholarship on the technique's history and contemporary status in dance music.

New media: New scale or new meaning?

Remix is often portrayed as a new practice and artifact. Journalist and advocate of "punk capitalism" Matt Mason (2008: 80), for example, presents remix as "nothing less than a new way to communicate." This obsession with the "new" as a source of cultural power and change is characteristic of modernist thinking and its preoccupation with breaking with the past and smashing traditions. Yet, as media theorist Charles Acland (2007: xv) argues, a preoccupation with the new also "betrays a concern about the past." Similarly, Ted Friedman (2005: 11) argues that debates about the present contain traces of the past. These two observations prompt two key questions: (1) What concerns about the past are submerged in the remix metaphor? and (2) If remix is a rhetorical response to current debates about copyright, then can an analysis of how remix is wielded yield insights about how we understand the recent past?

This dance between the old and the new is evident throughout *Remix.* In his book, Lessig presents remix as a new expression that is simultaneously a return to something familiar from the not-so-distant past. He would like to convince us that remix is a new form of expression, one made possible by technological progress and enabled by the mass uptake of digital and network technologies at the turn of the twenty-first century (2008: 18).

Simultaneously, Lessig wants to claim that this digital-remix culture also marks a return to something that was temporarily lost in the twentieth century, something "natural" that this new, technologically enabled cultural practice has reinvigorated. For Lessig, these new forms of expression mark a return to such core American values as free speech. He attempts to convince us that this evolution is made possible by technological progress, but is threatened by the copyright laws based on technologies of the twentieth century. As a new old thing, Lessig's conceptualization of remix attempts to naturalize current digital-media expression, while rendering other sorts of mediated expression artificial.

What kinds of assumptions about technology are implied by this characterization of remix as new? Lessig (2008: xviii) describes contemporary life as "a world in which technology begs all of us to create and spread creative work differently from how it was created and spread before." Even the language used in such a statement lends a sense of agency to digital technologies. Technologies have expectations and natural trajectories: They plead with us. What is new about remix is intertwined with assumptions that technology develops in an inevitable and progressive fashion—assumptions that are disputed by Friedman (1999, 2005) and others.

Lessig's understanding of remix as an inevitable consequence of technological change is based on an assumption that technology is progressive, that old technologies are rendered obsolete by newfangled ones. Lessig describes radio as giving way to TV (2008: 30), just as vinyl gave way to eight-tracks, then to cassettes, and so on (2008: 39). He assumes that if a technology is possible, it is inevitable—and that culture will be pushed forward in its wake. Friedman has argued that technological determinism such as this is typical of the libertarian ethic that dominates popular thinking about the Internet (1999: 27; 2005), and has become computer culture's "commonsense theory of history," despite evidence to the contrary (Friedman 1999: 105). Technological determinists, he argues, often speculate about the future by ignoring the past (Friedman 1999: 14), a tendency that is a particular problem for Lessig's understanding of remix as "new" in the face of its own lengthy history.

Schulz argues that "deterministic laden discourse enables the rhetor to make irrefutable prophecies, deflect responsibility when a technology proves deficient, downplay opposing positions and assert their own authority as seers of the future" (2002: 38). Friedman's analysis of cyberutopianism offers another insight into how technological determinism functions in an argument such as Lessig's. Writes Friedman, "Technological determinism functions as a cover, authorising a safe space in which to articulate utopian values" (1999: 7). Lessig's understanding of remix as an inevitable consequence of technological progress constructs what Friedman calls a "utopian sphere," a space where ideas about the future "can be projected and discussed without mockery or scorn" (1999: 5–6). The rhetoric of remix shelters Lessig from a key libertarian dilemma, one that copyright seems to bring to the fore: How can we simultaneously protect free speech and free markets? Writing about inherent contradictions between free speech and copyright in the U.S., legal scholar Rebecca Tushnet (2004) emphasizes how this libertarian dilemma brought about a troubling emphasis on transformative use over fair use. She writes, "By confining First Amendment analysis to the question of whether a particular use is an exception to a copyright owner's exclusive rights because it is transformative and critical, courts manage to preserve a libertarian vision of free speech fundamentally inconsistent with the overall structure of copyright. Paradoxically, the intersection of free speech and fair use serves to narrow both concepts rather than to preserve the multiple meanings and purposes of each" (2004: 547).

I will return to this question in my discussion of the emphasis on transformative use in Lessig's argument. But, for now, I want to highlight how Lessig's assumptions about technology and its effects allows him to imagine a future where individual expression is unfettered by corporate interests, a world where the little guy can compete with the multinational, the amateur with the professional, while copyright still acts as an incentive (even an inspiration!)[13] to create (2008: xvi), and where markets remain beyond question (2008: 121).

Lessig (2008: 18) dates this shift in production and distribution to "the turn of the last century;" that is, c. 2000. We can assume that Lessig is well aware that digital computers were commonplace personal and business technologies before 2000, and that the advent of the World Wide Web and related technologies in the early 1990s is understood to mark the rise of popular and commercial adoption of the Internet (Flichy 2007: 61–2). While Lessig is not explicit about the changes taking place c. 2000, it seems reasonable that this perceived break is related more to the improvement of existing digital and network technologies, and the mass adoption of relatively affordable high-speed broadband, than it is to the introduction of new technologies *per se*. That is, when digital computers and network technologies became cheaper, easier to use, and more efficient, more people

---

[13] Both copyleft scholars, such as David M. Berry and Giles Moss (2008: 8, 29), and advocates of "thin" copyright, such as Siva Vaidhyanathan (2003) and Rebecca Tushnet (2004: 541), are skeptical about claims that copyright acts as an incentive to create, given the existence of cultural works that predate copyright and nonmarket production today. Vaidhyanathan has also pointed out that the incentive assumption is not only untested, but untestable (McLaren 2004). In a critique of the Creative Commons, Berry and Moss also argue that the envisaged future looks a lot like the present. They write, "We argue that the Creative Commons project on the whole fails to confront and look beyond the logic and power asymmetries of the present. It tends to conflate how the world is with what it could be, with what we might want it to be ... . We find an organisation quick to accept the specious claims of neo-classical economics, with its myopic 'incentive' models of creativity and an instrumental view of culture as a resource" (Berry and Moss 2008: 29).

were inclined to experiment with and use these technologies. What the turn of the twenty-first century must represent, then, is participation on a larger scale—all thanks to improvements in digital and network technologies. So, while, on the one hand, the technology is seen to make us do things, on the other, its effects are not relevant unless they are en masse. Yet, it is under the cover of technological determinism that Lessig begins to highlight the fact that the tools of cultural production and distribution are now in the hands of the masses. Lessig (2008: 69) writes,

> Using the tools of digital technology—even the simplest tools, bundled into the most innovative modern operating systems—anyone can begin to "write" using images, or music, or video. And using the facilities of a free digital network, anyone can share that writing with anyone else.

For Lessig, these improvements in technology change the average person's relationship with both cultural products and cultural production. In the past, we merely watched Dorothy skip down the yellow brick road; now that *The Wizard of Oz* has been rendered digital, we can manipulate the video and audio components of the film. We can use the Scarecrow to "speak," or gain access to the man behind the curtain to "write." I will return to the special status afforded speaking and writing in understanding expression, as well as to the idea that reception is passive. But, for now, we should note that, for Lessig (2008: 18), this possibility, coupled with the increased scale of technological adoption (thanks to ease-of-use and efficiency), causes a shift in "cultures of creativity." The shift, technologically driven and determined in this view, is sure to do more good than harm. Cautions Schulz (2002: 191), "Determinism is manifest when history and time are used to demonstrate that technological change is empirically inescapable."

Drawing an analogy with computer memory or data storage, Lessig (2008: 20–31) describes this new culture of remix as "Read/Write," in contrast to the "Read-Only" media culture of the twentieth century. This analogy presents a highly oversimplified view of cultural engagement in the recent past. In the so-called Read-Only culture, Lessig claims that the available technologies of production, distribution, and consumption prevented the modification of either cultural artifacts or cultural commodities (e.g., vinyl records, televised broadcasts, etc.). Culture was something that was made by professionals (think Disney and EMI) and passively consumed by everyone else. It was the era of the couch potato.

"The twentieth century," writes Lessig (2008: 29), "was the first time in the history of human culture when popular culture had become professionalized, and when the people were taught to defer to the professional." As Lessig understands it, the mass adoption of digital and network technologies put an end to the privileged position enjoyed by professionals in the twentieth century, as these new and improved technologies enabled and prompted users—even "beg[ed] us" (2008: xvii)—to participate in a "Read/Write" culture, a new world constructed out of the digital "tokens" of the "Read-Only" culture of yesterday. This "new" culture of creativity might have been the result of the inevitability of technological progress, but it simultaneously marks the return of the influence of amateurs on culture. As such, Lessig wants to persuade us that remix is not so much a new cultural artifact as a natural one. And, as with the values that lay at the heart of the American Bill of Rights and its defense of free speech, remix represents natural rights that are not to be tampered with. Speaking of copyright reforms, Lessig (2008: xix) writes, "These alternatives would achieve the same ends that copyright seeks, without making felons of those who naturally do what new technologies encourage them to do." Elsewhere, Lessig (2008: 56–7) writes, "In the end, my aim is to draw all these forms [of remix] together to point to a kind of speech that will seem natural and familiar. And a kind of freedom that will feel inevitable." So, in mounting this very clever legal defense of the use of copyrighted materials within the existing understanding of copyright, Lessig is doing precisely what Schulz argues technological determinists do: He uses the assumption of technological determinism to naturalize remix, thus appealing to the concept of natural rights that sits at the heart of the U.S. Bill of Rights, a document that enshrines the right to free expression. This is not an argument for radical change, he seems to assure his readers, but a call for balance and reasoning in the face of technological change. What better event than technology to coax people from the couch?

Falling down the analog hole, or why we never were "read-only"

Yet, while Lessig would like us to understand "remix" as a kind of continuity (albeit one with a century-long interruption) and form of natural expression, the sense in which remix is new is also deeply intertwined with digital technologies. Using remix to signify the digital character of contemporary expression is common enough among popular commentators and critics. Recall Gibson's (2005: 18), pronouncement that "the remix is the very nature of the digital" which echoes Lessig's "Read/Write" metaphor. Others have similarly highlighted the digital in their definitions of remix (e.g., Diakopoulos et al. 2007: 133; Fitzgerald and O'Brien 2005; Hetcher 2009: 1872). However, the analog history of remix prompts us to ask whether the reliance on the digital in these arguments, the claim that remix is a new form of digital expression, is misplaced.

In Lessig's (2008: 51) view, remix is a quintessentially digital phenomenon, enabled by the existence of digital media and digital technologies. He writes,

> With the introduction of digital tokens of [Read-Only] culture and, more important, with the widespread availability of technologies that could manipulate digital tokens of RO culture, digital technology removed the constraints that had bound culture to particular analog tokens of RO culture. (Lessig 2008: 38)

Analog formats, such as vinyl records, were "naturally" constrained, explains Lessig (2008: 37), because consumer-generated copies were inferior to the original, reproduction technologies were rare, and, "for the ordinary consumer, RO tokens were to be played, not manipulated." These "natural" constraints of the analog world, he believes, were abolished by the birth of digital technologies (2008: 38).

This portrait fails to acknowledge the innovative use of analog technologies, and also seems to ignore their role in the creation of the first remixes and edits (as I will discuss in the next chapter). When Lessig writes (2008: 38) that vinyl records "really limited the consumer's ability to be anything other than 'a consumer,'" he overlooks the fact that it was DJs (end users; that is, consumers and not producers) who, in tandem with playback technologies, developed innovative techniques that liberated sounds found on fixed recordings to make on-the-fly compositions. These real-time sound collages, would inspire and shape the aesthetic of many of the earliest remixes and edits (Lawrence 2008). Lessig never acknowledges that the origins of remix as both production technique and cultural artifact were first shaped by analog technologies and formats—which is a fact, whether we are talking about a record label granting a remixer access to an expensive analog studio, clean master tapes, and a flat fee, or about a DJ making cheap tape edits, without permission, by transferring the sounds on vinyl to reel-to-reel tape and manipulating the resulting recording. Both these scenarios are evident in the development of remix as a technique and an artifact. This analog history of remix matters—and it troubles Lessig's narrative of progressive technologies.

Speak, memory: The generation of meaning and a history of reuse

Lessig's understanding of remix as a new kind of speech merits special consideration since this conceptualization directly shapes his understanding of remix as a generator of meaning. Remix is new for Lessig because it exemplifies this shift toward a "Read/Write" culture and represents, in his opinion, a new kind of compositional tool, by which he intends a new way to build and convey meaning. He writes, "Remix is collage; it comes from combining elements of RO culture; it succeeds by leveraging the meaning created by the reference to build something new" (2008: 76). Lessig is not alone in suggesting that remix, as a technique, is dependent on appropriation, arrangement, juxtaposition, and superimposition of meaning. But I argue that his preoccupation with the production of meaning as a way to understand remix suggests that his definition is not informed by the history and continued use of remix as a musical production technique in dance music, or with dance remixes as cultural artifacts. If Lessig's definition of remix is unable to accommodate its namesake's continued existence as well as its past, then his rhetorical use of remix as a signifier of the new is compromised. Also compromised and intertwined with his conceptualization of remix as new is the idea that remixes are digital.

Remix has a history that predates digital technologies, and, therefore troubles Lessig's understanding of remix as a digital phenomenon. The first recordings that were made and sold as "remixes" date back to the 1970s, in New York City (Lawrence 2003; Straw 2002), but the practice of commissioning and using alternate versions of a song also owes its origins to 1960s Jamaica, where one-offs, or dubplates, were commissioned by sound systems and record labels to create excitement on the dance floor in advance of a record's release—or to get customers into the clubs (Toynbee 2000: xvii). The birth of "remixes" in the discos of New York is closely associated with the ascendance of a new dance culture that used recorded music in tandem with playback technologies to create nonstop dancing; dance remixes also became a way to market a song to a different crowd. DJs were instrumental in the development of technique and remix aesthetics. Writes Tim Lawrence (2009: 129), "DJs had been using their specialist knowledge of the dance floor dynamic to remix twelve-inch singles for the commercial market since the summer of 1976." Not all alternate versions were commissioned and paid for by labels: Some DJs were also making unauthorized edits of songs and pressing them on acetate. As Lawrence has argued, this practice would have an impact on the growing aesthetic. As I will argue in greater detail in the next chapter, access is a key distinction between edits and remixes. Remixers and edit makers worked with a different set of sonic possibilities because they had access to different sets of sounds. Edit makers, who were constrained by the mixed sounds of the commercial release, would listen for certain sonic elements in a song such as a drum break. Remixers, on the other hand, had access to the multi-track master recordings and were thus able to isolate and manipulate individual layers in a mix, a fact that expanded their aesthetic options. Michael Chanan (1995: 147) explains: "With multi-track recording, not only could parts of different takes be edited together but individual parts could be altered without changing others played alongside. Each track can be manipulated separately; different effects can be added; the tracks can then be recombined and balanced with other tracks and the final mix sent to another recorder ... . it also creates new musical possibilities; the new mode of production therefore begins to turn the recording engineer—the mixer—into a musical creator of a new kind." Musical remixes work with the nature of "modern popular music as processive ... . It is constructed in a sequence of multiple takes, overdubs and editing" (Toynbee 2000: 55). A remixer makes a new version by adding and subtracting tracks, or by altering the pitch, equalization, dynamics, tempo etc., and rearranging the composition. Compare these definitions with Lessig's (2008: 69) understanding of remix as an act equivalent to quotation and occurring at different layers:

> They remix, or quote, a wide range of "texts" to produce something new. These quotes, however, happen at different layers. Unlike text, where the quotes follow in a single line—such as here, where the sentence explains, "and then a quote gets added"—remixed media may quote sounds over images, or video over text, or text over sounds. The quotes thus get mixed together. The mix produces the new creative work—the "remix."

Most of the creative work that Lessig cites in *Remix* combines fragments or samples from two or more media sources rather than from a single song or video. Referencing via juxtaposition and superimposition, as well as knowledge about the primary source, are crucial to his understanding of remix.

There are two problems with this understanding of remix. First, it conflates remixing with the technique of sampling—that is, isolating a fragment of some media source, or quoting it, within the mixing of layers. Second, if we consider the musical practice of remixing, we find that it is not necessarily dependent on quotation as such. When a remixer drops out the vocals, filters the horn sounds, or adds a percussion track, they are not referencing the tracks that make up the song, but using them differently (or not at all). Remixing doesn't have to be *about* the song; it can just be a new arrangement or iteration of the song.

Lessig's emphasis on the generation of meaning via the practice of referencing and his preoccupation with creating conversations *between* media sources and meanings are accompanied by a judgment about what constitutes a "good" remix. Lessig writes, "Remixed media succeed when they show others something new; they fail when they are trite or derivative" (2008: 82). In other words, for Lessig, "good" remixes build new meaning by playing with the meaning of old. Dance remixes, however, are derivative by definition. They are a new version. In dance music, remixes began as DJ tools, and the aim was to make a song easier for a DJ to *use*: The remix might make the song more danceable, or more suitable for radio play. A cappellas, dubs, bonus beats, and extended mixes were versions that made it easier for a DJ to mix such a track with other records (that is, to play them simultaneously), while other remixes appeal to certain styles or genres of music (e.g., a label might commission a house version of a song or a drum and bass mix), or hope for additional attention (and sales) by being attached to a well-known remixer. Complicating matters further, there are occasions when only the remix is released or known (some remixes can be seen as attempts to save bad songs from themselves), with no "original" for the listener to reference. My point is not that this technical meaning of remix has priority over the extension of the metaphor (and, of course, the techniques used to remix are indistinguishable from the tools used to mix any number of tracks), but that this "new" extended understanding of remix must also be able to accommodate the technique's origins and continued use. Remixes in pop music didn't leverage meaning; they hinged on use.

Another complication is that the form itself was shaped by reception. Lawrence (2009: 125) writes, "As the social ritual of nonstop dancing began to take shape, DJs realized they had to 'follow' as well as 'lead' their newly energized crowds." Remix began as a technique that was driven by the pleasures of the body—the desire to make a body move in time with the music and with other bodies. They were not predicated on a change in meaning, but on a change in use (e.g., more booty-shaking, more radio-friendly, easier-to-use). Lessig's argument, however, cannot accommodate or defend these remixes because they do not align with the values loaded into his definition.

By making the production of meaning central to his understanding of the practice of remixing, Lessig tends to value complexity and difficulty as a way to justify that practice's worth. He writes,

> But anyone who thinks remixes or mash-ups are neither original nor creative has very little idea about how they are made or what makes them great. It takes extraordinary knowledge about a culture to remix it well. The artist or student training to do it well learns far more about his past than one committed to this (in my view, hopelessly naive) view about "original" creativity ... . The form makes demands on the audience; they return the demands in kind. (Lessig 2008: 93)

So how does a popular dance remix fare when held up to these standards? Dance remixes are, by definition, not original. That said, unless the listener is familiar with the song being reworked, they may not be aware they are listening to a remix. Sonically speaking, a remix and an original are on equal footing, and remixes in dance music stand as a counterexample to the claim that remix as a form makes different demands on an audience: It doesn't necessarily apply. Nor does the idea that it takes "extraordinary knowledge of a culture" to remix (or to listen) well. While dance remixers who have a highly trained ear and are experienced at playing records to a dance floor are no doubt going to be better equipped to make good decisions about what aspects of song to alter or rearrange in order to find a new groove in the mix, there is nothing about the technique per se that requires knowledge about anything other than the song being remixed and the technology used to do that. (The time-stretching software used to generate musical mashups is popular precisely because it makes it easier to synch diverse recordings.) Complexity does not make a cultural phenomenon better or more valuable; it only makes it more complex. Valuing complexity over simplicity is a matter of aesthetic preference not unlike Lessig's preference for Girl Talk over Britney Spears. But I think there is more than taste at play in Lessig's preoccupation with generating meaning over works that are derivative, and it has to do with his faith in copyright and his desire to reform rather than abolish it. By aligning remix with cultural commentary and the established practice of referencing in art and literature, Lessig leads us toward the notion of fair use in copyright and builds a case that their use is transformative. There is a rhetorical reason to focus on the generation of meaning instead of a change in use, but, in doing so, creative use without permission may be left behind.

Won't someone think of the children—or, at least, the hobbyists?

At the same time as Lessig seems to turn a blind eye to recent history in popular culture, he reaches back to the turn of the twentieth century to argue that "remix culture" can be understood as return to what was lost when culture became professionalized (2008: 29). He writes, "Never before had the 'vocal cords' of ordinary citizens been as effectively displaced, and displaced, as Sousa feared, by these 'infernal machines.' The twentieth century was the first time in the history of human culture when popular culture had become professionalized, and when the people were taught to defer to the professional." Remix, then, marks the triumphant (if contested) return of the amateur, as well as the return of a participatory ethos, both of which can rouse ordinary folk from their "couch-potato stupor" (Lessig 2008: 254). But this characterization of culture as "Read-Only" is troubled by the particular music cultures that gave rise to the strategy of remix: That is, by the "Read/Write" media made with analog formats and technologies in Jamaica in the 1960s and in the nascent hip-hop and disco scenes in New York in the 1970s. It is also troubled by the flourishing cultures of sample-based music made in the 1980s and 1990s by professionals and amateurs alike (including artists who, like Girl Talk, composed their music entirely from samples) with such (then) relatively affordable digital technologies as samplers and sequencers (Toynbee 2000: 93–8), including house, hip-hop, and even mainstream-pop genres.

Music cultures present a problem for anyone who thinks twentieth-century culture can be neatly summed up by citing a division between professional performers and amateur audiences. After all, numerous popular-music genres, as well as cultures—from rock to electronic dance music—have benefited from both amateur and professional innovations and often have been forged in collaborations among self-trained, untrained, and semi-professional musicians and their "audiences" of listeners, dancers, and hangers-on. And while the return to a participatory folk culture is a common narrative in discourses about how digital and network technologies have changed culture, some scholars of pop music argue it was the circulation of *commercially* recorded music that increased participation in music culture. Toynbee writes, "The mass circulation of records led to a new kind of mediated orality, whereby young musicians learnt their craft listening to the phonograph as much as by reading music or watching performances [...]. This enormously extended the possibility of participation in music-making" (Toynbee 2000: 74).

The music industry in the twentieth century is less about the rise of the professional than it is about the commodification of culture—the commercial exploitation of music's objectification. Indeed, scholars such as Paul Théberge (1997) and Jason Toynbee (2000) have argued that the advent of low-cost digital technologies in the early 1980s (e.g., samplers and sequencers) mark a moment in which a "key innovation was the 'production' of musicians as *consumers* of high technology" (Théberge 1997: 70–1; italics added). While Lessig rightly asserts that the tools available today cost a fraction of what they once did, he fails to acknowledge that amateurs and starving professionals did rent studios, that they did buy low-cost samplers (McLeod 2004) when they became available in the late 1980s, that home studios were still within reach in the early 1990s—costing around $1,000 (Saunders 1993)—and that many artists (and some idle teenagers, too) made use of cheaper cassette tape technologies to achieve similar creative ends. As will be discussed in the following chapter, the practice of remixing was forged by these strategies of use, these situations of making do with whatever technology was at hand. Most importantly, this strategy was built on the *active* character of listening, viewing, and reading, and these functions continue to shape the aesthetic of reuse.

Lessig's failure to understand the particular cultures and series of events that gave rise to the remix as a larger cultural phenomenon outside of music is compounded, or, at least, further compromised, by his assertion that ordinary consumption or reception is passive. He writes of "simple consumption" (2008: 29), "passively listening" (2008: 106), "couch-potato stupor" (2008: 254), "just consumers" (2008: 25), and of television viewers' being channeled into following one programming mix over another (2008). This is a portrait of a recent past, where all the VCRs blinked 00:00, where the remote was forever lost in the couch, where warnings about home taping were heeded, and where, at 10 p.m., everyone knew where their children were. Laura Murray (2009: 5) offers a similar critique in her review of *RiP!: A Remix Manifesto,* a documentary based on Lessig's work. She writes,

> Lessig's vision of cultural history and creative process is almost laughably thin from the perspective of anyone versed in the most basic cultural studies and communications research; it manifests technological determinism of the crudest kind … . Lessig presents the twentieth century as a dark ages when people could only passively consume culture. It took the invention of digital media for us to be able to wake up and be creative, he says. This is, simply, ridiculous.

By denying agency and innovation to consumers/users of the past, we obscure an understanding of how their practices of consumption and use shaped both the technology we use today and our contemporary practices of consumption. As Murray points out, it is also an understanding of reception that only holds if one ignores scholarship in literary theory, musicology, film studies, and the visual arts—disciplines where a great deal of effort has been devoted to ideas about the work that readers, listeners, and viewers do to construct texts, music, and images, moving or otherwise.

While I think it is a mistake to attempt to defend amateur creativity by denying the role of everyday use in shaping culture, I agree that current copyright laws threaten creative usage and present a particular threat to amateur practice (or even to professional practice that does not have deep pockets). Given this history of an extant "Read/Write" culture, the assertion that remix is somehow the purview of teenagers and young adults, and that previous generations were passive (Lessig 2008: 109), is a misrepresentation of the practice.

Lessig never really backs up his generational argument about remixing, and his own book is populated by folk who are neither amateurs nor young. Johan Söderberg is a professional videographer and filmmaker who was born in 1962, Negativeland was formed in the late 1970s, and Breitz was born in 1972. Girl Talk alone counts as young—but, while his work is illegal, it is arguably the least innovative, following in the footsteps of artists such as Art of Noise, Public Enemy, Plunderphonics, and many others who composed music using hundreds of samples.

Sloppy examples aside, by equating remix with teenagers, Lessig entreats us to think of the children. It is an appeal to emotion and a rhetorical ploy, but, just like focusing on meaning, it overlooks the long-standing contribution of use and users to media innovation and creativity. Lessig's concern is that these laws "criminalize a generation" (2008: 294). My concern is that the current expansion of copyright criminalizes anyone who dares to use their culture by reproducing it. Among the problems with the rhetoric of remix is its tendency to avoid dealing with (or defending, or condemning) straightforward examples of expression involving replication and reuse (such as MP3 blogs) that were made possible by digital and network technologies.

In her work on the contradictions inherent in the First Amendment and fair use provisions in copyright law, Rebecca Tushnet (2004) draws attention to the debate's emphasis on transformative use and how this potentially devalues copying and overlooks its role in free speech. She writes, "The rhetoric of transformative use can then be applied in nontransformative cases to devalue pure copying" (2004: 561). She argues that emphasis on critical commentary over everyday use might leave many other kinds of speech acts vulnerable. "While using fair use to protect artists from censorship is appealing, other forms of copying are also integral to free speech today" (2004: 545). She warns that fair use and free speech are not the same thing: "Using fair use and free speech as interchangeable concepts thus has a profound and negative narrowing effect on the scope of fair use and in turn threatens First Amendment freedoms, because noncritical uses of copyrighted works have substantial value to society and to freedom of speech" (2004: 537). In Tushnet's opinion, not only does an emphasis on transformative use defend some practices and not others, but it might also play into the hands of the opposition. She writes, "An exclusive focus on transformation in thinking about copyright and freedom of speech is likely to support further expansions of copyright" (2004: 553).

The role of pure copying in expression is my concern in the two case studies that follow. Copying music was already an important consumption practice in music (Marshall 2004: 196) in the analog era, and the networked environment seems to amplify the role of copies in expression. I do not wish to dispute Lessig's assertion that what technology enables and what the law allows are out of synch, and that difficult policy battles need to be fought. My concern is that the rhetoric of remix distracts us from a deeper understanding of the affordances of copies and the particular affordances of digital copies. That is, if, as scholars of culture and media history, we proceed with Lessig's conceptualization of remix, we will build an argument on false premises. Remix is neither new nor digital. As is true for most artifacts and practices from music culture, the borders between amateurs and professionals, commerce and culture, young and old, performer and audience are all poorly defined. If we want to understand the role copies play in contemporary composition, we would do better to think not of their meaning, but of their use. Before I turn to use, however, I will look to two other key themes related to remix in cultural scholarship: First, the idea that remix is a kind of resistance; second, the idea that it is a new kind of cultural participation and empowerment.

THE RHETORIC OF REMIX

3.5 Remix as resistance

In this section, I turn to conceptions of remix that begin with different assumptions or that come to different conclusions. While Lawrence Lessig's activist position uses remix to normalize vilified practices by drawing parallels with accepted ones, he mounts his defense because he sees social value in remix as a kind of critique. Others take a different tack. Whereas Lessig's argument leads to conclusions about copyright reform and, ultimately, sits comfortably within the existing economic and social order, other scholars conceptualize remix as a *resistance* to late capitalism and commercial culture (e.g., Navas et al. 2015; Schütze 2003; Vautour 2006: 306). Bernard Schütze (2003), for instance, sees remix not only as a resistance to the status quo, but, by definition, as a subversive form. While Lessig views markets as beyond question and copyright as a policy that needs to be fixed and not done away with, Schütze's understanding of remix is one that challenges these same institutions and structures: He values sharing over ownership, openness over originality, and process over product. Remix, for Schütze, is "an aesthetic of impurity, and an ideology of unrestricted circulation" (2003). It is a challenge to existing orders and institutions, a strategy, and a process ("a verb not a noun" [2003]), rather than a category or a product.

Remix culture, then, is one "that is constantly renewing, manipulating, and modifying already mediated and mixed cultural material" (Schütze 2003). It encompasses a wide variety of subcultural practices, including "mix, mix again, remix: copyleft, cut 'n' paste, digital jumble, cross-fade, dub, tweak the knob, drop the needle, spin, merge, morph, bootleg, pirate, plagarize, enrich, sample, break down, reassemble, multiply input source, merge output, decompose, recompose, erase borders, remix again" (Schütze 2003). The emphasis on vernacular phrases, such as "tweak the knob," over remix practices that might be perceived as mainstream (à la Britney Spears's remixes) is intentional. Schütze (2003) seeks to distance the remixes he sees as acts of resistance from those that are in bed with the mainstream media industry and their pursuit of profit:

> A distinction must be made, however, between lucrative mainstream cultural "remixes" which are protected under copyright, and the remix methods of more marginal underground artistic practices and approaches. One could argue that mainstream culture has little to do with the remix as an open process—it is a "remake" culture that thrives on an endless parade of rehashes, repackaging, and repeats that do nothing more than recirculate the old in a new guise. Remix culture ... *upholds the remix as an open challenge to a culture predicated on exclusive ownership, authorship, and controlled distribution.*

Access is undoubtedly part of the remix story. However, I am not sure we can cast aside the music industry's role in the history of remix (or of remakes, in other areas of media) because of political agendas and preferences. What if the remake culture Schütze sniffs at and the underground practices he admires have something in common? For one, just as it is difficult to untangle listening from play, it is difficult to tease out the mainstream from the marginal: Some of the children who sat and watched repackaged Looney Tunes episodes on Saturday mornings in the 1970s were the same teenagers who bought Plunderphonics "Dab" tapes in the mid-1980s—surely the former artifacts were an influence on their understanding of the latter ones. Such material shares common characteristics, with respect to form, even if the intention of the so-called remixer differs. Schütze and Lessig may approach remix from different disciplinary traditions, and with different arguments and political agendas in mind, but they both value the potential for remixes to comment and critique. They value the narrative or discursive remix and disparage the nonnarrative (or, in musical terms, "musematic") version as derivative. Valuing narrative over other kinds of expression is not a problem in and of itself, but, in this case, it suppresses an important chapter in the history of remix—that of the musematic, or "repetition at the level of the short figure" (Middleton 1999: 146), as is common in dance remixing and editing. I will return to this, but, for now, it is enough to say that not all musical remix works on a narrative or discursive level, and that this preoccupation with comment is a problem for the rhetoric of remix in the context of cultural history.

In the visual arts, remix is often considered part of a continuum of reuse that had already surfaced in a number of modernist forms—collage, pastiche, bricolage, for example—but is also seen as quintessentially postmodern, a strategy of resistance borrowed from particular cultures of popular music (cf. Navas 2009). This flattening of a variety of forms and process into one— everything is remix—seeks to resurrect an association with the avant-garde at the same time that it declares its impossibility (cf. Krauss 1985). Resistance is seen as inherent to the process of fragmentation and reuse. For example, in a catalog essay for an exhibition of sample-based video artwork in Sydney, Australia from the 1980s to today, Mark Titmarsh asserts that "every form of sampling involves taking something from above and pulling it down to the underworld where the laws of gravity do not apply and the boundaries of copyright are not acknowledged" (Titmarsh 2006: 11). Remix, for Titmarsh, is underground and transgressive; the form lends it these qualities.

Video artist Dan Angeloro (2006), on the other hand, acknowledges that this assumption of resistance in the visual arts might have its limits. In her typology of what we might call "vernacular remixes,"[14] Angeloro notes that

---

[14] For an overview and discussion of vernacular creativity, see Burgess (2006, 2007).

this notion of resistance may no longer be overt, or even acknowledged. She writes, "What was once conceived as a tactical assault on commodity culture has, for many become a commonplace way of consuming culture … . The recent explosion of remix culture is not a dilution of the radical logic of the remix but rather its ultimate realisation: fragment by fragment the remix becomes the world (2006: 25)." The question is not whether fragmentation exists, but whether fragmentation (and variability) fundamentally disrupts. Does remix, as an aesthetic, infect the culture at large, as Angeloro suggests?

I will return to this question, but, for now, I want to highlight a possible historical problem with the idea that fragmentation is a resistance: That is, the professional aspirations of the various players who contributed to the aesthetic of remix, coupled with the commercial interests that helped to establish social and distribution networks among these players (Straw 2002), seem to challenge the view that remix as a form aims to oppose existing hierarchies and hegemonic power. The tendency to romanticize the contributions of the amateur over the professional in current scholarship does not entirely mesh with the history of remix in music. Many of the earliest edits and unauthorized remixes were treated like calling cards by marginalized professionals—DJs—who wanted to find a way into the music industry. While some would come to embrace their status on the margins, many aspired to the promise of musical stardom or industry power. However, we also know that unauthorized remixes—appropriations of image, sound, etc.—as Angelero (2006: 25) suggests, have been used as "a tactical assault on commodity culture" (and her own work as a video artist is a testament to this possibility).

Angeloro is right to ascribe "power" to the fragment: fragmentation is a kind of replication, isolation has aesthetic affordances and possibilities, and thinking about why this is so is a discussion we should be having. The history of fragmentation in music, however, complicates the valorization of remix as resistance—in a way that the history of fragmentation in the visual arts may not. In music, it seems that the aesthetic of remix stems from a number of parallel and separate music cultures and processes (dubs in Jamaica, disco and hip-hop in New York, musique concrète, tape edits, etc.). Yet, when we talk about remix as a metaphor, we tend to rely on a linear birth narrative—one that aligns the birth of remix with its ascendance in hip-hop culture, thereby associating it with the political struggles of Black America rather than with the marketing of popular culture and leisure, or with formal experimentation in high art, all of which are part of the history of musical remix. Fragmentation may be a more neutral strategy than the current metaphorical use of remix implies. The outlaw status of sampling as a musical process stems from its relationship to copyright law, not from its status as a fragment. Hence, the assumption that fragmentation has the status of resistance can only be attributed to certain remixes, but not all of them.

Remix as participation

"Remix culture" is also closely associated with the rise of social media in the twenty-first century. "Remix" is a used as a buzzword to signal the democratization of media production, a shift from the allegedly passive consumers of the broadcast era to the active participants and co-producers of Web 2.0. Many scholars and commentators see remix culture as a form of empowerment, a storming of the gates of corporate mass media by, what Jay Rosen dubbed, "the people formerly known as the audience" (Rosen 2006). For some, this empowerment is an opportunity to forge new business models that sit comfortably in the continuum of late capitalism, while for others, remix culture represents a wedge against corporate power structures and a challenge to the commodification of culture.[15] The notion of a remix culture is often aligned or associated with Henry Jenkins's conceptualization of a participatory culture (Wikstrom 2009). Indeed, Lawrence Lessig founds parts of his arguments about remix on the strength of Jenkins's work on convergence and participation (cf. Lessig 2008: 28, 78, 81, 94, 206, 207, 212, 276). Jenkins is not alone in his interest in identifying and understanding new modes of participation in media culture. For instance, Yochi Benkler (2006) has studied the efficacy and efficiency of nonmarket production in digital networks; Axel Bruns (2008) has developed the notion of produsage[16] to describe new forms of collaboration; and Jean Burgess (2006, 2007, 2009) has investigated the character and visibility of vernacular creativity in online discourse. Indeed, since the 2000s it has become common to discuss the "participatory turn" in media studies. The rise of new modes of cultural participation are often attributed to the very things remix is associated with; that is, the ease and affordability of access to digital-communication technologies and to fast digital networks. Jenkins (2009) defines a participatory culture as one in which the lines between producers and consumers are blurred; in which

---

[15] For Axel Bruns (2008), it represents a challenge to the notions of production and of products themselves.

[16] "In collaborative communities the creation of shared content takes place in a networked, participatory environment which breaks down the boundaries between producers and consumers and instead enables all participants to be users as well as producers of information and knowledge—frequently in a hybrid role of *produser* where usage is necessarily also productive. Produsers engage not in a traditional form of content production, but are instead involved in *produsage*—the collaborative and continuous building and extending of existing content in pursuit of further improvement. Participants in such activities are not producers in a conventional, industrial sense, as that term implies a distinction between producers and consumers which no longer exists; the artifacts of their work are not products existing as discrete, complete packages; and their activities are not a form of production because they proceed based on a set of preconditions and principles that are markedly at odds with the conventional industrial model" (Bruns 2007).

access is open; in which sharing is encouraged, and "members believe their contributions matter, and feel some degree of social connection with one another (at the least they care what other people think about what they have created)." This definition of a participatory culture is neither merely descriptive nor value-neutral. Instead, it draws on idealized notions of participatory democracy and offers a tacit critique of representation and specialization. Just as remix has a rhetorical role to play, the concept of a participatory culture seems driven as much by a set of normative goals and values about creating a more engaged digital citizenry as by a description of changes in cultural activity. This definition of participation also seems to imply that forms of media engagement in the past were passive by comparison.[17] The assumption of a passive audience however, seems to ignore the copious literary and cultural scholarship that has argued otherwise and as a result also misconstrues predigital consumption practices. This tendency also foregrounds another underlying assumption that merits scrutiny: the continued scholarly valorization of production and denigration of the cultural aspects of reception. By emphasizing the production of remixes over their circulation and use, we may be pushing an ideology of participation while simultaneously undervaluing various participants, and kinds of participation, in networked discourse.

3.6 Why the history of remix matters

Remix, as it currently circulates in popular and academic discourse, is best understood as a rhetorical trope rather than as a rich description of cultural practice. This usage seems to overlook or obscure the history of remix in dance music, and the vogue for using remix as a metaphor for all creativity carries with it a number of assumptions about technology and consumption that do not withstand critical scrutiny. Remix valorizes production by rendering reception passive and expression immaterial; it also seems to be based on debatable assumptions about the nature of technology as progressive and inevitable. Remix as rhetoric, aims to defend new modes of participatory media engagement by privileging production over use and, when viewed from the standpoint of situated users, fails to capture the

---

[17] Fitzgerald and O'Brien's characterization of remix is exemplary of this understanding of the concept. They write,

> New digital technologies along with the Internet have opened up enormous potential for what has become known as "remix"—cutting, pasting, mashing, sampling etc. No longer are end users or consumers seen as passive receptors of information, but rather in the process of distributed and peer production, consumers can take on the role of producers to become what Creative Commons legal counsel Mia Garlick calls "content conducers." (Fitzgerald and O'Brien 2005)

intertwined nature of production, distribution, and consumption. It fails to account for or acknowledge many other modes of participation. In its zeal to describe the potential empowerment of contemporary audiences through the use of digital technologies, the rhetoric of remix denies agency to users of the recent past and ignores the ongoing role played by consumption/ reception in the creation of meaning. Remix as a metaphor relies on obscuring this history in order to defend the use and appropriation of copyrighted material via digital technologies—at a time when efforts are being made to expand the scope and length of copyright beyond its intentions for policy. It is, in this sense, a thoroughly modernist gesture. It aims to use technology to secure a brighter tomorrow, by breaking free of the past: Don't look back.

By foregrounding remix as a rhetorical strategy, I aim to recover these recent histories of use and to highlight the role of copies and copying in these histories. Any theory of contemporary media culture must grapple with the persistence of the copy or fragment as a compositional unit because it is common to both analog and digital formats and technologies. Remix asks us to overlook the copy, to instead focus on notions of transformative use. Though there may be localized legal and political reasons to emphasize transformative use over replication, from a theoretical perspective, I am more interested in focusing on how this abstract property—a recording's status as a copy—facilitates repetition, and on what role repetition plays in circulation, production, and consumption. In the following pages, I will de-emphasize the remix as an explanatory or conceptual metaphor, and instead use "the copy" as a lens through which to study the hybrid nature of networks of reception and distribution, both today and in the past.

CHAPTER FOUR

Disco edits: Analog antecedents and network bias

4.1 What a difference a record makes

In this chapter, I turn to a close relative of the remix—the disco edit—a form of "extractive musical practice" (Fairchild 2014: 63) that is associated with the rise of disco in New York in the 1970s, and has enjoyed an enthusiastic revival by a new generation of DJs and producers in the twenty-first century. The hybrid nature of this revival—which has come in the form of a recent proliferation of unauthorized edits, usually made using editing software on computers, from either analog or digital source material, and then distributed digitally or on vinyl—presented an opportunity to read the history of the edit's material and cultural origins and its relationship with the history of remix as a related form and practice into current amateur and professional practices. This comparative approach, which bears some similarities to media archaeological approaches in media studies (Parikka 2012) and also borrows some of its interest in cultural poetics and new historicism from literary theory (Greenblatt 1987), allowed me to compare and contrast the digital production of edits with their analog antecedents, and to reflect upon the continued use of certain analog formats and technologies in a contemporary setting—as well as upon the hybrid nature of channels of discovery. This critical reading will reveal key ideas about the materiality of media, the history of use and reuse, and the affordances and biases of networked culture.

I show that all edits share a common compositional strategy, one that was initially shaped by the affordances of analog media and the contingencies of its use on the dance floor. Also shared is the questionable legal status of many disco edits: Most (but not all) are made without permission from the copyright holders, and the relatively unknown story of 1970s edits stands as another example of what Lee Marshall (2005: 4) calls the "historical continuities of piracy," part of its long history (cf. Johns 2010). I choose to study edits precisely because they are a significant compositional form and extractive musical practice that came into being without permission and authorization—they were born "illegal"—and because their story, though largely unknown outside of specialized histories of dance music, is one that had a significant influence on, and has significant parallels to, what has come to be called "remix culture," where remix is now used broadly to mean media made from extant media. Jonathan Sterne (2003: 337) prompts media historians to ask: "Why *these* technologies *now*? What social forms, what social relations, do they encapsulate?" For Sterne, media are "social all the way down." I would like to suggest that Sterne's social approach, while sensitive to the material dimensions of culture, can only ever tell part of the story. In this chapter, as an effort to consider both material and social histories I heed Sterne's call but at the same time pay close attention to form and structure as a way to understand the material affordances of recording formats. I ask: Why *this* form *now*? Why this format now? What social relations do they encapsulate and which material affordances shaped them? Regarding the recent fashion for vinyl and other analog technologies in an era of ubiquitous digital networks, I also join a chorus of voices asking why *vinyl* now? What are the rhetorical dimensions of analog formats and media in network culture?

This chapter uses the disco edit to focus on questions about social and cultural continuities and change in an era of digital networks. It asks how analog and digital copies are the same, in what ways they are different, and what the possible answers to these questions say about materiality, media use, and the production and circulation of meaning. Using competing narratives about the "disco edit" I explore the relationship among reproduction technologies, storage/playback formats, and forms of composition in popular music. Disco edits as an extractive musical practice are media artifacts made from other media artifacts—copies made from copies. Like remixes, they are reworked compositions but, as a less-known form, with its own hazy history in the annals of dance music, the disco edit offers an alternative path to thinking about the origins of remix culture, troubling many assumptions about the significance of digital technologies and copying practices. Edits came into being as part of a gray market in recorded music, records made in small numbers that were played by marginal-industry professionals in the dark of night—as such, they are an under recognized form, one with a shadowy history marked by competing birth narratives, fallen heroes, spent media artifacts, and faded memories. Contemporary edits, those made in this decade with digital tools, are perhaps more visible—thanks to the proliferation of network technologies—but, this visibility has not made them any better understood. My aim is not to present a history of disco edits as a form, but rather to use its particular histories to contemplate how both listening practices and artifacts are shaped and informed by a format's materiality. By selecting two cultural moments in the production, distribution, and reception of disco edits—their origins in 1970s New York (Lawrence 2003,

2008) and their popular revival on the Internet in the 2000s (Beta 2008; Drever 2009; Lech et al. 2008; Rowlands 2008)—I highlight overlooked histories of reception, and am able to foreground the dispositions of copies—their possibilities[1]—and prompt a more nuanced consideration of repetition, reuse, and reproduction as historical engines of innovation, continuity, and change. Rather than focusing solely on the production of recordings, I foreground their reception and the role that listening to them plays in music cultures, thereby bringing existing cultural histories and the media artifacts of music culture into dialogue in order to better understand each.

Following Lisa Gitelman (2006: 13), I focus on the way in which "media and their publics co-evolve," using what she calls the "data of culture" as a starting point: that is, the "records and documents, the archivable bits or irreducible pieces of modern culture that seem archivable under prevailing and evolving knowledge structures, and that suggest, demand or defy preservation" (2006: 12). For edits, this includes vinyl records, reel-to-reel tape, and acetates, as well as digital sound files and networked metadata about recorded sound in a variety of media formats.[2] By focusing on the use and production of media objects in the past (e.g., vinyl records, acetate records, and reel-to-reel tape), and comparing that history with the contemporary culture of edit-making born of hybrid media use (i.e., made with digital technologies but distributed via analog and digital means), I hope to enrich our understanding of use, replication, and circulation as creative strategies, social tactics, and aesthetic experiences.

4.2 Interrupting the rhetoric of remix

Scholarship that is critical about copyright's overreach (e.g., Demers 2006; Lessig 2008; McLeod 2007; McLeod and DiCola 2011; Toynbee 2004; Vaidhyanathan 2003) has also raised awareness about the importance of

---

[1] Jonathan Sterne (2003: 341), in his conclusion to *The Audible Past*, suggests that we treat possibility as a central historical problem. Sterne asks, "How and under what conditions did it become possible to manipulate sound in new ways? How and under what conditions did new practices of listening become possible?"

[2] To study the contemporary production and use of edits, I used a mixed-method approach, creating an archive of approximately 200 documents by monitoring both the scant music journalism on the phenomenon in mainstream publications and the more effusive offerings on self-published blogs during the first decade of the twenty-first century. I also followed and participated in discussions on key online forums—two Australian forums where I live, two based in the U.K., and one in the U.S.—frequented by DJs, producers, promoters, collectors, and dancers between 2006 and 2009; surveyed the offerings of online music retailers; conducted formal and informal interviews with participants in dance-music scenes in New York, London, and Sydney (where I live); and participated in the local dance-music scene. This research was not intended to be exhaustive; instead, my approach was critical and theoretical.

musical borrowings and reuse in many of the twentieth century's innovations in popular music, with stories about the blues, folk music, Jamaican
dub, and hip-hop now on high rotation. In raising awareness about the
long history of copying practices, we also have established a canon of birth
narratives. The repetition of key narratives in the service of arguments
about copyright's overreach, however, may also overshadow other significant stories of media use and obscure the role copies, replication, and
everyday users play in our understanding of forms and the agency of users
in the production of meaning. That is, in the process of defending today's
media users, we may overlook evidence of their agency in the recent past.
Although legal and economic questions pertaining to copyright are not
the focus of my analysis of remix, edits, and MP3 blogs in the chapters
that follow, they make a deeper investigation of aesthetic forms and music
culture more urgent.

As the previous chapter suggested, the rhetoric of remix reveals unsettled
questions about the place of consumption and circulation practices and the
materiality of media in the generation of meaning. The history of remix
as a compositional technique and a musical artifact does not always mesh
with the participatory, open, collaborative, and noncommercial values we
ascribe to remix as a metaphor for digital production. Nor does this history
necessarily share the cyber-utopian hopes for a "more just, egalitarian,
democratic and creative society" (Friedman 2005: 220) that are sometimes
associated with digital remix. That "remix" came to be shorthand for these
values, and to represent these dreams, seems to have had less to do with
its history, and more with the aspirations the rhetoric obscures. I see the
rhetoric of remix as opening up a space for utopian thinking about digital
and network technologies, that space "made possible by the curious logic of
technological inevitability, which shuts down critical engagement with the
social causes of technological change, while opening up room to imagine the
future that 'inevitable' technological changes might deliver" (2005: 209).

Remixes, edits, and other popular musical forms based on extant
recordings are difficult historical subjects because they are both practice and
product. They are recursive and reflexive; a compositional house of mirrors.
Chronological narratives about the origin of such postproduction techniques
and artifacts can be misleading and timelines identifying significant contributions to the contemporary notion of remix can sometimes read like a
list of modernism's greatest hits, populated as they are with 1920s collage
artists; avant-garde art movements (e.g., Dada, Fluxus); concepts like the
cut-up technique used by William S. Burroughs in literature and jump cuts
in film; jazz improvisation and *musique concrète*—alongside the usual
popular-music suspects: Jamaican dub, hip-hop, disco, house, etc. Yet, in
casting a wide net, we may confuse when we intend to clarify. Indeed, many
of these art forms, styles, and cultures did not necessarily know about,
follow from, or even influence other ones. It is worth recalling that, while

remix is often presented as a linear narrative in the potted histories that populate academic treatises on remix—with origins in 1960s Jamaica, in the Bronx streets of the 1970s, and, later, in bedroom studios worldwide—many of these moments were unconnected, or, at least, the participants were not aware of their predecessors. As music journalist and DJ Bill Brewster noted, "Early disco remixers wouldn't have been aware of what was going on in the reggae scene. Things happened independently" (Lynskey 2004). Both Hillegonda Rietveld (2007: 99–100) and Tim Lawrence (2008) have drawn attention to disco and hip-hop as parallel innovations. For Rietveld, such examples of media "parallelism" should make us suspicious of easy linear histories. Rietveld (2007: 101) writes, "An increasing global synchronicity implies that choices of 'zero moments' and 'seminal inventions' in linear historical narratives may be mostly a matter of cultural politics and economic resources, a matter of whose voice is documented, distributed and heard." Such parallels are an opportunity to study the zeitgeist from a material perspective, focusing on the material dimensions, formats and technologies that these diverse practices and artifacts.

Though disco edits qualify as a lesser-known chapter in narratives about the origins of sampling and remixing, they are not the only recordings that deviate from or complicate our treasured potted histories: Buchanan and Goodman's 1956 hit *The Flying Saucer,* a parody record made from reel-to-reel recordings (McLeod 2007: 74); Bill Holt's 1974 self-produced sample-fest, *Dreamies*; Montreal-based PAJ's cassette-tape "pause" edits, starting the same year (Kent 2010);[3] the pause tapes made and used by Bronx DJs in the 1970s (McLeod and DiCola 2011: 53–4) are just a few examples that do not fit neatly into the existing birth narrative of remix. Yet, all made use of recording technologies that were at hand to produce new compositions. Writing about the 12-inch single, the format that introduced extended remixes to the commercial dance-music market, William Straw (2002: 167) argues, "Like other media histories, that of the 12-inch has spawned one set of narratives fixated on a moment of punctual discovery and others which recount minor mutations from within a set of possibilities." A focus on edits might seem like one such minor mutation: However,

---

[3]Writes Kent (2010), "It all started in the fall of 1974: Pierre Gagnon and Jean Barbeau, two young DJs from Quebec, invested in a pair of Sony cassette decks and started experimenting with the pause buttons. Within a year, the duo, guided by Pierre's drummer-friend Allen Vallières, who taught them music theory, were creating primitive edits. Initially, they were simply making one complete song from parts one and two, found on both sides of a 45. But, as their timing improved and their imaginations wandered, they began trying more complex chops: extending sections of songs, rearranging, and repeating parts. One of their earliest edits made this way extended the intro to Esther Phillips's "What a Difference a Day Makes" before dropping straight into the break. This sounds simple. But, in its time, it was something of a revelation: They had no idea that DJs in New York were doing similar things on reel-to-reel recorders."

in choosing to focus on this particular narrative, one in circulation among dance-music afficionados at the time of this writing, I mean to interrupt the narrative arc upon which the rhetoric of remix depends and thereby recover copying as a tactic and creative strategy, by way of considering what is similar about these activities—focusing, copying, and fragmenting—when the material and technological conditions of their reproduction differ.

4.3 Disco edits, a technical distinction

Disco edits are reworked compositions, new versions of a song made from a preexisting recording; an edit (sometimes called a re-edit) is composed using extant copies of the commercial recording, often without seeking permission from the copyright holder. The first edits were made from early through to the mid-1970s, as a part of the birth of disco as a musical genre (as opposed to its earlier meaning as a place to go dancing). Beginning in the 2000s, edits became closely associated with a renewed interest in, and fashion for, dance music from the 1970s and 1980s (Beta 2008; Drever 2009; Lech et al. 2008; Rowlands 2008). This revival coincided with the advent of the Broadband era, and edits are sometimes viewed and referred to as a genre or subgenre in contemporary dance music.[4]

The distinction that practitioners and aficionados make between edits and remixes centers on the relationship between the source material and the new composition. DJ and producer Greg Wilson made his name as a DJ in the U.K. in the 1980s when he was a key player in the early Electro scene in Northern England. Wilson was rediscovered by a new generation of dancers in the 2000s and is now well-known for his writing as well as his disco edits and live performances with his trusty Revox B77 reel-to-reel tape machine as a part of his DJ set up. In 2007, at a time when edits had become as fashionable as they were controversial, Wilson was asked to explain the edit/remix difference and to rehearse their histories in an online interview. He highlighted this relationship between source material, and ways to access it. He said, "In a strict sense [an edit] is taking an existing recording and altering the arrangement ... . In the original sense, an edit involved the stereo master only, whereas a remix was when you worked with the multi-track tape of a recording and were able to access all the separate elements, allowing you to add effects and change the EQ's of each

---

[4]The edits revival also runs parallel to rise of the mashups—a loose term that is often defined as a vocal track from one song set to the instrumental of another, but has also been extended to refer to other forms of recombination, synonymous with remix. Charles Fairchild (2014: 77) argues that this definition marginalizes the history of sample-based music and had led many academics to focus on the humor and rebelliousness made possible by the practice, rather than its musicality.

individual sound" (Le Tan 2008). Although Wilson also argues that, today, "the lines [between edits and remixes] have become increasingly blurred" (Le Tan 2008), and notes that the term was not used by producers then (Le Tan 2008),[5] the interview's focus on the question of how to distinguish edits from remixes suggests that the distinction has currency.

Pinpointing shifts in usage and meaning is notoriously difficult. However, as the interview with Wilson exemplifies, considerable discussion takes place among DJs and record collectors over such distinctions and boundaries.[6] Lay listeners should beware the record collector who begins a sentence with, "Actually ...". Knowing the differences among genres, forms, and techniques—indeed, realizing that there were ever differences, or that they persist—contributes to the culture of connoisseurship that underpins DJ practice and many dance music cultures. Dance music, Straw (1993: 180) says, does not "embody the postmodern assemblage of random fragments," as many have claimed. Rather, he suggests, DJs can be seen as participants in "one of the last modernist art worlds" (1993: 181). Straw's insight compounds when considered in tandem with Kembrew McLeod's argument that the proliferation of subgenres of dance music can be understood as a gatekeeping mechanism: "[S]pecialized knowledge is a way of maintaining clear boundaries that define in-group/out-group relations," he wrote (2001: 72). The hierarchies produced by cultures of connoisseurship, however, tend to be overlooked in discussions that use the DJ as a heroic figurehead for democratized cultural production—a tension to which I will return. These rituals of distinction, Fairchild (2014: 63) argues, underpin the legitimation of musical practices in communities. Writing about *The Grey Album* as part of a tradition of "extractive" musical practice, Fairchild (2014: 63) explains that such practices "are legitimated publicly through constantly evolving debates and contests over what counts as music that people who already know and understand similar forms of music can recognize and accept as being within that tradition." And it is clear that participants in various dance-music cultures make a distinction between edits and remix as extractive practices and forms of composition, and, edits, in particular, are subject to a great deal of debate. A recent round up of the best edits of 2015 on Vinyl Factory's website began with the caveat "Not always strictly official and a divisive issue among DJs, collectors and the ethics committee alike, edits remain a staple of every dance music record shop."

Both edits and remixes are part of this tradition of extractive musical practice; they are compositional forms that employ strategies and techniques that can be referred to as "cut-and-paste"—that is, sections are selected, fragmented, and repeated via re-recording or sampling (i.e., copying).

---

[5]Wilson was discussing his first tape edit, made in 1983.
[6]Distinctions and boundaries are a common source of debate and discussion in online dance-music forums, as my archive of online forums bears out.

The cut-and-paste approach makes it possible to omit parts of a song, extend other parts through repetition, alter the sequence of parts, or layer sounds on top of one another. It takes a trained ear to identify parts of a recording that are suitable for looping—editors listen for sections that are "not covered in a mix by other instruments or voices" (Fairchild 2014: 91). Remixes have a wider set of sonic qualities that can be altered because they have access to the multiple tracks that were mixed together to make the song (in some cases, remixers even have access to outtakes from the recording session). So, in addition to making sequential changes, and having access to more clean sections of a recording, the use of multi-tracks gives a producer access to "texture and space as a compositional device" (Toynbee 2000: 91).

But these distinctions between the two creative strategies are retro-active—that is, after the forms or strategies have come to be seen as such. As situated innovations, editing and remixing grew out of a set of companion activities in a number of unrelated music cultures that revolved around the creative and social use of recorded music in the early 1970s in New York City (Lawrence 2003, 2008; Straw 2002). These activities included collecting and listening to records, playing and mixing between them, and responding to the playing of records through dance, repetition, and repro-duction. Edits, perhaps even more than remixes, I argue, are a musical form anchored in a culture of media use: an artifact that owes its existence as much to the dance floor as the studio. Or, as New York DJ/producer Lee Douglas put it in an interview, "Edits made disco" (Beta 2008).

4.4 Hang the DJ

Digital sampling has received considerable attention in the study of popular music and culture (notably, Fairchild 2014; McLeod and DiCola 2011; Rose 1994; Schloss 2004), as well as with regard to its legal status (Demers 2006; Lessig 2008; Vaidhyanathan 2003). Indeed, it is common to hail the digital sampler as the technological catalyst of remix culture.[7] This emphasis on digital sampling has meant that creative reproduction predating the arrival of the affordable digital sampler in the 1980s is often overlooked or under-emphasized in our understanding of remix. Tim Lawrence's scholarship on the DJ, producer, and bootlegger Walter Gibbons (2008), and his history of American dance music in the 1970s (*Love Saves the Day*, 2003), are notable exceptions—and the discussion in this chapter of the relationship

---

[7]Richard Middleton, for instance, claims that the prevalence of remixing and sampling "as a means of generating material is of course rooted in the development and spread of digitized production technologies" (1999: 153).

between materiality and form relies on a close reading of Gibbons's story, as told by Lawrence.

Musicologist Richard Middleton argues that "'form' has always come into being in a dialogue between particular 'instances' and the larger body of work or 'tradition.'" For Middleton (1999: 154), this implies that "question[s] of form" should be located "at the point of reception." This assumption invites us to relocate questions about compositions made from existing composition, away from composers as *producers* of organized sound, and toward producers as listeners[8] (i.e., as consumers of sound). Listening is a kind of specialized attention to the moment: always fleeting, but as crucial a part of the generation of an aesthetic experience as the "instruments, machines, hands and actions" (Hennion 2001: 2). The work doesn't "do" something to its listeners; listeners "do" something with the work.

To place the question of disco edits as a form at the point of reception, we must place ourselves in the position of someone listening to a record being played, whether on the dance floor or from the DJ booth. The rise, in 1970s New York, of edits as a compositional technique-cum-form was shaped by a cast of listeners—DJs, dancers, and hangers-on—in tandem with the material qualities and functional properties of vinyl records and other analog technologies. As the largest city in the U.S., as well as an important center of production and distribution for the music industry, New York was also a place where records, new and old, were plentiful—a factor that contributed to the growth of various pop-culture movements in the city including disco (Straw 2002: 165–6).

Once considered a parasite in the music industry, dance DJs are often held up by theorists and critics today as paradigmatic creative figures in "remix culture," special individuals who unearthed the secret to turning mass-market consumption technologies into DIY production tools (cf. McLeod and DiCola 2011: 54; Miller 2004). Art theorist Nicolas Bourriaud's (2000: 13) theory of postproduction, for instance, positions the DJ as a Pied Piper for the aesthetics of reuse. He writes,

These artists who insert their own work into that of others contribute to the eradication of the traditional distinction between production and consumption, creation and copy, readymade and original work. The material they manipulate is no longer *primary*. It is no longer a matter of elaborating a form on the basis of a raw material but working with objects that are already in circulation on the cultural market, which is to say, objects already *informed* by other objects. Notions of originality

---

[8]Examples of scholarship that puts listening first include Antoine Hennion's work on the sociology of music (2008) and Simon Frith's (1998: 278) reminder that "memories dance with the music too."

(being at the origin of) and even of creation (making something from nothing) are slowly blurred in this new cultural landscape marked by the twin figures of the DJ and the programmer, both of whom have the task of selecting cultural objects and inserting them into new contexts.

Similarly, Kembrew McLeod (2007: 72) has drawn attention to the DJ's role as a sonic alchemist who transforms consumption practices into production techniques—a seeming realization of Jacques Attali's prophesies:

> Afrika Bambaataa's sonic collages echoed Attali's technique, in which the cultural consumer—the record buyer, the DJ—morphed into the cultural producer. The turntable is an object of consumption that was reimagined by DJs as a technology of production, and today's software programs now allow anyone with a computer to collage and compose.

For McLeod, this urge to break it down was in the zeitgeist but, if we reach back to Barthes' critique of authorship and his position that it is readers who construct meaning, then, just like Dorothy, we have always had the power to go back to Kansas. We must remind ourselves that no actual authors were harmed in the writing of *The Death of the Author*; instead, Barthes (1977: 142–8) reinterpreted what was there all along.[9] In the dialectic of production and consumption, reception, although distinct from production, was always active, even when that agency was ignored or overlooked by critics.

Dance DJs were key players in the development and popular use of remixes, yet, their heroic status in theories of remix culture seems to stem from this perceived hack—flipping consumption on its head and transforming it into its more valorized counterpart, production. "The turntable is an object of consumption that was reimagined by DJs as a technology of production ..." writes McLeod (2007: 72). But DJs don't necessarily characterize their practice in this way: Their concerns are finding records, keeping the dance floor moving, getting another gig, guarding secrets,[10] etc. It is worth considering how a practice, whose (admittedly noble) ambition is to ensure that we can get our groove on, came to represent such heady aims. How—and why—did it come to describe so much more?

Lisa Gitelman (2006: 6) argues that media exists at the intersection of authority and amnesia, that media becomes authoritative when the social protocols governing its use are forgotten or ignored. While Gitelman's observation was more about how we come to a kind of tacit consensus

---

[9]Toynbee (2001: 6) reminds us that, when Barthes wrote the essay in 1968, "it was a polemic intended to undermine the then hegemonic notion that the author is the source of meaning in literature."

[10]For an early discussion of the DJ culture of connoisseurship, see Straw (1993).

on how we use a medium, I think it also illuminates what has come to be known as the creative misuse of media and technology, and how such tactics develop their own protocols and forms. Both DJs and edit producers challenge the *authority* of the medium at the precise moment they enact it: It is by sitting up and attending to "His Master's Voice" (as the old RCA Victor slogan would have it), by listening, that the authorial control the record conjures and represents is also submerged. The listener, caught up in the moment of sonic reproduction—its playback—simultaneously constructs and forgets the artist represented by the recording; the author becomes lost in song. Yet, simultaneously, by performing the sounds on the record, the DJ makes an undeniable authorial gesture, even a romantic one. Writing about the culture and production of rock-music bootlegs, Lee Marshall (2005: 60) asks whether dance music, with its seeming lack of regard for authorial authenticity and control, could be marked by the same romantic rejection of romanticism that he finds among the bootleggers: "The rejection of Romanticism is itself a Romantic gesture as one of the key Romantic traits is a rejection of earlier voices in order to discover one's own expression." To echo William Straw (1993), the DJ, it turns out, was never postmodern.

This heroic interpretation of the DJ as an economic alchemist able to turn passive, feminized consumption into heroic, masculinized production has preoccupied theories of remix, and digital culture does seem to be characterized by precisely this sort of romanticism. But is all this hocus-pocus really necessary to account for the agency of DJs as creative figures? If we assume that reception and use already imply agency, if we begin with the idea that consumption is always already active then we need to find some other way to understand the romantic character of copying practices, whether it involves playing a record or recording one. Romantic notions about genius, originality, and authenticity still remain our commonsense understanding of expression and creative communication: Why? What do we do with these ideals? How do they animate our culture? What kind of pleasure do we seek in them?

Rather than view the DJ as a subversive figure, I adopt a less heroic assumption: That of the DJ as an expert listener/user. By shifting the focus onto consumption (and, as will become clear, circulation), I do not mean to deny the performative nature of what a DJ does, nor do I mean to render the DJ's role uncreative. Instead, a position that assumes consumption is an active part of meaning making, offers a way to recover the significance of the copy in the foundational narrative of dance edits and remixes—and to sharpen our understanding of the affordances and limitations of a medium's materiality so we do not treat this relational property—copy—as incidental.

4.5 Walter Gibbons, the break, and the edits that made disco

An infectious reworking of The Temptations' "Law of the Land" was the first edit to wind its way through New York nightclubs in the early days of disco in the 1970s[11] (Lawrence 2008: 288). The unauthorized recording was cut on acetate in 1973 by DJ Walter Gibbons, and then snapped up by other DJs in the nascent scene (Lawrence 2008: 289–91; McMillian 2002). Rich Flores, Gibbons' business partner and then-boyfriend, told Tim Lawrence that the nineteen-year-old DJ's revision of the Motown song took its compositional cues from the dance floor; Gibbons often played the track as part of his DJ set, mixing between two copies of the same record to extend parts of the song that were particularly danceable. Reports Flores, "'Law of the Land' starts with clapping and [Gibbons] used to extend that section in real time but there were a few fuck-ups, so I said, 'Why don't we record the song over and over again, just the beginning of it, and then splice the magnetic tape together?' ... Then we pressed it to acetate" (Lawrence 2008: 288).

Acetates are less durable than vinyl records, but they could be produced on demand, in small numbers, and could be played on an ordinary turntable—qualities that made the fragile discs attractive to DJs. Angel Sound Studio owner Sandy Sandoval told Lawrence (2008: 289),

> [DJs] would get these tapes together, but the tapes couldn't be used for DJing [because the clubs were only equipped with turntables], so they came to us to have the music put onto disc. They would exchange recordings and make compilations ... . They were all striving to have something that was a little bit different.

According to New York DJ Danny Krivit, making edits or cutups was common practice among DJs at the time. Krivit recalls going to Sunshine Studios to have acetates made: "And for some reason they weren't considered mass-produced thing[s] like bootlegs were, so people weren't

---

[11] Whether there was another record that beat Gibbons to the punch would be of no consequence, and pinpointing firsts is notoriously difficult. As Will Straw (1993) wrote, in his critical reading of the history of the 12-inch single, "Disagreement about these various events is unsurprising, given the compressed time period in which they occurred. This uncertainty is symptomatic, as well, of the hazy distinction between limited-run 'test pressings,' produced for local disc jockeys, and full-fledged promotional copies produced as part of the larger release strategy for a disco single. Histories of the 12-inch single have been troubled by the overlapping of experimental prototypes and official releases, something common in the case of those industries (like that producing computer software) for whom professional insiders constitute an important market."

chasin[g] you down" (McMillan 2002). While very few of these efforts were officially released, many were played in the clubs. "It just seemed that all the DJs who were somebody did it," Krivit told music writer Neil McMillian (2002). "Alongside these early re-edits, more commercialized 'disco mixers,' bootleg records segueing together up to 50 songs, began to appear around 1975."

Other club DJs were the primary market for acetate edits and bootlegs (Lawrence 2008: 291; McMillian 2002), and, today, DJs continue to be the target market for edits as well as the major producers of the form. Many DJs view edits as a tool of the trade. A participant on an online music forum in 2008 expressed this view when he wrote, "One thing I like about edits is that they are a kind of DJ specialist item. It ... says, I am the DJ, I have special versions of tracks for dance-floors that are somewhat rare and hard to find." Comments from many edit makers and DJs echo this sentiment of functionality. Duncan Stump, a British DJ-producer told video magazine *The Art Pack*, "We make it a little bit more playable; a little bit more deejay-able" (Lech et al. 2008). Stump's statement suggests that an edit is understood by producers as a particular kind of recording: one that is made with future compositional use in mind. An edit is made to serve a functional purpose in the practice of playing and mixing between recorded music; an edit might make a song easier to mix into other tracks by extending the song's beginning ("intro") and end ("outro"); one might extend and repeat the parts of a song that are thought likely to elicit a dancer's response (often, by extending a drum break); one might create an exclusive version of a well-known song—working with a dancer's paradoxical longing for both familiarity and novelty and the DJ's desire to create a sound all their own—in order to attract and interact with an audience, secure a gig, etc. In the history of recorded music, the disco edit is yet another example of how reproduction and recording technologies can facilitate stylistic innovation and the formation of genres and cultures such as disco.

That said, as a compositional technique, editing is impartial to style of music and original storage medium: Edits are the end result of the process of re-recording an existing sound recording and editing the copy or the resulting recording, often (but not always) without the permission of the copyright holder. Re-recording—copying—is an essential step in recomposition. Notably, early disco DJs such as Gibbons played danceable songs from many different musical genres and relied as much on old records (and bootlegs of rare records) as on new ones (Straw 2002: 168). "Reggae, afro-funk, old and new soul and other forms were pulled into the repertory of dance clubs: the constant difficulty of finding these recordings was bemoaned in various press accounts of disc jockey work," writes Straw (2002: 168). Acetates were also an easy way to copy or "bootleg" a record that was no longer available, and DJs used studios like Angel Sound to make copies of rare recordings so they could play them in their sets (Lawrence

2008: 289, 291; McMillian 2002). Flores even admitted that the idea for his acetate label, Melting Pot, was inspired by the number of records he saw being copied to acetate by DJs at Angel Sound at a cost of seven to eight dollars an acetate. He thought he might make use of Gibbons's "impressive" collection and copy some of the most sought-after records for other DJs to buy. (Melting Pot only ever released two edits. The rest, Flores says, were "direct copies"; that is, bootlegs [Lawrence 2008: 291].)

Given the significance of recording to the form, it is tempting to focus on Gibbons's makeshift home studio—perhaps at the moment when Gibbons began recording a vinyl record on reel-to-reel tape and cutting the resulting tape—or on distribution, with DJs in the know clamoring for acetate copies of rare recordings (Lawrence 2008: 289). Flores's narrative arc is telling. His story opens in a nightclub, with Gibbons mixing between two copies of the same record, no doubt in the company of people on the dance floor (Lawrence 2008: 280, 288). To focus on the medium that shaped the content, then, we must rewind this narrative and consider Gibbons's habit of buying two copies of commercially released records that met certain sonic criteria. McLeod writes, "With their two turntables and a mixer, early disco DJs stretched tunes from three minutes to twenty, crafting entirely new versions of songs—all without involving the original songwriters and musicians" (2007: 70). Mixing between two copies of the same record, Lawrence explains, enabled a DJ to "intensify the experience of the dance floor" (2008: 282) and "keep their dance floors moving" (2008: 292).

This media use might not have altered the record—it remained "read-only," as Lessig would have it—but it could trump the notion of the work itself, since the song seemed to disappear through its use. When Walter Gibbons played "Happy Song," for instance, François Kevorkian (a.k.a. François K), a well-known New York DJ and producer, told Lawrence, "[You] would never hear the actual song. You just heard the drums. It seemed like he kept them going forever ..." (2008: 281). For DJs, recorded songs are both finished products and raw materials, building blocks that can be deployed to create new musical moments in real time. As ready-made modules, these recordings can be fragmented in any way the user chooses—breaking down a song into parts without altering the original, for instance. The *challenge* to "the master" is made all the more powerful since it is uttered by its own voice and played back in high fidelity: a faithful, but unintended, reproduction of recorded sound.

Gibbons was not alone in his obsession with and use of breaks. Isolating the break is often seen as "the central innovation of early hip hop" (Schloss 2004: 31), and pioneering hip-hop DJs like Kool Herc were also playing records in this manner.[12] (Herc called his technique the "merry go round".)

---

[12] Writing about hip-hop DJs, David Toop (1991: 60, in Schloss 2004: 31) observes that "a conga or a bongo solo, a timbales break or simply the drummer hammering out the

Lawrence's (2008: 277) work on Gibbons aims to recognize the disco DJ's contributions to popular music and to "open up a conversation about the relationship between disco and hip-hop." Why was it that, "within the space of a few short months, the break had assumed a central position within New York's nascent dance scene" (2008: 282), while the same technique was simultaneously killing it with dancers uptown? The intersecting histories of hip-hop and disco warrant further scholarly attention, but for the purposes of this inquiry, I only want to note that vinyl was being similarly used by multiple DJs in different musical contexts.

In focusing my attention on format, I do not mean to deny the individual contributions to culture—as Schloss (2004: 27) stresses, we need to take care to remember that *people* create culture, "each of whom had volition, creativity, and choice as to how to proceed"—but, rather, to use these cultural histories as a way of highlighting how consumption practices including copying and play, were key drivers in uncovering previously unknown possibilities of media formats and technologies. As Schloss (2004: 27) reminds us, musical cultures and genres do not "emerge fully formed," but grow, "through a series of small innovations that [are] later retroactively defined as foundational." Isolating the break, or playing doubles, is one such innovation; Gibbons's tape edits are another. Little by little, copy by copy, edits made disco.

Many discussions about copies revolve around their relationship with an original even when none exists as Benjamin warned. When we speak about most popular music recordings, there is rarely an original event, but a series of them, as Evan Eisenberg (2005) and others have noted: The mixed-down master recording is made to stand in as the "original," in the sense of its being that which is copied. Yet, it is not the existence of a master recording that made new musical moments possible, but the existence and procurement of *two copies* of such a recording that enabled Gibbons (Lawrence 2008: 279–80) and other DJs to isolate the drum break (Toop 1991: 60, in Schloss 2004: 31). This novel musical moment was enabled by multiples, by copies as abundance and copies as instances. Two copies of the same recording contain functionally identical content, but, as media artifacts, they can only be said to be similar because they are distinct objects, not one and the same. When DJs took two records and played part of each back-to-back, they exploited copy as a property that designates two things as being similar, but distinct, and copy as a property that indicates identity. But it is the former, the property of copy as similarity, that made the interruption, the innovation, possible. Or, to highjack Jonathan Sterne's (2003: 221) observation about sound recording, in the case of playing doubles,

---

beat—these could be isolated by using two copies of the record on twin turntables and, playing the one section over and over, flipping the needle back to the start on one while the other played through."

reproductions preceded and enabled that elusive quality: originality. It was the effect of playing records in this way, by seamlessly mixing between the playing of fragments of a recording that Gibbons would attempt to record to tape and then, in some cases, etch onto acetate. By isolating part of a fixed recording (often, the drum break) and fragmenting the record through repetition of part of it, Gibbons was able to unearth a groove that was new, yet that was also in the physical groove all along.

Vinyl, a storage and playback format, afforded users with a set of possibilities that had not been considered by its producers or manufacturers. They were put to a different use, changing their function without altering the material qualities. The potential properties of copies, together with the affordances of vinyl (and later tape and acetate) were possibilities that users discovered. DJs exploited vinyl's material characteristics to produce this novel effect. Copies of the same mass-produced recording could be relied upon to be physically alike and to sound identical (as long as they were cared for)—as noted, they are two instances of the same type. Vinyl records contain audio signals in a continuous spiral groove, a material property that makes it possible for users to begin and end play whenever (or wherever) they choose to do so. Though precision is difficult, practiced users employ a combination of auditory and spatial cues and cognitive capacities that draw upon their musical lexicon—their knowledge of the song itself—to find their chosen points of entry and exit. It is a musical dissection made possible by the character of vinyl as a medium of sound reproduction: The perfect parroting of *part* of a recording made recomposition a creative possibility, while it left the source copy unaltered. Fixity enabled recomposition.

4.6 Let your body talk

Vinyl's materiality made recomposition possible—copies as instances enabled repetitions that altered that which was listened to—but, to understand the cultural innovation, we cannot focus on materiality independent of its history and social use. "Playing doubles" and other pioneering techniques were situated practices—DJs exploited the possibilities of the media format in tandem with sound-reproduction technologies (mixer, turntable, and sound system) in a social context (nightclub, street party, etc.). It was in a particular time and space that a DJ played and listened to records in the presence of dancers listening and dancing to records. The space is communal, the moment is shared, and the media experience—listening to recordings in this space—is interactive, marked by several intersections of human bodies with media technologies. It is in this shared space and time that DJs are able to observe and interact with bodies in motion, and attempt to elicit response through the choice and use of recorded sound. *Simultaneously,* dancers and other listeners respond to the music, to the sonic event, as well as to the movements of other dancers and other sensory stimulations in space itself (lights, voices, romantic intrigue, etc.), with motion and sound (e.g., hand clapping, foot stomping, vocalizations, etc.). There is no point of omniscience: it is the people, in the space, in conjunction with the media played, who constitute the musical event. Dancers, like the DJs, *use* the music. For music sociologist Antoine Hennion (2001: 1) there is no reason to deem listening passive: that both DJs and dancers listen in the space simultaneously, and that both can be said to be involved in performances of listening. Why should the dancer's physical participation in the music be seen as passive, while the DJ's action of playing a recording is understood as active? Hennion (2001: 10) theorizes that music lovers use music as a technology to reach alternate states. He writes,

> Listening is a precise and highly organized activity, but its aim is not to control something or to achieve a specific goal: on the contrary, its objective is to bring about a loss of control, an act of surrender. It is not a matter of doing something, but of making something happen [...]). What should happen is not planned or intentional: we must allow ourselves to be carried away, moved, so that something can take place. I have done everything necessary to make something happen but it is imperative that I do not try to control what does happen.

Hennion (2001: 15) argues that dance and other uses of music "cannot be disassociated from 'music itself'". That said, in histories of dance music and in music journalism, we privilege the DJ's actions when accounting for the content and mood of a night because it is the DJ who manipulates the "data of culture" (Gitelman 2006: 13)—it is he or she who selects the records and manipulates the sound—and it is the data of culture that we can pin down, observe, and document.

According to Lawrence (2008), Gibbons was revered as a DJ: He was a skilled selector and mixer, his collection was extensive,[13] and he was sensitive to the subtleties of "working the room"—that is, of eliciting and reacting to interpretation and responses from dancers. It is all a part of the DJ's performance of records—of their knowledge of those records and of what makes a dance floor move. Although some would like to deny them their status as performers, most DJs do describe their efforts as "performance." New York DJ François K recently talked about what it means for him as a DJ to perform records:

---

[13] Lawrence (2008: 280) notes that, when the eighteen-year-old Gibbons met Flores in 1972, he had already collected over 1,500 7-inch singles.

I'm "performing" records right on the mixing boards ... I'm trying to take any record and treat people to a new version of it. A version that I'm dubbing out right in front of them. You will find me performing a record, not just letting it play out. I can take that aesthetic to pretty much anything I'm featuring. In that sense, it's easy to move beyond trends or fashion. Whether it's an old Quincy Jones track or just something that came out last week, it's about the treatment you apply to make it make sense. (Tregoning 2010)

Great DJs like François K or Walter Gibbons are able to communicate something about their own experience of listening—Can you hear what I hear?—and then respond to the mood of the room and the reactions of other listening bodies and minds—Can you feel it?

"In the end, the essence of musical performance is being able to convey emotion," wrote Daniel Levitin (2007: 204) in his discussion about cognition and musical expertise. Gibbons brought his expertise as a listener to his musical *use* of vinyl recordings. His performance of them in a social context, it seems, led him to the production of his first tape edits (Lawrence 279: 288). Records alone did not beget tape edits; Gibbons did.

This is a pattern worth noting: It is the *use* of recordings, rather than their *production*, that gave rise to edits as a compositional strategy and that shaped the resulting content and aesthetic. To borrow a digital metaphor, "extending the break," "playing doubles," and mixing between two records are analog hacks[14]: a user's interruption of the continuous signal embodied in the fixed groove; a tacit assertion that, for users, playback's past and play's present are indistinguishable as sonic events. Users "hacked" mass-produced vinyl records—objects of consumption—by exploiting the nature of records as copies that can be repeated and as copies that are only similar: Each record is independent and unique, even when it contains the same content as another one. Lessig (2008) would characterize vinyl records as "read-only" because they are fixed objects of consumption that cannot be altered, but it is this characteristic—its *fixity*, as well as its existence as both instance and multiple—that DJs used to isolate a fragment of song and repeat it in real time, to forge a compositional strategy that worked with the reliability of the storage medium to reproduce a fixed recording at will. Through repetition, DJs, as users of vinyl, were able to access the

---

[14] For Mackenzie Wark (2004: 160) a hack is, "the production of production: Production takes place on the basis of a prior hack which gives to production its formal, social, repeatable and reproducible form. Every production is a hack formalized and repeated on the basis of its representation. To produce is to repeat; to hack, to differentiate." The "hack" differentiates by taking advantage of what is already available or possible—recall that Marx thought consumption was already production, and vice versa (1978: 228).

compositional possibilities of the "'changing same'—that is, the constant variation of collectively owned, repeated materials" (Middleton 1999: 143).

Mixing between records in this manner requires physical and mental dexterity and Gibbons's skills were impressive. But vinyl also had its limitations, and so does the body. According to nightclub patron Mark Zimmer,

> [Gibbons] was working with these short little records which were two or three minutes long with maybe a two-measure introduction, and he had the mixing down pat. He would extend the break until he got exhausted or until the people on the dance floor became fatigued. (Lawrence 2008: 281)

If it was bodies in motion on the dance floor that prompted DJs to extend the break, it was the body's own limitations that drove Gibbons to explore the use of another analog format, reel-to-reel tape. DJ Tony Smith recounted:

> These quick-fire mixes were *work* … . There were so many short songs where he had to do this mixing technique that after a while he started to put his beat mixes on reel-to-reel at home. Walter became really adept at reel-to-reel. (Lawrence 2008: 288)

If playback and play are indistinguishable from the listener's standpoint, then it seems reasonable to consider the creative possibilities that rerecording a recording might open up. As a strategy for composition, crossing media formats empowered users to augment and compound the effects and results of the DJ's compositional skill set of selection, repetition, filter, and mix with the physical properties of reel-to-reel tape—which can be cut and looped, sped up, slowed down, and recorded again ad infinitum. Each time an edited composition crossed back to the turntable via vinyl or acetate, yet another user-created feedback loop became possible—a mediated call and response that continues to this day.

Dancers made dance music

It could be argued that the contribution of dancers to edits as a compositional form is only incidental; but to omit dancers is to omit the body from the story of dance music. I argue that edits, as a compositional strategy, were forged by this intersection of human bodies with electronic technologies and copies of recordings. The network among dancers, DJs, recordings, and playback technologies highlights the active nature of listening, and troubles theories that code reception as passive. Yet, in some academic cultural analysis of dance-music cultures, both dancer and dance floor as communal events are often sidelined: Discussions of "remix culture" (sometime "DJ Culture") look to the DJ as the heroic figurehead, but not to the community of dancers. Jeremy Gilbert and Ewan Pearson (now a well-known producer and DJ) consider academic anxieties when theorizing about the role of dancing in dance music and culture. They write, "Dance seems to resist discourse; and some discourses have resisted writing about dance—failing to deal with the dance at the heart of dance culture whatsoever" (Gilbert and Pearson 1999: 6). Sociological approaches, they argue, tend to view "the current dance mania as a part of modern man's revolt against being a perpetual spectator" (1999: 16), as well as a tendency to want it to "signify" (1999: 15). Dance can be taken seriously if it is a resistance or a code, but not if it is a pleasure.[15] Gilbert and Pearson disagree and suggest we move beyond thinking about dancing as an activity that has "a message to reveal," that is a "mirror" of some social phenomenon, or that is "'mere' escapism" (1999: 16). Dancing is a way of experiencing music. They write,

> Music is specifically registered throughout the body, it is not simply a matter of mental cognition. This aspect of musical experience is manifested most vividly in the case of dance music; the dancer received music through the body in a manner whose directness is manifested in the very act of dancing ... Nowhere is the physical reality of music made more obvious than on the dancefloor, where particular configurations of sound (i.e., Records) are judged by their success or failure in "making us" dance. (Gilbert and Pearson 1999: 45–7)

DJs don't just perform records: The best DJs aim to work the floor. "The DJ is utterly directed towards getting people on to the floor. In effect s/he has to construct dancers, by playing music which will articulate bodies in dance. It ought to do so with maximum force—one wants to be carried away by the music—but also without prescribing how one moves" writes Toynbee (2000: 144). For Toynbee and others this makes the dance floor a bit of a puzzle, since it is a space at once free and programmed. Regardless, our understanding of music culture is impoverished if we leave out key participants. Early DJs do talk about how their style was shaped by dancers—Kool Herc, for instance, noticed that dancers were "waiting for certain parts of the record," prompting him to shift his attention to finding the best breaks

---

[15] Gilbert and Pearson (1999: 15) write, "Any suggestion that we might consider dance to be what Paul Spencer has called 'an end in itself that transcends utility' is strongly resisted ... all such accounts agree that there must be a function, or a telos, in the activity of dance ... social dance is evoked in terms of the symbolic reinforcement of community structures and the regulation of social behaviour."

(Chang 2005: 79). Given this, it seems imperative that we underscore the interaction between DJs and dancers and acknowledge their contribution to the origins of the form.

4.7 Are samples copies?

I have used the story of Walter Gibbons and the rise of edits to highlight the analog antecedents of today's digital edits and remixes and trace their material origins. In this narrative, playback and re-recording prompted innovations in form and style; they serve as examples of how something that is just the same, that is a copy, a repetition, can bring something new into the world. But are these analog reproductions and repetitions similar to or identical with our current notion of samples and sampling? Keeping in mind that identity and similarity are different relationships, I ask: Are samples copies? Recall that my approach in this book is to tease out what the property of being a copy may (or may not) tell us about historically situated mediated experience (where experience spans modes of production, distribution, and reception) and help us better understand the relationship between media technologies and cultural change. So, if samples are one and the same as their source (that is, they are identical), or if they share many, but not all, properties with their source (that is, they are similar), what does this distinction tell us about re-recordings/samples as historically situated artifacts and re-recording/sampling as a historically and socially situated practices? How do relationships with recorded instances and abundance shape these experiences? That is, how do copies influence copying, and how does repetition shape what is repeated?

The word *sample* as it relates to electronics and sound recording is a relatively recent sense[16] of the word. This sense means "any of the numerous momentary values in the amplitude of an analogue signal that are obtained when it is sampled for conversion to a digital form"; another sense means "an excerpt of recorded sound or music reused or modified as part of a new recording or performance; a sound excerpt stored in digital form for this purpose" (sample, n.). *Sampling,* as a verb used in electronics and sound recording, indicates "the action or process of sampling sounds (cf. sample, v.) in order to convert an analogue signal into a digital one; *spec.* the technique of digitally encoding sound for subsequent electronic processing, modification, or reuse, esp. as part of a recording or performance; the incorporation of an excerpt from one musical recording into another" (sample, v.).

---

[16]Per the OED the sense of sampling that refers to electronics and sound arises in 1970 and the musical sense dates to 1985 (though it seems likely it was in circulation among music technologists prior to this documentation).

Ever since the early 1990s when Grand Upright Music successfully sued Biz Markie for copyright infringement related to a sample he used on his album *I Need a Haircut,* the digital sampler has held a place in our collective consciousness as the technological catalyst for the struggles over copyright and fair use. Following on from these conflicts, scholars have offered critiques of copyright that question whether it is an aesthetically neutral policy, or whether the law favors some creative acts over others. In the introduction to their edited collection *Music and Copyright*, Simon Frith and Lee Marshall expressed concern that copyright now restricts more musical activity than it supports (Frith and Marshall 2004: 16). This concern was the subject of musicologist Joanna Demers's (2006) study of the relationship between intellectual property law and musical creativity, in which she examined key copyright battles and how they have altered the aesthetics of popular music. She writes, "IP laws have influenced the careers and compositional choices of many artists who either allude to or duplicate other compositions in their own works. For instance, expensive litigation has fundamentally changed Public Enemy's sound by making the group unwilling to sample anymore" (2006: 11–12).

Public Enemy came to prominence in the late 1980s, a part of hip-hop's second wave. First, by creating "pause tapes" and tape loops, and later by using a SP-1200, a 12-bit digital sampler,[17] the group created dense, wall-of-sound collages—a kind of musical realism stitched from a wide variety of extant recordings. While many listeners and music critics felt an affinity for this new sound in much the way an earlier generation heard echoes of the city streets in bebop's chaotic dissonance, Public Enemy's collages were made up of re-recordings of copyrighted material, selected from records they had collected and then sampled. Chuck D and Shocklee say that the enforcement of strict copyright laws in the early 1990s fundamentally changed Public Enemy's style and their sound, by altering the sonic possibilities available to them. Chuck D told Kembrew McLeod,

> Public Enemy's music was affected more than anybody's because we were taking thousands of sounds. If you separated the sounds, they wouldn't have been anything—they were unrecognizable. The sounds were all collaged together to make a sonic wall. Public Enemy was affected because it is too expensive to defend against a claim. So we had to change our whole style, the style of *It Takes a Nation* and *Fear of a Black Planet*, by 1991. (McLeod 2004: 24)

When the group stopped working with existing recordings, their sound changed—not only because they couldn't afford to sample so much

---

[17]For a discussion of the SP-1200 and how hip-hop producers exploited the sampler, see Milner (2009: 330–5).

(although this was a factor), but also because sampling allowed them to work with sonority. Shocklee explained this shift to McLeod:

> We were forced to start using different organic instruments, but you can't really get the right kind of compression that way. A guitar sampled off a record is going to hit differently than a guitar sampled in the studio. The guitar that's sampled off a record is going to have all the compression that they put on the recording, the equalization. It's going to hit the tape harder. It's going to slap at you. Something that's organic is almost going to have a powder effect. It hits more like a pillow than a piece of wood. So those things change your mood, the feeling you can get off of a record. If you notice that by the early 1990s, the sound has gotten a lot softer. (McLeod 2004: 24)

These sonic possibilities are often overlooked in discussions about sampling technologies[18] in media and cultural studies where samples are often thought to be synonymous with citation or quotation. While samples can be used to signify, samples also offer producers "sonic flexibility" (Porcello 1991: 69). As Schocklee's comment suggests, artists can work with different dimensions of a recording—in addition to capturing and redeploying vocals, melodies and rhythms, artists can work with the sonic qualities of recordings as well as the technologies they are using to manipulate those sample. Hip-hop DJs loved the SP-1200 for qualities that its inventors thought were faults. Shockley told Greg Milner: "It quantified sound very abruptly ... It was the thing that gave the SP-1200 its soul." This shift, according to Shocklee, was "more like DJing" (Milner 2009: 334). Performing recordings could bring its own sound.

The musical uses of sampling were user-led innovations—Milner (2009: 332) documents how the engineers of the SP-1200 were baffled by the success of what they thought was inferior technology—and these unintended uses appear to have been shaped by the practice and use of analog technologies and recordings by DJs in that era. Demers work shows us, in case after case, how limiting the repertoire of sounds with which one can work, and restricting the possible uses of a technology, in turn limits the parameters for expression and performance. The obvious rejoinder is that samples can be used, but they must be cleared. The often sampled New York electro group ESG released an EP in 1992 entitled "Sample Credits Don't Pay Our Bills"—and it is often pointed out that copyright holders have a legal right to their rent and it is often the small independent players that have the hardest time collecting. Licensing, however, can be an expensive prospect

---

[18] The aesthetics of sampling is an under-researched area in the study of popular music. For notable exceptions, see Fairchild (2013), Rodgers (2004), Schloss (2004), and McLeod and DiCola (2011).

that, as Marshall (2005: 135) points out, "effectively censor[s] the use of found materials by small-time musician[s]." Given that nonprofessional and semi-professional music makers have also been a source of innovation in popular music in the last forty-plus years, particularly in the use of technologies such as samplers, synthesizers, and drum machines, this becomes illustrative of how the protection of expression can simultaneously prevent new expression. Or, more accurately, given that it is common knowledge that sampling is widespread in an era of cheap digital technologies, it deems a good deal of everyday expression as deviant, illicit, or for personal use only. It sends expression underground, out of the glare of publicity. In such cases, copyright restricts access,[19] use, and new possibilities.

Copyright may have been designed as an incentive to create, but Jason Toynbee (2001) argues that the romantic model of creativity copyright was founded upon continues to privilege some forms of musical creativity while it sidelines others. Copyright doesn't protect the interests of all artists; It protects the interests of a particular subset of artists. Toynbee critiques copyright for its failure to account for the social nature of many modes of creativity and, with regard to music making, for its disregard for the mediated character of creativity in twentieth- and twenty-first-century popular music. Almost all aspects of music making today necessarily involve, or are shaped by, recorded sound. They shape genres, influence styles, and create communal experiences. Recordings are often the end product of a long chain of mediated musical practices and making music and making recordings are often one and the same activity. "In much popular music, the musical work is the recording," argues Toynbee (2004: 127). Which is to say that the composition takes place *during* the process of recording, not prior to it. In copyright, composition and performance are conceptualized as different functions, yet "in an important sense the two are intertwined in most forms of popular music making," writes Toynbee (2004: 127). In contemporary dance music, for instance, there is often no composition that exists apart from the record the producer creates, and it is usually the producer, once thought of as a technician, who is now considered the creative force behind the record over and above any samples or musicians that were recorded. Indeed, it is the producer who will now claim "writing" credits in order to exploit copyright. While dance producers may have found a way to access copyright protection, Toynbee (2004: 124) argues that copyright unfairly privileges certain kinds of musical production over others and "fail[s] to take account of an increasingly important characteristic of music in the twentieth century and after; the renewed convergence of the functions of writing and performance through techniques like improvisation, repetition-variation

---

[19] For an in-depth discussion on this problem, see McLeod and DiCola (2011).

and sampling." Copyright fails contemporary musicians, Toynbee (2004: 124) argues, because it fails to mesh with popular practices—in particular, those that aren't that easily viewed as a kind of writing and are instead entangled with the affordances of recorded sound and its performance. Writes Toynbee (2000: 69), "With sound recording the writing of music takes on a different form." When Public Enemy's Shocklee, tells us that sampling is more like DJing, he's telling us something about how composition and performance are intertwined. Listening is the practice that binds them.

The privileging of writing in copyright overshadows the significance of listening in musical practice. It also fails to account for the influence of recording technologies and formats on that which is recorded. In popular music, when discussing the role that early and mid-century recordings played in shaping music, style and training are often acknowledged as instrumental. Many musicians, from the Jazz Age onward (Toynbee 2004: 126), have told stories about how records not only inspired, but loomed large in their musical training, talking about how listening to records taught them to play. When asked how he taught himself to play,[20] the eccentric guitarist and recording artist John Fahey said: "Well I had a lot of old records around ... and I listened to those and tried to imitate them as best I could" (Duncan 1969).

In later decades musicians speak less of how recordings enabled them to learn to play songs, styles or fragments, and more about how listening to records taught them how to make their own recordings. That is, they listened to sonic qualities and sought suitable samples in the same way an earlier generation listened for musical patterns. Today, after decades of multi-track recording and sample-based genres, enthusiastic listeners are said to spot samples as sport, a colloquialism suggesting that more listeners are now attuned to the electronic composition of recordings—the way they are made up of layered tracks, each of which has its own sonority as well as a relationship in the mix. As Tara Rodgers (2004: 314) has highlighted, the specialized skills and musicality involved in sampling are often overlooked in the academic appreciations of sampling that view it primarily and exclusively as a practice of resistance.

Considering reception is crucial to understanding edits as a form. Vinyl as a storage and playback format made repeated play possible, and playback in real time made it possible to fragment in real time. Through repetition, a DJ could recompose on the fly. Grandmaster Flash describes "playing doubles" to Kembrew McLeod (2007: 71):

---

[20] For example, John Fahey discussed the role records played in his musical education on an episode of *Guitar Guitar* (Duncan 1969), as did Joan Baez, in a documentary on her career (Wharton 2009).

You know the percussive part that you wait for—before they called it "the break" it was "the get-down part." What pissed me off was that part was so short, so I just extended it with two copies to five minutes.

Repeated play could extend "the get-down part"; re-recording created new possibilities for further extension, time-shifting, and manipulation. However, the practice of sampling is not only the recording or repetition of a phrase; to understand sampling, we also need to emphasize the role of *close listening*. Rodgers argues that, all too often, discussions of sampling are connected either to anxieties about borderlines between humans and machines or to questions about copyright. She argues that the *musicality* of sampling is overlooked. Samplers are often misunderstood as effortless and automatic, with little credit given to the listening practice, skill, and effort it takes to find a sample and capture it in the first place. Explains Rogers (2004: 314–15), "[E]vidence suggests that the gathering and manipulation of samples is one of the most time-consuming (and thus, central) aspects of electronic music production ... . Like the practice of learning and playing almost any musical instrument, sampling is a laborious, and eventually habitual, embodied physical routine." This requires extensive listening to and collecting recordings, as well as understanding what kind of groove the repetition might produce.

Rodgers asks how sampling resonates with, or diverges from, other musical practices. She identifies four key steps in the sampling process: selecting, recording, editing, and processing. In general, she believes there has been a lack of focus on the goals of the samplists—specifically, on their musical goals. Rodgers considers digital technologies to be a new family of instruments and set of musical possibilities (2004: 313). At the same time, she cites other musical precedents for sampling:

> It is well documented that sampling is not a new musical practice, nor is it linked to the advent of the microchip. Roots of sampling extend throughout Afrodiasporic musical practices including Caribbean "versioning," bop "quoting" and dub and reggae production techniques. (Rodgers 2004: 313)

The practice of sampling is connected to the place of listening and repetition as key musical practices and their long history. Gibbons, and others who made tape edits of commercially mixed recordings on vinyl, were engaged in an activity that was very similar to sampling. These recording activities— whether they were Gibbons's dancefloor-ready acetates or cassette-tape edits, like those made by PAJ, a trio of DJs in Montreal (Kent 2010)[21]—

---

[21] According to the liner notes on a recent re-release of PAJ's efforts by the Glaswegian DJ Al Kent, PAJ "produced all of these edits between 1975–8. Some made it onto acetates, cut at

required expert listening, an understanding of what was usable and repeatable, of how that would play to a dance floor, and of how to make use of re-recording to fragment and recompose. They were able to use recording and repetition to perform connections they had made while listening to music. Tara Rodgers argues that "samplers, arguably more than other instruments offer musicians the opportunity to articulate a personalized 'aural history'—an archive of sounds that can be employed to express specific musical and political statements" (2004: 315); re-recording and later sampling gave experienced listeners an outlet for sharing their attention to detail; these practices enabled what we might call a performance of listening.

The existence of such early tape edits suggest that listening and production practices were transformed prior to the widespread use of samplers. PAJ's cassette-tape edits suggest that recorded music was already heard as a possible engine for recomposition, via fragmentation and layering, prior to the availability of digital sampling technologies. Sampling, as Rodgers highlights, was part of a pop-music continuum. It can be argued that some of these practices, in turn, inspired innovations in DJing and turntablism, as well as the edit-making that informs this chapter. Sample-based music is not unique in its use of repetition—as Middleton (1999) emphasizes, repetition is a part of all music, including high-art music—but it can be said that all recordings are potential samples as repetition and replicability are affordances of the technology. The earliest disco edits that concern this chapter were user-driven innovations that built on the performative aspects of the DJ's playing and mixing between records. The early 1970s mark a moment when people had been hearing music produced with multi-track recordings for almost a decade and they'd been playing with records for decades. The audience was listening.

Levitin explains that much of the pleasure we derive from music comes from the way it plays with timing and with the brain's sensitivity to "timing information" (2007: 108). "Perhaps the ultimate illusion in music is the illusion of structure and form," he writes. "There is nothing in a sequence of notes themselves that creates the rich emotional associations we have with music, nothing about a scale, a chord, or a chord sequence that intrinsically causes us to expect a resolution. Our ability to make sense of music depends on experience, and on neural structures that can learn and modify themselves with each new listening to an old song. Our brains learn a kind of musical grammar that is specific to the music of our culture, just as we learn to speak the language of our culture" (2007: 108). Levitin recounts

---

New York's Sunshine Sounds Studios and were distributed through David Mancuso's New York Record Pool. Some got no further than reel-to-reel tape (some were even only originally recorded on cassette!). But they all got club play thanks to PAJ Disco Mix's relationship with Canada's top DJ of the time, The Limelight's Robert Ouimet" (Kent 2010).

how, in 1969, his own experience of listening to records while wearing headphones forever changed his relationship with music. He writes,

> The new artists that I was listening to were all exploring stereo mixing for the first time. Because the speakers that came with my hundred-dollar all-in-one stereo system weren't very good, I had never before heard the depth that I could hear in the headphones—the placement of the instruments both in the left-right field and in the front-back (reverberant) space. To me, records were no longer just about songs anymore, but about the sound. Headphones opened up a world of sonic colors, a palette of nuances and details that went far beyond the chords and melody, the lyrics of a particular singer's voice ... . The sound was an enveloping experience. Headphones made the music more personal for me; it was suddenly coming from inside my head, not out there in the world. This personal connection is ultimately what drove me to become a recording engineer and producer. (Levitin 2007: 2)

Levitin's anecdote is evidence that listeners, even eleven-year-old listeners, could hear the shift from what Toynbee refers to as the "documentary" and "ventriloquism" modes of recording to the construction of new sonic environments that came with the widespread use of multi-tracking and effects (Toynbee 2000: 68–101).[22] The other notable part of Levitin's story is his claim that listening to records fueled a passion for wanting to produce and engineer these created soundscapes. Writing about his education as a young sound engineer, Levitin explains that he learned to hear the difference, not only between different microphones, but between *brands* of magnetic tape. "Ampex 456 tape had a characteristic 'bump' in the low frequency range, Scotch 250 had a characteristic crispness in the high frequencies, and Agra 467 a luster in the midrange" (2007: 3). Critical to my argument about the relationship among material, form, and listening is Levitin's revelation that the parts making up the whole could be perceived, and that it was through repeated listening—that is, reception—that his desire to manipulate these fragments seems to spring. This intimacy that Levitin experienced is a common one—the voice, after all, is inside *your* head—and sound recordings tend to produce an intimacy between listeners and, indeed, a shared history of listening.

---

[22] Toynbee argues that this begins with techniques such as tape echoes in the 1950s, Phil Spector's Wall of Sound series in the 1960s, and, finally with the time-shifting and experimentation that multi-tracking made possible as it began to be used in the 1960s, but that they required a new perception of the technosphere. Toynbee, curious as to why sound recording was so slow to employ such techniques when compared with filmmaking, theorizes that this was because music was already invested in, and defined by, the manipulation of time. Real-time play was adequate; time-based innovations in recording were not initially necessary (Toynbee 2000: 68–101).

For Rodgers, sampling uses "'reality' as a point of departure to an alternative, metaphysical sonic vocabulary" (2004: 315). Sampling is often discussed in terms of its ability to comment on reality—that is, in terms of its narrative potential. Paul Théberge (2003: 94) observed that most pop-music scholarship focuses on the "disruptive" uses of sampling and overlooks many other common uses of samples in media production. Théberge wanted to draw attention to the common use of licensed sample libraries, but I'd like to apply this observation to edits. These early edits— repetitions intended to extend the best bits of a song, or to elicit bodily response from dancers in order to keep them dancing—do not disrupt in the same way a satirical mashup does. It does not offer comment, instead, repetition is used to unearth a groove. According to Levitin (2007: 170), "Groove is that quality that moves the song forward, the musical equivalent to a book that you can't put down. When a song has a good groove, it invites us into a sonic world we don't want to leave. Although we are aware of the pulse of the song, external time seems to stand still, and we don't want the song to ever end." (Recall one edit maker's explanation for his craft: "When you hear something great, you want it to continue" [Beta 2008].) Levitin (2007: 170) argues that groove seems to come from "a particular performer or a particular performance, not what is written down on paper." Groove varies from performance to performance, and not all listeners agree on which grooves are "good."[23] Middleton (1999: 143) writes that groove "marks an understanding of rhythmic patterning that underlines its role in producing the characteristic rhythmic 'feel' of a piece, a feel created by a repeating framework with which variation can then take place." (Or, as the pop group Dee-Lite would have it, "Groove Is in the Heart.") Though Levitin (2007: 171) explains that musicians tend to agree "that a groove works best when it is not strictly metronomic—that is, when it is not perfectly machinelike," it is clear that the perfect repetition enabled by technology, first by mixing between two records, then through tape-recording, and, later, through digital sampling and sequencing, contributed to aesthetic developments in musical form (it is also clear that electronic producers are well aware of the appeal of imperfection, with many boasting about how they manipulate their samples to produce this particularity Levitin discusses). But, as Toynbee points out, even the "robotic" sound of sequencers could be embraced by producers and composers—there are a number of dance genres premised on such a sound.[24] This convergence of timing and copying—repeating the past in the present, and thus

---

[23] "The brain needs to create a model of a constant pulse—a schema—so that we know when the musicians are deviating from it. This is similar to variations of a melody: "we need to have a mental representation of what the melody is in order to know—and appreciate—when the musician is taking liberties with it," writes Levitin (2007).

[24] The poet Tan Lin proposed an alternate definition of groove, one based on the poetics of

changing the future—is one of the affordances of recordings that producers work with.

If we take the material dimension of media seriously, however, we have to acknowledge that copying and sampling are not synonymous. Sampling, and, indeed, the practice of re-recording on tape that preceded digital sampling, are dependent on the copying processes; but, more crucially, the resultant aesthetic is predicated on encounters with copies of recordings and on repeated listening. That these techniques followed on the heels of a decade of multi-track production and its technosphere of sound possibilities, that records were cheap and plentiful and listeners could become intimately involved in this technosphere as a result of repeated play and the existence of various playback technologies, were crucial elements in identifying possible samples and then turning them into useful ones. "Playing doubles" was an innovation made possible by the sonic equivalency of two distinct records that contained the same content, but also the DJ-listener's imaginings of the song and its possibilities. Dee-Lite's 1990 pop-dance song "Groove Is in the Heart" is said to be about the infatuation one can experience when hearing a new song for the first time; echoes of this sense of infatuation can be heard when contemporary edit producers explain why they talk about loving a song so much they never want it to end. Dancers also contributed to the aesthetic—a groove prompts dancers to move; it offers them a way of experiencing the sound. By excising a fragment from its whole, an editor or a sampler may or may not create links between both. Writes Toynbee (2000: 128), "The musician's urge to repeat produces difference just because that initial experience is unrecoverable, an aspect of the lack in which all human subjects are constituted. The point is that in trying and failing to repeat an ideal experience, variation creeps in."

Samples require more scholarly attention on aesthetic grounds. As both Fairchild (2014) and Rodgers (2004) have argued, their *musicality* merits more research and thought; so too does their materiality. Middleton (1999: 154) has observed that samples provide an opportunity to consider the relationship of "individual pieces to the larger repertory." I would like to suggest that they are also opportunities to think about the material dimensions of technology and listening. We must acknowledge and think through how analog listening experiences, formats, collections, and fragmentation shaped sampling as a digital technique, and then grapple with the reality of particular instances, material encounters, and situated listening. We should also consider the growing trade in vintage digital gear from the 1980s and 1990s—including early samplers and Digital FM Synthesizers—and listen closely to users reports about the sound of the machines that move

---

digital reading as replication. He writes that "a 'groove' is disco's 'description' of data copying itself, ad nauseam" (2008: 94).

them. Giving credit to the edit is one small gesture towards these material histories.

4.8 Parasites, pirates, and permission

Though Gibbons's edits and later remixes are now respected and revered as trailblazing, such reverence was not always forthcoming. In the early 1970s, club DJs were, as Lawrence (2008: 295) notes, "widely regarded as musical parasites," and there was some resentment in certain parts of the recording industry when such lowly figures were courted by the labels. When DJs like Gibbons began to receive paid commissions from labels to create remixes, and when those studio versions began to outsell the original recordings, some writers, artists, and (even) producers felt slighted and maybe a little insulted—if not downright threatened (Lawrence 2008: 295, 218). "The mixer cut-up the lyrics and changed the music … . It was as if the writers and producers were nothing," songwriter Allan Felder told Lawrence (2008: 295). This sentiment, that edits and remixes are derivative creations and that their makers are parasites, continues to be leveled against edit makers today, although perhaps not for the same reasons. The mid-1970s-era disdain centered on a perceived lack of musicality in the role of DJs, engineers, and other knob twiddlers; today, though this might continue in some circles, the disdain for edit makers often comes from more established players in the same music market or culture.

Spirited debates continue to take place online. One such debate took place on the website DJHistory.com in the height of the renewed fashion for edits over a then-unknown edit maker who released his digitally produced edit on vinyl without initially licensing the track. The dressing-down he received from the producer and copyright holder of the source track is illustrative of this continued sense that edit makers are parasites and their efforts uncreative:

> [Y]ou need to leave the making of records to people who have something original to contribute. In case you hadn't noticed, the business of selling recorded music is in serious flux and we are taking hits left, right and center. Now would be the time to treat copyright-holders and authors of intellectual property with respect, proper licensing protocol and kid-fucking-gloves, not to bootleg and re-sell their shit to boost your own profile.

There is a deep irony to these tussles over permission particularly in light of how permission played in the origin of edits as a form. Shifts in attitudes about permission also provides us with an opportunity to reflect on the "historical continuities of piracy" (Marshall 2005: 4).

In narratives about the origins of remix, the birth of the 12-inch single and Gibbons's contribution to extended-dance formats, it is easy to overlook that some of the practices and artifacts that helped build his career were unauthorized. Gibbons made (and, in at least two instances, sold) his edited compositions *without* permission from the copyright holders. As I mentioned earlier, Melting Pot, the label he ran with Flores, also bootlegged rare records from Gibbons's collection for other DJs to use (Lawrence 2008: 291). Gibbons was also not alone in this small black market for recordings on acetate. Angel Sound's Sandy Sandoval told Lawrence that, by the mid-1970s, about 20 percent of his business was cutting acetates for club DJs (Lawrence 2008: 289). And, although most of these artifacts are difficult to account for, given their short lifespan and questionable legal status, contemporary private collections—such as that of Patrick Lejeune (a.k.a. Disco Patrick)—provide evidence of the prolif-eration of this specialized media artifact and the greater culture of which they were a part. These illicit artifacts and unauthorized practices paved the way for the later commercial success of extended-dance formats, such as remixes. For Gibbons, in particular, it was his success as a DJ and the energy his edits seemed to ignite on the dance floor that prompted the invitation from Salsoul to produce remixes for the new disco label. Working with the multi-track master tapes—and in a studio, assisted by an engineer (at a fixed fee)—rather than with the premixed and mastered commercial record (Lawrence 2008: 292–300) widened Gibbons's creative scope. However, as Lawrence notes, Gibbons's style as a remixer, like his style as an edit maker, continued to be influenced by the on-the-fly sound collages he made as a DJ, and by the moments he shared with a roomful of dancers (Lawrence 2008: 294). Permission might have been "vital, legally" (Yoko Ono, in Lessig 2008: 11), but it was by no means vital to the innovations that Gibbons and other users forged by working within the possibilities recordings and recording technologies afforded. Although I am primarily interested in aesthetic innovations and their relationship with materiality, I think it is also worth noting that Gibbons's subsequent success as a remixer also expanded the possibilities for DJs within the music industry—and that this success hinged on work he began doing without permission. Writing in 1986, *Billboard*'s dance reporter Brian Chin explained that "studio mixing, one of the first realistic career diversifications available to a club DJ, has become pervasive in the record industry" (1986). DJs knew things about songs, and how they worked in a dance context, that others did not. That the origins of edits were unauthorized does not mean they occurred in opposition to the music industry, or as a resistance to the commercial music industry. Indeed, edits could be seen as a technique that DJs used to get noticed within the recording industry. The coding of remix as a resistance is a highly problematic, if not wholly romantic, gesture. Toynbee has argued that it was the circulation of *commercially* recorded music that increased participation in music culture. When musicians became consumers of recording and playback technologies, as well as recordings, new kinds of participation became possible. This is not to say that every DJ or producer who makes music wants a major-label record deal. But, in the history of popular music, it is very difficult to cast off the industry that subsists on the culture—even when we would like to, given the track record of some of the major labels toward artists and consumers. Recall that Schütze's answer to this cultural dilemma is to distinguish the remixes that were made for the recording industry, dismissing them as "remakes": My concern is that, if we do this, we are gerrymandering cultural artifacts along political lines, rather than "carving the beast of reality along its joints" (Plato 1973: 265e). The history of remix aesthetics suggests that we could develop an approach that could account for innovations, whether they come from above or from below, and, thus, one that deals with both the materiality of media, the situated nature of mediated experience, and aesthetics of circulation.

4.9 Digital revival and an analog persistence

Despite the copious column inches devoted to their demise, vinyl records did not vanish with the introduction of the compact disc in the 1980s, nor did the format disappear with the advent of the MP3 in the late 1990s. New vinyl records continued to be manufactured and sold (albeit in smaller numbers than in their heyday) and while some old records gathered dust in basements, thrift shops, and other venerable institutions of cultural waste (Straw 2000), others are actively sought out, traded, sold, and collected, in person and online. In recent years, articles on vinyl's revival in the network era have replaced the stories about vinyl's obsolescence in the mainstream press. In 2015, for example, the Recording Industry of America reported that U.S. sales of album-length vinyl records were at their highest since 1988. Although new vinyl is still a tiny fraction of the market for recorded music, a $416 million market can't be ignored (particularly after two decades of ever dwindling sales.) Vinyl's comeback is an opportunity to ask: Why this technology *now*? To begin to unpack this contemporary moment, to understand the meaning of vinyl in networked culture, I turn to a related revival: The return of the disco edit in the 2000s and the phenomena's attachments to vinyl.

The dawn of the twenty-first century witnessed the widespread uptake of affordable digital-editing software and broadband Internet access in the developed world; it was also when, in certain circles, the edits and the disco they helped create, enjoyed a 'revival' of their own (Beta 2008; Drever 2009; Lech et al. 2008; Reynolds 2001; Rowlands 2008). In the late 1990s and early 2000s, as the market for what came to be known as Electronic Dance Music expanded and became increasingly commercialized, there was a simultaneous interest in the roots and histories of underground scenes and the genealogies of samples, as well as a growing global conversation, facilitated by email lists, newsgroups, and online forums, organized around genres (and rapidly multiplying subgenres), DJs, and producers. This new globalized outlook for dance music's many genre cultures refocused the narratives about dance music culture away from place, scenes, parties, and clubs, and towards genres, DJs, and producers. It is in an environment of networked communication that particular groups of participants began to consider their histories, and to some extent reenact them (or perhaps to recognize their culture's readymade rituals.) It is also at this moment, after over two decades of remix culture in the dance music sense, that edits as a particular form are invoked, produced, and put to use. A curious aspect of the edit's renewed popularity was that while most were made with digital tools, the parameters of the technique were, for the most part, unchanged and vinyl continued to shape the form with many edit makers turning to secondhand vinyl for source material, and some choosing a vinyl release for their efforts. As such, edits offer an alternative pathway into interrogating the uses and affordances of analog formats and technologies in network culture.

Despite the expenses of manufacturing[25] and difficulties with distribution, vinyl remained a popular format for edits (Lech et al. 2008; Rowlands 2008), and a small but significant number of contemporary DJs continued to play and collect vinyl, either exclusively or in tandem with digital formats. Producing edits to play to dance floors and collecting records, (i.e., "digging in the crates") are companion practices. Joseph Schloss, in his 2004 ethnography of sample-based U.S. hip-hop producers, stressed the significance of finding records, playing them, and producing them as companion practices. DJing was central: "Many producers will argue that the entire production process is, at its foundation, simply a more elaborate form of deejaying" (2004: 53). But record collecting was also seen by participants as expected, and essential, education and training (2004: 52)—to the extent that "most [hip-hop] producers take the position that to have a true understanding of the culture, each hip-hop producer should, to some degree, reproduce its history" (2004: 52). Recordings enabled and facilitated this eternal return, this ritual of belonging. In oral cultures,[26]

---

[25] According to the Vinyl Factory Australia's January 2009 price list, pressing 200–300 copies with white labels costs about $10 AUD per record (Vinyl Factory, 2009, pers. comm., May 15, 2009). Prices may be lower in the U.S. and Europe, but distribution remains problematic for independents everywhere.

[26] For a discussion of secondary orality see Walter Ong (1991), *Orality and Literacy*.

rituals of repetition are used to maintain and perpetuate a culture: poems, stories, and rules are preserved through their telling and retelling; incantations are known through their use; instructions and recipes are passed down through their instantiations and practice. For contemporary makers of disco edits, pressing their compositions to vinyl inserts them into a tradition that they had come to admire—they become part of the history of vinyl— and also perpetuate its use.

As a compositional technique, the production of edits, like the collecting of recordings, is closely related to the DJ's practice. Edits expand a DJ's arsenal of tracks. Walter Gibbons's story is illustrative because his edits began as an attempt to simulate how he played records in real-time, to capture the effect of playing doubles in a communal space. The point was not to document a past but to facilitate an intensified future. Gibbons went to the trouble of recording with future use in mind, creating records he could use to facilitate real-time composition and, hopefully, to keep the dance floor moving. Mediated listening as a practice is inscribed or embedded in compositional forms. Disco edits are artifacts of specialized practices of listening, de facto documents of use. For some, the edit is a new way to occupy or inhabit a favorite song. Said DJ-producer Prince Language, "When you hear something great, you want it to continue" (Beta 2008). Kathleen Williams (2014) in her study of recut movie trailers, adapted the concept of "desire lines"—those well-worn shortcuts we come across in urban environments that show us how use can so often deviate from the designer's intentions—to analyse the phenomena of recut film trailers and other networked media objects and practices. Williams (2014: 275) writes, "Desire lines reflect how individual and collective desire feed into one another; once one path is created, it encourages other users of that space to take it." DJ edits deviate from the fixed track, and hope that others will follow. Said edit-producer Greg Wilson: "I like the DIY aspect [of edits], which allows DJ's to put their own slant on a particular track via their home computer, then take it out and play it to others in a club environment" (Harkin 2008). Like the recut trailer aficionados on YouTube, edit-makers participate in the "give and take" (Tiessen 2004: 4, in Williams 2014: 140) of the networked environment.[27]

Rather than focus on transformative qualities, as discussions of digital remixes often do, I want to highlight how the properties of *copy* continue to be central to form. Edits help us ponder how something that is just the same can bring something new into being. At the edit's heart is dissemination, the migration and movement of copies through propagation or replication; fixed recordings are interrupted by users through the reproduction

---

[27] Writes Williams (2014: 140), "Thus, desire lines are not merely about the role of human desire, but more about the give and take that already exists between people and their environment" (Tiessen 2004: 4).

of a fragment of fixed sounds (or images or text). The advent of digital technologies—in particular, digital samplers—simplified the process. But all recordings make new use possible by isolating a sound fragment and reproducing it—by turning an individual's focus, or attention, into a fixed object or module that makes repetition (resulting in a new composition) or manipulation (resulting in a new sound that can be inserted into a new composition) possible. As edits illustrate, multiplication is a potential source of innovation and further potential was unearthed when these media objects were moved from one format to another—as when sounds on vinyl were recorded to tape.

Edits are often seen as a subversion of a work's fixed nature, and, as a disrespect for authorial control. In most cases, they *are* a violation of copyright—but, when considered as a creative practice adjacent to vinyl use, edits also reveal a reverence for the recording, a migration of fixed points of view, an object-oriented compositional technique that exists at the intersection of copies and their paths of distribution and dissemination. As edit maker Jacques Renault put it, "Every edit is an ode to the artist ... . You admire this piece of work so much you want to make it even better" (Beta 2008). Edits are not examples of so-called slippery texts—if anything, it was the vinyl on the turntable that was, literally and figuratively, slippery. Instead the edit objectifies, fixes, or records, the seemingly ethereal and subjective experience of listening.

Digital technologies did not give rise to either the remix or the edit, but they did give more people access to the tools necessary to enact such practices, as well as the ease and speed for producing results. Network technologies also increased access to source material and radically changed distribution. Given the ease of access to both digital tools and networked music, the recent proliferation of edits in contemporary dance music comes as no surprise; the popularity of releasing these efforts on vinyl, on the other hand, can appear puzzling.

Harold Innis (1949: 457) wrote, "Our knowledge of other civilizations depends in large part on the character of the media used by each civilization in so far as it is capable of being preserved or of being made accessible by discovery ... ." Networked information about vinyl records has created new paths of discovery, new desire lines left for others to follow. An underground dance culture that took place in the dark of night, behind closed doors, that actively encouraged a culture of connoisseurship, is now partially accessible to new listeners via the recordings left behind. This access may occur through information about records available online, through digitized copies of music found on vinyl, and through market trade in secondhand records, both online and off. The possibility of encounter with remixed records, Straw (2002: 165) highlights, would become a defining aspect of the 12-inch single as coveted object. He writes,

As objects, 12-inch singles moved across music markets and cultural spaces at speeds distinct from those of other recording configurations. In doing so, they produced lines of fracture within musical culture, as parts of that culture came to change at rates which challenged the ability of other parts to profit from that change. As an object which was characterized, much of the time, by its scarcity, the 12-inch single highlighted inequities of access between center and periphery, and, more broadly, between the U.S. market and national musical markets elsewhere.

This dynamic between the center and periphery is often overlooked in arguments about remix that see it as a form of free speech, or as a resistance to the market. Today, edits exist both inside and outside the commercial exchange of recorded music; they thumb their nose at the music industry as they are, at the same time, a part of its margins. Music users in networked culture do post their edits online in the hopes they will find like-minded listeners who will deploy their efforts off the network and on the dance floor—but we also see users releasing edits as promotion. An informal survey of online music forums and blogs finds users doing just this. Links to downloadable edits are common in various online spaces for musical discourse. Some well-known edit makers even lament this ease of access: "What's annoying is how much people hype them on the Web ... . People do edits for the sake of copping a name for themselves" (Lee Douglas, in Beta 2008). Others complain about the ease of production: "People don't put quite enough effort into it. It's easy to attempt, but it's not easy to get it right with computer technology" (DJ Harvey, in Beta 2008).

When producers who are known for making edits are critiquing that very activity, there does seem to be an appeal to what Gilbert and Pearson (1999: 23) pinpointed as a nostalgia "for a moment of primal unity and oneness—a unity that is quickly revealed to be a valorization of the small scale, of the nascent dance forms and the lives, values and activities of small elite vanguard of producers and consumers." There can be an elitism in marginality, and a kind of border patrol among the marginal elite, "scorning all those behind the times, those who were not party to their particular cultural dislocation" (1999: 24). Hence, some edit makers lament the ease with which others join their ranks. It is in this climate of suspicion that we should consider the choice to release edits on vinyl: While it is difficult to quantify the market for records whose legal status is questionable, in 2008 at the height of the fashion for edits, one U.K. music retailer told the *Guardian* that unauthorized edits made up about 40 percent of their stock in vinyl (Rowlands 2008), and unauthorized edits (sometimes labeled 12-inch vinyl promos) are easy to obtain from many dance-music retailers.

Market factors—in particular, the desire to secure paid DJ gigs—motivate some. Just as Greg Wilson has said he made his edits in the 1980s as an attempt to get paid remixing work, DJs can, and do, continue to use edits as a promotional product today. According to Todd Terje, a Norwegian DJ known for his prolific production of edits,

> This is a good commercial tool thing ... [t]here's no cash in selling music, so I think this is the best way of making money. You let your name flow freely on the internet and let people book you ... and it's the DJ money that enables you to produce music, so there's a circle. (Drever 2009: 11)

Edits contribute to the commodification of the DJ's identity by circulating a media object; the edit serves as a representation of DJ practice, independent of his or her interaction with dancers, sound systems, and space. It helps to build the DJ's brand and turns the ephemeral into a document that can be preserved and discovered. Todd Terje cannot clone himself, but his edits can multiply and spread the word of his listening prowess, his sound. When an edit circulates in a networked environment, distribution can serve a dual purpose: It can be the product and the promotion all at once. An edit mythologizes a DJ as an identity—he or she becomes a *producer*—but it also makes it easier for other DJs to play the song in a certain style. In a culture that values the freedom found at the margins, edits on vinyl were a new line of demarcation between "us and them."[28]

Edits made with digital tools, but released on vinyl, were, in De Certeauian terms, an analog tactic in a digital environment. As a tactic, moving audio from one format to another can be viewed as a way to gain access to fixed sounds in order to manipulate them in creative ways. By pressing relatively few records, editors working in a climate of hostility from copyright holders can create a space to work below the radar, where they can go relatively unnoticed, or, at least, be perceived as not representing a major financial threat. Edit maker Cosmo Vitelli sees an explicit connection between the use of vinyl and a lack of permission: "It's about records. You can't download them on Beatport because you don't have the rights. It's still vinyl-oriented[,] the edits market" (Lech et al. 2008). The small numbers of pressings—a typical pressing is around 300–500 records (Lech et al. 2008)—adds to the allure of the edit as a collectible object, an aura that is often enhanced by creators with hand-stamped labels, edition numbers, and other indicators of the bespoke and handmade.

An edit may also serve as a way to remember what was forgotten: a performance of listening. And, with authority, the unauthorized editors repeat, redistribute, and play back the long-dormant sounds on a vinyl record they perhaps found, covered in dust, at a garage sale, or that they

---

[28] Steve Jones observes, "If, as Grossberg [...] noted, 'rock is a differentiating machine (that) continually separates Us ... from Them', then important new lines of demarcation are being drawn by Internet technology" (2002: 214).

downloaded from a fellow collector. In doing so, they preserve, forget, and become the artist all at once. An editor might want to recirculate a rare record or show off their collection. As one forum participant in 2008 put it,

> A lot of edits are basically rare records ... in the past they would have been bootlegged ... nowadays ... you've got the software why not just extend that intro ... so you can mix it ... or get rid of that wack middle bit ... [or] if you find a killer record that no-one has, you can play it out, or bootleg it, or do an edit and then press that and you get your name associated with the edit.

Gitelman observed that "the history of emergent media ... is partly the history, of what (and who) gets preserved—written down, printed up, recorded, filmed, taped or scanned, and why," and she cites James Lastra's argument that inscription and personification are the two "tropes for understanding and normalizing new media" (Lastra 2006: 6–7, in Gitelman 2006: 25). In a sea of digital copies, the extra effort and expense can be read as an attempt to normalize these practices—to make something that seems lasting out of the ephemeral experience of listening. It seems that analog representation afford users qualities of personification that digital representation does not. As one edit maker said, when promoting a collection of edits on an online forum,

> We've put our money where our mouth and shoes are ... and put the [dance crew's] sound to wax ... . With all of us vinyl buyers and collectors—we can tell you it is all killer.

Vinyl is a show of commitment to one's own efforts, as well as to vinyl as a medium. The release of a record inserts the contemporary edit-producer into the history of vinyl—and, thus, into the history of contemporary dance-music culture, a culture that has the 12-inch vinyl record at its heart. It serves to perpetuate and honor the centrality of the format to the development of the culture, and to remember the material format that has made the intervention possible. We must also ask whether metadata about vinyl recordings is networked differently from those released only via digital means. In short, because information about a record is not the record itself, the networking of metadata gives rise to a new and complex relationship with documentation, as well as with the things themselves, a subject I will return to in the following chapter.

I would like to suggest that, in a networked digital culture, vinyl and other analog technologies can be used as a wedge against forms of power that might undermine creative intentions and innovative use. For example, if the glare of publicity proves problematic, turning to the analog might be a way to evade the network's culture of surveillance while still taking advantage of its public affordances. The persistence of vinyl in the digital era was made possible through its continued use: That is, because people continued to play it long after it was abandoned by the majority of the music industry, and because participants continued to document a vinyl culture without recourse to authority, or without seeking permission, vinyl culture did its best to document itself with vinyl records.

4.10 Credit to the edit

The story of disco edits suggests that we need to rethink the role and influence of analog technologies in "remix culture." Edits help us to understand the interplay between use and production, and among bodies, minds, and material media. The history of edits foregrounds the materiality of media, and, as such, it troubles an understanding of expression as immaterial and storage format as aesthetically irrelevant. If, as the history of the edits suggests, materiality shapes expression at the same time that it helps disseminate, then the materiality of networked distribution, with its disposition towards movement via multiplication, merits further exploration. I will turn to the cultural question of distribution in the following chapter.

I have argued that "remix" may serve a rhetorical purpose in the defense of creative reproduction, but, when we consider the history of its close relation, the edit, we must admit that it does so by obscuring the social and political implications of media use in the past and by missing something crucial about creative media use in the present. The preoccupation with remix as a metaphor to describe any media made by combining existing media focuses our attention on the *production* of meaning, at the expense of an examination of encounter, use and circulation. To understand how contemporary music is shaped by digital networks, we must confront the proliferation of perfect copies and fragments, their documentation, their circulation, and their use.

After all, the history of edits is a history of use—use that changed the content by working with the properties of being a copy and the material properties of media. Reproduction preceded originality (Sterne 2006); edits made disco (Beta 2008); production was already its opposite (Marx 1978). While most edit producers today rely on digital tools to record and manipulate sounds (often, these tools are the same digital technologies they might use in the service of remixing or creating an original production), I have focused on how the origins of editing as compositional techniques were analog, initially born from the use of analog recording technologies to imitate or represent the use of vinyl in a real-time, real-world social situation and from the possibilities and limits of the body working in conjunction with technologies of sound reproduction. To understand the aesthetic of the edit as a musical form and its possibilities and priorities, I have argued that we must account for the materiality of vinyl—its functional properties as an analog medium of sound reproduction and its physical existence as a copy and an artifact that can be encountered and accounted for—as well as other analog formats, particularly acetate and tape if we want to understand extractive musical forms.

The materiality of media also has a rhetorical dimension, and the small but significant persistence of vinyl in our era of digital networks is neither an anachronism nor a resistance to these technologies. Vinyl is a digital tactic, one that understands the biases of the network towards fixed artifacts and that acknowledges that, contrary to popular opinion, digital technologies do not make texts more slippery, or less fixed, but tend instead to reinforce the copy and help propagate and move fixed points of view through use. This, in turn, prompts a consideration of networked discovery and the remediation of encounters, ideas that the next chapter aims to explore in greater depth.

CHAPTER FIVE

The new romantics

5.1 Piracy's long history

Piracy is copyright's double; at once its evil twin and its angelic other. Like copyright, piracy has a history and as recent scholarship (cf. Johns 2002, 2010) has shown, contemporary concerns about music downloading bear an uncanny resemblance to earlier debates about unauthorized reproduction and circulation. While it comes as no surprise that the rhetoric for and against the proliferation of MP3 blogs in the mid-2000s was shaped by earlier debates about file sharing on Napster in the 2000s, home taping in the 1980s, and bootleg rock records in the 1970s, the ability to map early twentieth-century debates about sheet music (Johns 2002) onto our own concerns about digital technologies in the twenty-first century should give us pause. It is as if our debates are on repeat; or just skipping like a broken record.

In this chapter, I suggest that in order to understand the persistence of these tensions surrounding everyday copying practices, easily reproducible media and, of course, copyright and piracy, we would do well to acknowledge and examine how meaning is produced in *circulation*, how that meaning is related to the *material* dimensions of digital artifacts and networks and their social *use*. I also suggest that we need to consider how and why romantic ideals about creativity, authorship, and authenticity continue to animate our cultural conflicts and celebrations. In doing so, I offer a way of understanding how copies as artifacts and copying as cultural practices have become intertwined with ideals of authenticity and new modes of expression and sociality and begin to build a case for the scholarly study of the aesthetics of collection, encounter, and distribution in the networked environment.

Shifts in modes of cultural consumption, distribution, and production associated with digital and network technologies are thought to challenge romantic notions of creativity, originality, and authorship, undermining the traditional distinctions made between producers and consumers and disrupting extant modes of exchange (Bruns 2007, 2008; Jenkins 2006a).

As earlier chapters have noted, a range of scholarly theories and explanatory frameworks seek to describe, understand, and, sometimes, defend these new practices. For example, Lawrence Lessig (2005, 2008), Lev Manovich (2005, 2007a, 2007b), and many others use "remix" as an explanatory metaphor for contemporary culture (Navas et al. 2015). Curator Nicholas Bourriaud (2000) writes of post-production, and Henry Jenkins (2006a, 2006b) and Yochai Benkler (2006) suggest we concentrate on the convergence of media forms and the participatory nature of these changes. Many of these theories offer either implicit or explicit critiques of romantic authorship, discarding old-fashioned ideas about the misunderstood artist-genius in the garret, and instead foregrounding collaborative understandings of authorship and social aspects of creativity (Benkler 2006; Toynbee 2001), gift economies (Hyde 2007), and nonmarket production (Benkler 2006).

New forms of born-digital expression, discourse, and exchange such as MP3 blogs, mashups, and peer-to-peer technologies, seem to exemplify these theories and prompt us to examine long held assumptions about authorship, creativity, and making meaning. Streaming technologies, on the other hand, appear to sidestep the issue by obscuring the copy from the users' view while relying on its functional affordances. However, in the lived experience of everyday media users, ideals of originality, self-expression, individuality, and authenticity persist alongside an enthusiasm for creative reuse, collaboration, free access, social authorship, and sharing. This seeming contradiction has prompted some scholars to revisit romanticism and to probe how it functions. In the wake of Napster's court-ordered demise in 2001, for example, Lee Marshall (2004) drew attention to how the rhetorical contours of the Napster legal battle mirrored earlier conflicts over bootlegged rock records and suggested that if we want to understand this cultural *déjà vu*, we should consider how both "sides" of the debate were premised upon romantic understandings of authorship and creativity. It wasn't that digital technologies were disrupting laws and customs, rather it was that existing tensions related to the strong tradition of romanticism and romantic thinking in popular music culture were bubbling to the surface. Romanticism, Marshall (2005: 2) theorizes, is not capitalism's "other." Instead it offered a modern world view capable of both complementing commerce and rebelling against it. It is "a way of coping with the contradictory experience of art in a social formation dominated by rationalism and utilitarianism," and "it also emphasize[s] an understanding of subjectivity and aesthetics that exacerbates the apparent schism between capitalist rationalization and aesthetic experience." Similarly, Thomas Streeter (2011) has pondered the dominance of romantic individualism in late twentieth century computer culture, arguing that contemporary romanticism is a world view that is strong enough to bend back the bars of Max Weber's iron cage of modernity: "In our day romanticism has become a kind of cultural toolkit, a grab bag of cultural habits, available for use in a variety of contexts" (2011: 46). In the face of technological predictability, bureaucratic efficiency, and market-oriented rationality, Streeter argues that romanticism revives the possibility of enchantment and freedom.

My aim in this chapter is to unpack how romantic ideals about creativity, authorship, individuality, and art continue to animate both our conflicts and celebrations of networked culture. In doing so, I consider how the binary between modernist ideals about romantic authors and postmodern celebrations about collaboration and creative reuse plays out in a diverse range of scholarship on new forms of networked communication and expression. To think through some common tropes about digital culture and interrogate the notion that the Internet era might be seen as a kind of folk revival, a return to a more democratic, direct, intimate, authentic, and even *natural* experience of art, community, and each other, I consider MP3 blogs in the mid- to late 2000s, as a form and phenomenon. Although the practice of blogging generally and MP3 blogging specifically endures, the meaning of MP3 blogging as a form and practice has changed since the height of its popularity. Reflecting on this particular period, post-Napster but simultaneous with other avenues and platforms for downloading and peer-to-peer music sharing (i.e., Limewire and Pirate Bay) prior to on-demand streaming, offers an alternate understanding of the meaning of copying practices in popular music culture.

It is worth noting that the now-defunct file-sharing platform Napster was among the network technologies that gave rise to a new expectation for music lovers: that is, the expectation that the all music should be accessible by anyone, at any time. The celestial jukebox had arrived and with it the desire for unlimited, frictionless access. The everyday conflicts that came about as a result of these new expectations and capabilities pitted rights holders and consumers against one another, but they can also focus our attention on previously overlooked questions of distribution and access. The rhetorical contours of these arguments about artists' and users' rights and responsibilities continue to shape and have repercussions on present day debates.

MP3 blogs proved to be a fruitful site of study as they were among the forms of networked expression and discourse that increased the visibility of everyday music practices such as collecting, ordering, listening, *and* copying. Their brief history of influence (or in some cases intentional obscurity) also offers an important reminder that though such practices were once less visible or private, this didn't mean that these practices weren't already significant engines of individual and collective notions of cultural experience. People don't just listen to music, they use it and do things with it.

Music users have a long and storied history. Music users held rent parties in Harlem in the 1920s, and in the 1950s music users stayed up late listening to the radio and trying to learn to play the blues (Wharton 2009). Music users have multimillion-dollar record contracts and music users give their recordings away for free. They are commuters streaming Spotify, they are promoters out to make a buck, they are the squat parties out to make a point, they are worshipping their God, and they are lost in the supermarket, humming along to the Captain and Tennille. Music users are the young people who are trying to stand out from the crowd and the teenagers who are desperate to fit in. Music users are the couples in the suburbs playing something nice to go with dinner and they are also the weekend warriors heading out on the town in search of the perfect high. Music users are the stores and cafes that can't quite tune in the radio station, they are the people at the concert who never shut up. They are as distracted as they are dedicated. Music users turn on the radio "for company," they argue about their favorite songs on the Internet, they post pirated videos on their Facebook page, they kill time in record stores, they collect acetates they will never play, they want to get the girl, they want to feel one with the crowd, they are dancing in the kitchen, they want to lose themselves in the music. Music users are the best minds of their generation; music users are those people planting stories in the press.

In the following sections, I use my study of the MP3 blog to critique common understandings about how digital technologies and networks give rise to new kinds of participatory cultures and highlight the ideological and normative dimensions of this understanding of networked discourse. I highlight how MP3 blogs were shaped by existing participatory practices and ideals, and explore how these relate to persistent ideas and ideals about authenticity. Finally, drawing on the considerable body of popular music scholarship about the ideologies and myths that have long sustained popular-music cultures, I consider the parallels among discourses of authenticity, folk ideologies in popular music, and the suggestion that networked culture is a participatory culture that constitutes a folk revival. I also look back to earlier "folk revivals," considering how and why we might consider Harry Smith's *Anthology of American Folk Music* as the MP3 blog's analog antecedent, and part of the long history of collection and circulation as meaningful cultural practices. Along the way I will tease out the tensions and romantic ideals that underpin these claims with the hope of identifying some aesthetic dimensions of social distribution and network visibility.

5.2 MP3 blogs as social media

A wide variety of music-focused sites including MP3 blogs came into being in the early to mid-2000s with the advent of Web 2.0 technologies such as free blog platforms (i.e., Blogger and Wordpress), file hosting services (i.e., the now defunct Megaupload), and improved access to fast broadband. MP3 blogs followed on from Napster's popularity and demise in 2001 (Wolk 2002) and, like the fanzines, mixed tapes, and playlists that preceded them, MP3 blogs tended to be highly personalized (and often specialized) articulations of knowledge, taste, and emotions that draw upon the aesthetic possibilities of text, enumeration, juxtaposition, reproduction, and redistribution (Novak 2011; Wolk 2002). The output was diverse: There were blogs that covered the cutting edge of the underground and those who collated information on a particular genre or period in music history (i.e., Rare soul 45s); there were bloggers who used songs as a springboard for creative writing; there were bloggers who took a personal approach, outing their eclectic collections, and sometimes recounting stories about how a song featured in their personal lives. MP3 blogs were the citizen journalists of music criticism, the know-it-all record store clerk, and the obsessive collector rolled into one. They were pirates and players; an affront to the industry, perhaps, but also the indie marketing team's best friend. Their contradictions are as interesting as their contributions and, in this section, I highlight a few common characteristics of the form and practice, drawing on a small study I conducted at the height of their influence and popularity in the late 2000s.

As with most social media, the practice of MP3 blogging is premised on the possibility of connection: Connecting text to sound, music to listeners, and people to each other. The practice is linked to new kinds of sociality and a technology used to represent the self in an online environment. As a networked form of discourse, MP3 blogs produced a new visibility for previously private practices of music consumption. This visibility is an opportunity to consider how MP3 blogs, present us with an intriguing tension—one that, arguably, also lurks in the DJ booth and in the remixer's studio—while bloggers, like DJs, create an aesthetic experience using preexisting recordings and attempt to elicit response from those who encounter their use of these recordings, they simultaneously rely on, enact, and seek pleasure in romantic ideals of creative expression and gestures.

For scholars, such as Henry Jenkins (2006a), who are interested in fan practices and media convergence, MP3 blogs would seem to exemplify and make visible the emergence of a "participatory culture"—an open culture defined by the contributions of all participants, rather than by dichotomies between production and consumption, artist and audience. However, an "ethos of participation" (Reynolds 2009) is also typical of marginalized or underground music scenes—and it is the margins, rather than the mainstream, that tended to be represented on MP3 blogs (O'Donnell 2006). It is notable that the participatory ethos preceded the mass uptake of broadband and digital technologies, and, as such, undoubtedly shaped the online practice of MP3 blogging (as well as the anxieties that have bubbled up around the online outing of once-underground scenes [Borschke 2010;

Reynolds 2009]). Explicit comparisons to the self-published zines of the 1990s and earlier were made in popular coverage of the new form. In a *Spin* article, "MP3 Blogs become the new Zines," the critic Douglas Wolk (2002) explains:

> Here's how it used to work, before the Internet: There was commercial, mainstream culture, and then there was everything else. Newspapers and glossy magazines were the voice of the mainstream; the voice of everything else was zines—initially short for "fanzines," eventually shorthand for any scrappy pop-culture rag you'd never find at a proper newsstand. Zines were obsessive and adventurous about their subjects in a way that bigger publications couldn't possibly be. In other words, they were blogs. On paper. Kinda.

Although blogging and file-hosting platforms could have hosted any kind of content, the musical genres and styles encountered on MP3 blogs in the 2000s had a particular character: they tended to represent niche genres (e.g., indie rock, freak folk, underground dance, and the like) and obscure or forgotten recordings and genres (O'Donnell 2006). Blogs focused more on the so-called long tail than mainstream hits and because of this shared drive to represent the under-represented, many blogs were shaped by prenetworked countercultural practices and ideals. David Novak's (2011) study of the labels and MP3 blogs associated with the redistribution of older regional styles of popular music including Turkish Rock and Cambodian psychedelia—an eclectic range of rediscoveries that he dubs World Music 2.0—is a case in point. In this study, Novak (2011: 611) shows how these new cultural formations "are strongly derivative of 'old media' aesthetics developed in the American musical underground of the 1980s and 1990s." For example, Novak considers the American rarities label Sublime Frequencies known for retro pop sounds from Asia and Africa such as "Radio Java" and "Radio Niger," and connects the dots between this project and the founders' previous work as the Sun City Girls, a celebrated underground recording duo. One of the band's side projects in the 1980s and 1990s was a cassette exchange that facilitated the circulation of "weird music." Explains Novak (2011: 612), "A listener connected to this underground 'cassette culture' might receive a tape from a fellow trader compiling North American experimental groups juxtaposed with tracks of Tuvan throat singing, Bollywood film music, or Inuit versions of Rolling Stones hits." Novak (2011: 614) argues that these projects have a shared aesthetic of discovery, one that embraces "a blind encounter with pure mystery, a punk transcendence of negotiable meaning," and an ideology of redistribution, that "recognizes that media are limited by their own structures of reproduction, that appropriation is multidirectional, and that any attempt to regulate access is an attempt to control public consciousness" (2011: 616).

Many of the bloggers I spoke to also connected their MP3 blogs to previous subcultural practices and values. Said one New York-based blogger, "I grew up on bootlegs and punk zines and weird fanzines and white labels, all of that. [My blog] was just more of that" (telephone interview, June 19, 2007). Many MP3 blogs were made up of zine-style accounts, including conversational reviews of recordings; highly opinionated reports on musical and cultural trends; interviews with lesser-known or forgotten artists, label owners, and—in the true network spirit—other bloggers. A New Jersey blogger in his mid-forties told me he had been writing about music in zines and newspapers since the mid-1980s; when access to the Internet came along, it seemed only natural to move his activities online. Younger bloggers may have missed earlier eras of DIY media, but they were aware of and inspired by these histories. They contextualized their blogs as a continuation of their participation in musical communities and public discourse, rather than their first foray into a culture that valued participation. These continuities are a reminder that when we call new forms of networked expression "participatory," we should also consider the values and cultural formations that they remediate. In order to understand MP3 blogs in the mid-2000s we should acknowledge that many bloggers came from, or were interested in, music scenes that already valued participation—cultures that celebrated openness and access, where participants wore many hats, and brought their capacities and enthusiasms to bear on a particular collective project, 'a scene.' Of course, in practice, these ideals were not always met in underground scenes, but it was a constitutive ideal, one that shaped and connected many and varied "underground" music scenes in opposition to a perceived corporate mainstream.

MP3 blogs, then, allowed us to glimpse the social use of music. Alec Austin et al's (2011: 5) research on attitudes about file sharing foregrounds two social functions of sharing media: the desire to be part of an engaged media community and/or conversation and the desire to share the pleasure that a media property induced in its user. Social connection was a common theme in the discussions I had with bloggers. They all said that they hoped to engage with other music lovers, whether to discuss music or to act as enablers, enticing others to listen to their favorite sounds and songs. Early bloggers, danah boyd (2006: 28) observed, were generally "concerned with blogging to those that they know and the potential of like-minded strangers who stumble across their site," and MP3 bloggers were similarly interested in communication and social connection. For music lovers, these connections were understandably related to their interest in music. For example, one New York-based blogger I spoke to said that he turned to the Internet when he tired of burning CDRs for friends in an informal CD-swapping group; a London-based blogger started his blog as a way to promote his DJ crew (and, he hoped, to secure DJ gigs); a Sydney-based blogger told me she launched her career as a music journalist on her blog;

and a San Francisco-based blogger I spoke with told me his group blog began as a way for a few far-flung friends to gather, as they once did at music shops and nightclubs when the lived in the same city. MP3 blogs could also extend a person's existing online relationships: One pioneering blogger told me that his blog's name was also his screen name in online music forums. He began his blog when he was fresh out of college and not yet working. At the time, he was deeply involved in a couple of small online social communities, and that these online acquaintances were a natural audience, once he decided to start writing about his life and music online. The blog was like an open letter written to his online friends.

Forging new kinds of social connections with like-minded strangers was a common goal for bloggers in the 2000s (boyd 2006: 26). One of the bloggers I interviewed began his MP3 blog in 2004 when he found himself a long way from other, like-minded music lovers, living in a small town in Florida, caring for an aging relative, and working part-time. He said,

> I got there and discovered that being in your late twenties in a retirement community can be a little isolating. I ended up reaching a point where I desperately needed to sort of speak to people and have some sort of connection with what was going on. I was isolated enough that I wasn't going to be able to get new music any other way but this. This was it and I was really excited that someone was taking time to do it. (Telephone interview, July 10, 2007)

After spending considerable time in the comment sections of other people's blogs, he decided to launch his own. He said,

> I would go around and I would get my eight or ten songs and I would listen to [them] about five or six times, get intimately familiar with that music and then I would kind of join in with what I knew. It became a necessary round for me. (Telephone interview, July 10, 2007)

Other bloggers told similar stories about how their own consumption of networked music inspired their MP3 blogging activities. One blogger talked about how a DJ's website inspired his site; another said he had been commenting on other people's music blogs, and an invitation to contribute a post sparked his own efforts. Many bloggers cited websites and proto-blogs that confound our origin story of MP3 Blogs, predating sites that are often celebrated in the press as first past the post. One such blogger started and hosted a group-authored site. This project began in 2000, as a way for him to maintain connections with a small group of friends who had moved to other cities after graduating from college. He explains, "It became a way to say, 'Hey, what are you listening to now that I don't talk to you so much?'" (telephone interview, July 24, 2007). By 2007, the blog had grown to a community of about fifty-five people who were posting and discussing music with each other. "It was just kind of a way of exploring new music," he says. Such anecdotes illustrate boyd's theory that "networked publics" can create a space that is social and public in very familiar ways. She writes, "Social network sites like MySpace and Facebook are networked publics, just like parks and other outdoor spaces can be understood as public. Collections of people connected through network technologies like 'the blogosphere' are publics, just like those connected by geography or identity are" (2008: 16). The group-blogger's comments also highlight that, through the blog, he and his fellow bloggers engaged in a conversation, not just *about* music, but *with* music. Shared asynchronous listening was a key part of their networked communication: It created a kind of intimacy and shared activity for the group. This is not entirely novel or unfamiliar—music sociologist Simon Frith (1981b: 7) has argued that popular-music cultures were already marked by a sense of simultaneity that could arise from individuals' listening to the same records independently of one another. And boyd's "public" is in part inspired by political philosopher Hannah Arendt (1998: 50, in boyd 2008: 17), who wrote, "the presence of others who see what we see and hear what we hear assures us of the reality of the world and ourselves." MP3 blogs were a new way to socialize through music: They are a new take on Frith's (1998: 4) contention that "such conversations are the common currency of friendship and the essence of popular culture." Or as boyd (2007: 155) pointed out, "digital networks will never merely map the social, but inevitably develop their own dynamics through which they become the social."

In his blog, my interviewee in Florida created a space to participate in a music-oriented community that his geographic isolation would have otherwise prevented. A blogger in Portsmouth, England, echoed this sentiment. He told me, "In my circle of friends none are into the same music [as me.] Online I can find all sorts of people [who are]. I connect with like-minded people. We all meet online through posting on forums and we went to Sonar festival together" (telephone interview, July 26, 2008). Such sentiments illustrate Mark Deuze's (2006: 71) observations about the sense of community that digital discourse can create. He writes, "What is amazing about a digital culture—rather than a print, visual or information culture—is that it fosters community while at the same time can be fueled by isolation."

MP3 blogs appear to chronicle that peculiar intimacy that recorded sound can create; that is, the feeling that the voice is indeed inside your head, and of how networked music augments this aura of intimacy. Many of the bloggers I spoke with used words such as "personal" and "intimate" to describe their mediated music experiences. The website that inspired a New York-based blogger to start his list-style blog in 2004 was a DJ's website that included the latter's favorite tracks from the 1970s. He said,

He'd ripped them all [to MP3] himself—and he was saying, "This was in my crate back in the day and this is what I consider to be the primo dance floor disco tracks." … I thought it was also really personal thing to do—like putting up your own mix. (Telephone interview, June 19, 2007)

This social desire to connect is woven into the blogger's digital identity. Building on McLuhan's idea that technologies are "extensions of man," boyd (2006: 11) theorized blogs as a kind of digital body, a technology that would "allow people to extend themselves into a networked digital environment that is often thought to be disembodying. The blog becomes both the digital body as well as the medium through which bloggers express themselves." They are a partial representation of the blogger's persona and their interests in the digital sphere, an online identity made out of preexisting and newly created media. They are examples of Henry Jenkins's (2006a: 3–4) observation that "each of us constructs our own personal mythology from bits and fragments of information extracted from the media flow and transformed into resources through which we make sense of our everyday life." But, as boyd (2006: 16–19) explains, blogs are simultaneously public bodies, and they create a space that is premised on what Georgina Born (2005: 25) calls an "anticipation of social connections." For MP3 bloggers, this persona, or digital body, is an explicit effort to construct an identity from preexisting media; that is, an identity made from recorded music. It is a body that is assembled by its users; popular music is, to appropriate Adorno's (1990: 311) phrase, its "social cement."

That people use network technologies to communicate and connect, that social media is, well, social, is unsurprising to us today. The emergence of new forms of expression like MP3 blogs and playlists in the 2000s not only served to confirm theories about the relevance of consumption practices but they also highlight the cultural dimensions of distribution and how it is interwoven in practices of production and consumption. The MP3 blog as a form, is simultaneously a space of production, consumption, and distribution. Arguably, this can be said of many media formats—the previous chapter drew attention to how vinyl functioned in such a manner—but distribution is often neglected by scholars as a site for making meaning. Like David Novak (2013: 18), I am interested in how circulation is culture-making and thus pay special attention to how the affective dimensions of MP3 blogging, like many other social media practices, are premised on technologies of distribution and circulation and their material affordances.

5.3 Material media: MP3 blogs as artifacts and practices

Listening is a cultural practice and the character and complexity of listening to music is not only a matter of what was listened to; rather, it is enriched by a consideration of how music reaches a listener (Jones 2002). Listening to music today is, by and large, a *mediated* experience, one that is shaped by and dependent upon recordings and media technologies. Sociologist Antoine Hennion (2001: 12) contends that, if we want to understand everyday music practices, then, rather than start with the musical content, we should "start with its media." In this section, I draw attention to some formal characteristics of blogs and MP3s as media forms and formats in response to this call.

At the heart of every MP3 blog is a digital sound file—an MP3—which has been assigned particular coordinates on a server that is connected to the Internet, a network that is digital and distributed. In most cases, the blogger is not the artist or the producer of the recording—although they may have produced the MP3 in the sense that they copied or "ripped" it from another analog or digital recording—and they often, but not always, post the song without the copyright holder's consent. Nonetheless, bloggers (as well as downloaders) have argued that their practice is a form of expression, and they view their actions as creative communication rather than piracy. They make use of the affordances of networked media to represent, connect, and distribute; they follow its customs. As Yochai Benkler (2006: 218) explains, "On the Web, linking to original materials and references is considered a core characteristic of communication. The culture is oriented toward 'see for yourself.'" Or, in the case of MP3 blogs, toward *listening* for yourself, as visibility becomes a precursor to audibility. This visibility, it seems, is part of the format's rhetorical potential, shaping the content in particular ways. As one blogger I spoke with asked, "Why spend 3,000 words talking about how something sounded when the advent of the technology allowed people to just listen to it?" (telephone interview, July 10, 2007). In this way, the authority of the blogger is also tied to the use of the blog; as a document they have an instrumental purpose, akin to what Lisa Gitelman (2014: 1–2) calls a document's "know-show function," and its functional role in the production of knowledge. They are also an art form in tune with the affordances of the media with which they are working. Form follows function.

boyd (2006: 33) theorized that all blogs, regardless of their content, can be understood as a framework for expression—as both a medium for expression and a by-product of it. MP3 blogs play along; they are a mixed-media practice centered around two key actions: the uploading, or "posting," of an MP3 on a regular or semiregular basis, and the creation of a textual record of this networking activity on their blog, rendering the digital sound file findable and thus available for download by a third party. The media format at the core of the practice, the MP3, shapes both the "medium for expression" and the "by-product" in a particular way. The MP3s rhetorical potential is intertwined with the format's materiality and affordances. Media formats or delivery technologies cannot be reduced to "simply and only technologies," as Jenkins (2006a: 13–14) and others suggest. Delivery technologies such as MP3s (or eight-track tapes, or vinyl records) are not somehow neutral and outside of culture; they are not *merely* containers for content (although they also are just that). As the previous chapter argued, users can work with the affordances of particular media formats to innovate and create in ways the designers of these technologies would never have imagined; they can also work with and amplify the designer's intentions. If materiality of media matters, then the frictionless digital network should offer opportunities for new forms of communication and cultural change that were previously unimaginable.

The question remains, however, of whether it really makes any sense to speak of the materiality of digital objects—or whether their materiality is simply constituted by an absence. Gitelman (2006: 128) argues that the electronic document,

> [...] cannot be identified with any exclusive material property, any bibliographic differences that distinguishes it from other electronic objects; it can only be identified according to its cultural standing, its meaning, within the social network of its potential circulation. An electronic document is any electronic object that is used to document, that stands as a potential ally in explanation.

This does not mean that electronic documents are immaterial—there continues to be a host of *matter and energy* that makes a digital object possible (as is teased out by Jean-Francois Blanchette [2011] in his material history of bits and analysed by James Allen-Robertson [2015] in his genealogy of the hard disk drive). Instead, the digital renders all kinds of electronic documents as similarly material—the materiality of an MP3 and the materiality of a WAV file can be said to be indistinguishable; so, too, the materiality of a JPEG is indistinguishable from the materiality of a text document or an MP3—making their technological context and their social and cultural histories more urgent. So, if we are to start with the media, we must consider the affordances and assumptions of the MP3.

Jonathan Sterne's (2006, 2012) work on the social history of the MP3, documents and explains how and why particular assumptions about "good" sound, listening, and the ease of exchange were incorporated into the design of the format. Sterne (2012: 148–83) recounts how specific commercial recordings were used in the listening tests used to set sonic standards—for instance, Suzanne Vega's spare *a cappella* vocal on "Tom's

Diner," was used by the engineer to refine the compression algorithm—and suggests that a considerable number of aesthetic judgments and assumptions about listening subjects were baked into theses listening tests, events that Sterne (2012: 149) calls a "performance of objectivity." MP3s, says Sterne (2006: 838), are cultural artifacts encoded in "a form designed for massive exchange, casual listening, and massive accumulation." MP3s are software that we treat like objects (Sterne 2006). Replication is in the format's DNA; the MP3 was made to be copied.

On an MP3 blog, the "post" is not the only artifact left behind by the practice; by networking an MP3 file and making it available to a third party for download, the blog enabled the generation of new instances— new copies—of the MP3. This new digital artifact is identical, but *distinct,* from the networked copy, stored as it is on the downloader's hard drive for future playback, future replication, and, thus, future distribution. This concert of actions, in conjunction with the playing of a copied file, generates both a digital artifact—a copy—and, as I will unravel, its *provenance.* These properties—copy and provenance—are related, and may well be, at most, coextensive, but they are not the same property. Every copy is the same as the thing it replicates, but each copy is an instance, and thus is capable of having a distinct history of origin and custodianship.

Hence the visibility of the blogger's performance of taste—that is, what the blogger decided to draw attention to at a particular moment— generates a site for new possibilities of encounter and future listening. In Foucauldian terms, they serve as initiators of discourse (Foucault 1977). The blog need not be an accurate representation of the blogger's actual listening practices or collections: It is an idealized performance of that practice, enacted for public consumption. Bloggers use the Web to make their (previously ephemeral) taste visible and available; it becomes a possible present, a hope to share their listening experience and their tastes with others. Attali (1985: 3) may have called for us to listen to the world rather than to look upon it, but it seems that, in the twenty-first century, audibility has become something to behold. MP3 blogs, like edits, appear to behave like Williams' (2012, 2014) recut trailers—they express enthusiasm and lay out a new desire line to follow. They offer an alternate route, yielding to what Foucault might call the enchantment of enumeration.[1] Writing about the fictional Borgesian list that inspired *The Order of Things,* Foucault asks, "What is impossible is not the propinquity of the things listed, but the very site on which their propinquity would be possible ... where could they ever meet, except in the immaterial sound of the voice pronouncing their enumeration, or on the page transcribing it?" (2010: xvii–xviii).

---

[1]Foucault (2010: xvii) writes, "... the mere act of enumeration that heaps them all together has a power of enchantment all its own."

On that page, a new Leviathan is raised; the "blog becomes both the digital body as well as the medium through which bloggers express themselves" (boyd 2006: 11). Digital bodies are modular, made up of "posts"—units of composition that themselves are made up of mixed media (text, images, sound files, links)—as well as the relationships between these posts and their consumption. MP3 blogs, like Web pages, are texts that exist only in the present tense, events that are generated by a Web server when each user calls. Blogs may represent an individual's online identity, but, as boyd (2006: 47–57) explains, blogs are simultaneously public bodies—a space that invites and awaits its own assembly, via known and unknown third parties. For individuals encountering the blog, this digital body is assembled when they call up the URL, and through their reading of all or any parts of the blog, whether they read every post or just download a single song without regard for the text. This archival vitality, this co-production between the blogger and the reader-listener-downloader, is the process by which digital bodies are brought to life. Where else could this seemingly random assortment of songs ever meet, except in the body of the blog or, to use Foucault as a refrain, "in the immaterial sound of the voice pronouncing their enumeration or the page transcribing it?" (Foucault 2010: xviii). While some blogs offer a great deal of biographical detail in between their thoughts about music and collections of MP3s, others are more journalistic and still others are simply lists. Yet, even in a collection that is embellished with relatively little textual information, a digital body—a personality, an identity—can be perceived through the blogger's enunciation of the songs and their transcription. Benjamin described book collectors as individuals who have "a relationship to objects which does not emphasize their functional, utilitarian value—that is their usefulness—but studies and loves them as the scene, the stage, of their fate" (2007c: 60). The blog sets the scene for a song's unknown fate. It is a new possibility.

In an MP3 blog, all elements of the post are intentionally intertwined with the sonic content of the MP3s, and, necessarily, they include coordinates for the digital copy. It is difficult to separate the blog as a Web page from the document or digital object it gives context to—here, a musical recording stored in MP3 format—but this object can easily be pried from its context. (The Web page as a new artifact begets a new instance, a replica of the MP3.) The blogger's performance of taste, to use Hennion's (2001) concept, is premised on playback, an event that is, in turn, dependent upon prior replication. MP3 blogs are a generative form of expression, one that generates both provenance and copy. It is the use of MP3s, in tandem with the documentation of that possibility, that raises digital bodies from distributed archives (archival vitality is, akin to Hennion's [2001] conceptualization of music as a "coproduction" between the audience and the author, an unpredictable mediated event.) Digital bodies and musical events can be raised from distributed archives because, as Sven Spieker theorized, "archives do not record experience so much as its absence; they mark the point where an experience is missing from its proper place, and what is returned to us in an archive may well be something we never possessed in the first place" (2008: 3). The blog may stand as an account of what was listened to or worthy of note, but it also documents and networks as a way to engender future listening. It is a call that awaits a response.[2]

MP3 blogs stand as much as a form concerned with the future of the musical work, as they do as a document of some past experience, or as a thing in itself. MP3 blogs generate as well as the digital artifact, and this history—these partial stories of origins, discovery, and use—are offered up as a potential future for another listener. The blog anticipates that others could, and *should*, listen, too. It facilitates distribution via replication and with each multiplication of the MP3, the blogger distributes a part of itself; its taste is put into motion.

5.4 Provenance as metadata

Provenance is a kind of metadata—it is data about data—and as such it is a concept that can help us account for the meaning produced by our trails of enthusiasm (cf. Williams 2012, 2014), both intentional and otherwise. I start with the assumption that while consumption was always a meaningful cultural practice and site of scholarly inquiry, networks have also made these practices and their meanings more visible. Sometimes this visibility turns practices of consumption into ones of distribution. Sociologist Antoine Hennion (2001: 10) theorizes about the great lengths to which music lovers go to make music "happen," and, in this section, I ponder how listeners use their recordings in the MP3 blog framework to feather the nest for future play.

Provenance is an archival concept that may seem unlikely in a digital context, where copies are generated and destroyed as a matter of course. As metadata, provenance is both part and parcel, playing both structural and descriptive roles in the life of a digital object. That said, provenance is a particular kind of metadata—it is a story about origins, on the one hand,

---

[2] I nod here to Charles Keil's (1966) concept "Engendered feeling," an idea that characterizes "the aesthetic used in performative music, particularly that with African origins," that is premised on interaction, and it is intended to contrast with "the romantic position of 'embodied meaning'" (Marshall 2005: 98–9). According to Marshall, "An aesthetic of engendered feeling means that the emphasis is on producing a response from a listener and that there is an ethical commitment to social participation rather than purely individual or 'random expression' ... and listeners also have a responsibility—to engage with the music (rather than just to contemplate it), to follow the musicians' decisions as they are made, and to respond to them." (Frith 1998: 137–8).

and a history of ownership or movement on the other.[3] As such, it is a concept that we can use to help account for how a blog's textual and other nonmusical output (i.e., images, links etc.) contribute to the production of the copy and its subsequent play, while avoiding issues of style and content.[4] MP3 blogs have the potential to generate what we might call a registry of understanding, a visible record that is open to interpretation and allows us to glimpse the cultural history of the propagation and circulation of copies in digital networks.

In the realm of art, antiquities, and archival practice, an artifact's provenance refers to "the origin or source of something" and "information regarding the origins, custody, and ownership of an item or collection" (Pearce-Moses 2005). These definitions emphasize the social history of the object, as well as the real people who occupy that story. The *OED* records four different usages, two of them relevant to the discussion at hand. The first usage dates to the late eighteenth century and means "the fact of coming from some particular source or quarter; origin, derivation ('provenance, n.')." This usage emphasizes spatiality and temporality—the notion that an artifact's history can be accounted for if we track its movement through space and time. (Where did it come from? Where did it end up, and where did it happen to be in between?) The other contemporary usage of *provenance,* dating to the late nineteenth century, is associated with art and antiquities and uses ownership and custodianship as a guide. It defines *provenance* as "the history of the ownership of a work of art or an antique, used as a guide to authenticity or quality; a documented record of this ('provenance, n.')." The provenance of a work of art, for instance, will include documentation that proves that it is what it purports to be (i.e., you can rest assured that you bought a bona fide Rothko because its path from painter-genius, to primary market, to secondary market, and so on is documented and, hence, verifiable[5]). It should be noted that provenance as an idea and ideal develops in parallel with romantic notions of authorship (the ideal upon which copyright depends).

---

[3]As I am using provenance metaphorically, overlooking the distinction between provenance and the archaeological term provenience, which refers to where an object was found. (International Art Research Foundation) It is possible that a mediation on these differences would be productive and future scholarship might consider this distinction in a digital environment of abundant copies.

[4]This is not to say that style and content don't also influence how the blog is produced and used—both my own work and David Novak's (2011) shows us otherwise—but simply that if we want to understand the influence of the media formats and technologies, we stand to gain some perspective from considering what all blogs have in common regardless of their content.

[5]This can also apply to mass-produced objects: Sometimes, in fact, collectors are more interested in who owned the object than they are in the object itself. In an episode of *Seinfeld,* George Costanza thought he had bought the actor Jon Voight's Chrysler LeBaron, only to find that the car had belonged to a *John* Voight. The gag here centers on the folly of valuing provenance.

Provenance is used forensically to authenticate files,[6] but we might also use it to account for cultural life of networked digital artifacts, to bring cultural questions about distribution to the fore—not by denying the importance of production, but by ceasing to privilege it. By considering how the generation of provenance is related to the multiplication of copies, we stand to gain a deeper understanding of how digital and network technologies, as Steve Jones (2002: 214) has suggested, "have consequences for how people get to music, and for how music gets to people." We stand to develop a deeper understanding of how and why circulation is culture making.

Provenance can help to explain why different senses of the property of copy—copy as instance, and copy as identity—matter in the digital realm where, as Gitelman (2006) theorizes, we often tend to use instances as an index for identity. Provenance offers a way of understanding how these differences animate the archive. When we speak of digital *copies,* we tend to bring the sense of copy as abundance to the fore; an MP3 participates in a multiplicity (in this sense it is an index that points to the recording as a work) and yet it is also an independent instance. In the digital environment, we often refer to a particular sense of copying, one that stems from computing architecture: that is "to read (data stored in one location), or the data in (a disc, etc.), and reproduce it in another. (Const. *from* the first location *to* (or *into*, etc.) the second.) ('copy, v.1')." Digital automation is dependent upon the proliferation of copies in data structures. Every "movement" of data from one register to another, generates a new instance of the data (i.e., a copy), and each of these instances are independent from the others with which it is identical. This process of proliferation would seem to erase a relevance of the history of transmission and ownership; Copia in the digital environment appears to produce a gap. Yet, writes Gitelman, "Each lacuna in provenance (the discomfort of not knowing where a digital object comes from) can't help but put provenance on the table" (2006: 147). Provenance, is the cultural process that we use to fill the gap, that is, it is how we write our own histories onto media objects such as MP3s, via the blog page that transcribes and inscribes it.

Each MP3 blog is an ad hoc archive, a framework for expression that is seemingly in tune with the architecture on which the framework depends, random access memory. (RAM allows you to store things anywhere so long as you record where you stored them.) As Sven Spieker (2008: 18) notes, "The [principle of provenance] reminds us that in an archive, it is never just a question of what is being stored but rather of what is being stored where. Archival storage has something to do with topology, and the authority of

---

[6]There is a body of literature on digital provenance in computing that centers on questions of authentication and information forensics (i.e. Paskin 2003). Though I am aware of this research, my discussion is not directly influenced by its use in these fields. However, future research might examine the cultural assumptions behind this work.

the archivist derives from his or her ability to interpret texts in relation both to their place in the archive and to the place from which they emerged." The MP3 blogger produces their own topology of taste in the body of their blog. These topologies can convey a number of possibilities including where the song has been, where you can find it now, and where it might take you. This, in turn, invites other listeners to explore the map (or, at the very least, to zero in on the coordinates of the copy), to generate a copy of their own, and thus to begin overlaying their own listening practice onto the copy created. How a particular MP3 came to be on one's hard drive includes a partial history of its reproduction, production, and use. Each copy of a recording, including those that were unauthorized, have their own histories and each of these histories informs the history of the work and its uses. Copies compound at the same moment they disconnect. They are at once instance and identity.

Last night a blogger saved my life

Thinking about the provenance of digital artifacts makes explicit the idea that ownership or custodianship, as well as reproduction, plays a starring role in a media object's history. There is a parallel between the blogger's performance and the dance DJ, a figure who plays prerecorded music in the company of others, creating novel musical moments through the juxtaposition and manipulation of existing recordings, the experience of shared listening, and the novel moment of mixing two records together. A London-based blogger-DJ suggested that, for him, the practices were related. He said,

> It's always the same thing—blogging or DJing—I want to share music. All I gained when I was DJing was being able to share that song. I was never that good at the [dancefloor.] It fits me well blogging—it's about me putting records out for people to listen to. I have more records than I can listen to. One day the blog will end but for now, I'm going through my record collection. (Telephone interview, July 12, 2008)

These two practices are connected, not only by recording, but through shared listening as a valued practice. DJs can and do become synonymous with recordings that they did not produce but that they play with some frequency and aplomb. They have "signature" tracks. However, unlike a dance DJ, who uses recorded music as the building blocks for a live event in the company of dancers, the listening event produced by the blog is asynchronous—separated by space and time, but connected by the MP3's possibility of perfect reproduction and repetition. So, while shared listening may motivate both activities, the blogger's blogging generates a capacity that their DJ practice does not: the propagation of copies and their potential distribution. Borrowing and expanding upon provenance as an archival concept makes it possible to account for the diversity of nonmusical content generated by the blogger and linked to the sound file: that is, any textual or visual content in the blog post, as well as any metadata attached to the MP3 itself (for instance, many bloggers add their blog's name alongside the artist's name and the song title). If we reconsider boyd's (2006: 27–39) notion that blogs are digital bodies constructed from posts and the relationships among those posts, then the concept of provenance also must be able to account for the context the blog creates by virtue of its nature as a networked set or collection. Provenance, then, accounts for these sets of related data, these ready-made epistemologies that are unleashed by the body of the blog as a whole. As a form, blogs connect each expression with previous expressions (boyd 2006: 29). In the case of MP3 blogs, that identity can, in turn, come to be associated with the music that is found there.

One blog that I followed was simple and elegant, nothing more than an ordered list. Each line consisted of the date, the track name, the name of the recording artist, and a link to the sound file. Many of the MP3s posted here, the New York-based blogger told me, were digital recordings of his collection of secondhand vinyl. Many tracks were hard to find, or were no longer commercially available. Only the most recent links were active, and there was neither commentary nor explanation: yet, a discernible style was produced by this curated list. It is here that I believe provenance can be a useful concept, one that can help us account for and explain how a recording can come to be associated with its inclusion in a particular set or collection, maintaining its identity while simultaneously becoming associated with the identity of its user. It will help us to explain why new authenticities can build out of something that is just the same.

This particular blogger included the name of his blog in the file's metadata. When I listened to songs from this blog on an MP3 player or a smart phone, for example, the blog's name appeared on the screen, along with the name of the artist and the song. Metadata such as this marks the copy with a partial history of its reproduction. It reminds us of a digital artifact's provenance by telling us not only what it is, but where it came from, and who caused that to happen. Not all digital artifacts wear their history, but they can still be understood as having one. Long after the links on the site are broken, the textual record that the blog leaves behind still stand as a representation of the blogger's tastes and listening habits. This set, this collection of previously unrelated songs, creates a personal archive and generates relationships among songs by virtue of their inclusion. Just as DJs are often said to have their own unique sound, despite the fact that they use extant recordings to make that sound, this list-style blog also came to be identified with a certain sound, inspiring a number of blogs that were similar in form, style, and content.

By turning subjective ways of knowing and understanding into digital objects—in this case, the blog—previously secret histories of media use and reuse can enrich our understanding of media use in everyday life. Collections reveal something about the collector, as well as potentially altering our understanding of the things they contain. As Foucault (2010: xvii) noted, enumeration itself can be enchanting. Networked collections also reveal something about how the blogger's performance of taste enables future listening, and about how they imbue the distribution of music with a history of their use. These epistemologies of listening become ready-made responses to Frith's (2003: 101) call for ethnographic research "that would try to map in detail people's timetable of engagement, the reason why particular music gets particular attention at particular moments and how these moments are, in turn, imbricated in people's social networks."

In blogs, we find precisely this sort of data, with music lovers outing their collections and/or their ways of understanding the music they've collected, and explaining the intimate details of their listening practices while simultaneously performing that practice by making new listening experiences possible through a process of copy and playback. MP3 blogs generate provenance for individual copies—but, as a form, MP3 blogs are also shaped by the provenance they generate. That is, the blog, as a whole, can be seen as a registry of understanding. Bloggers play their collections, or some part of them, through their blogs. In doing so, they play the network. In addition to documenting their own history of listening (yesterday, I listened to this; last week, I went to this concert by this band; today, I'm thinking about my favorite song from high school), the blogger is also performing, motivated by the possibility that somebody—possibly many bodies—might be listening, too. Indeed, the blogger's actions seem to indicate, not only that someone *might* listen, but that someone *should* listen. This insistence is evident in the very possibility of duplication. The underlying message—not merely "Listen to this"—is, "You *must* listen to this." For Sterne (2006: 838–9), this insistence is a part of the MP3's design. He writes,

> The primary, illegal uses of the MP3 are not aberrant uses or an error in the technology: they are its highest moral calling: "Eliminate redundancies! Reduce bandwidth use! Travel great distances frequently and with little effort! Accumulate on the hard drives of the middle class! Address a distracted listening subject!" These are the instructions encoded into the very form of the MP3.

The insistence is palpable: Play. Propagate. Preserve. Play back. Jason Toynbee's (2001) definition of "social authorship" offers a musically inflected understanding of the curatorial impulse. He writes, "Creativity can be conceived as authorship because creative action consists in the authorization of a particular choice and combination of possibles. 'Hear these sounds like this!' is the unstated injunction of the social author in popular music" (2001: 12). Offering the copy provides networked music lovers with a new rhetorical move—a digital one—in their effort to persuade listeners to concur with their tastes. Frith (1998: 16) argues that the "essence of popular culture practice is making judgments and assessing differences", and that, within this process, we establish our identities. Frith (1998: 16) writes,

> Pop judgment is a double process: our critical task, as fans, is first to get people to listen to the right things (hence all these references to other groups and sounds), and only then to persuade them to like them. Our everyday arguments about music are concentrated on the first process: getting people to listen the right way. Only when we can accept that someone is hearing what we're hearing but just doesn't value it will we cede to subjective taste and agree that there's no point to further argument. Popular cultural arguments, in other words, are not about likes and dislikes as such, but about ways of listening, about ways of hearing, about ways of being.

If we apply this logic to networked discourse, we must account for this use of MP3s as discursive tools within what Frith (1998: 3) calls "the dialectic of liking things." What benefits are gained by reducing the rich diversity of content to the more abstract concept of provenance? What light does this shed on the practice of MP3 blogging, and how does it help elucidate the roles played by copies and copying in the practice? In part, provenance, with its emphasis on what is being stored where, and who put it there, helps us focus our attention on media use and distribution, rather than on privileging production as a site of critique. It avoids reconceptualizing reception or consumption as a new kind of production—a tactic that attempts to raise the value, or status, of the practice by perpetuating the valuing of production over use. Provenance allows for different, yet identical, objects to have different stories to tell, since they have different histories of discovery and use. Provenance helps focus our attention on the copy's status as an instance that has relationships at once with the song it plays, with the collection in which it is found, and with its use by the collector.

The generation of digital provenance creates a number of possibilities, and duplication is certainly one of them. For, when a blogger networks an MP3, it becomes available to a third party, who can then make a copy from the copy without altering the content of either. Duplication is an unquestionable possibility. However, the metaphors of sharing and stealing—the metaphors that the debate surrounding copyright rely upon (Loughlan 2007)—fail us. Copies are socially propagated—that is to say, a copy begets more copies through its use—and that propagation can be said to be coproduced, a consequence of the actions of both uploader and downloader. This propagation is at once social (i.e., information produced by social actions) and alienated (i.e., the blogger and the downloader can remain completely unaware of each other, and any textual or visual content the blogger has posted in association with their sound file can be ignored). Nonetheless, the copy remains dependent on the provenance generated by the blog. Provenance generates copy. Documentation makes the reproduction of documents possible.

What kind of information is produced or reproduced by these actions? What kind of information can be lost? In the case of the MP3 blog, the act of copying can create social networks, extend social relationships, and enrich knowledge networks by making detailed patterns of knowledge accessible for interpretation and use. Copying—generating something that is exactly like something else, but that is not the same thing—also makes it possible to escape the network, both literally and figuratively. The new instance of the MP3 can literally be moved off the network and used on any number of unnetworked MP3 players. Figuratively, because copy and provenance are related, but not the same property, the new digital instance need not carry its provenance along with it. Indeed, a copy can seem to shake off provenance and the weight of history without altering its relationship with the sonic content. Strip an MP3 of information about a song, its artists, and its origins, and it will still sound the same when played. A copy's history—its provenance—might prompt its replication (the download could only be prompted by the blogger's upload and textual record), but, once duplicated, the new copy is a truly modern object, one that need not look back to tell a meaningful story.

Whether the blogger admits it or not, the MP3, not its provenance, always takes center stage. One of the bloggers I spoke with was also a great chronicler of the early days of MP3 blogs as a form and a growing community of interest. Many of this blogger's entries have helped enrich musical discourse on a number of subjects, but he readily admits that, just as the liner notes are not the record, his MP3 blogging practice was not animated by text. Writing may provide a source of satisfaction for the blogger and the site's visitors, but we must not ignore the possibility that one might download a file and ignore the blogger's musings (indeed, popular MP3 blog aggregators, such as the Hype Machine and Elbows, facilitated listening and downloading so a listener did not need to visit a blogger's site at all). The blogger in question says this does not bother him. In a post on his blog, he asked, "Why should I tell you what to think about something you can just as easily listen to on your own and form your own opinion?"

In part, this position on interpretation is a familiar Internet trope. It is the emancipatory note nailed to the critic's door: Make the information available, and let individuals make up their own minds. However, this blogger's desire to connect people to music—the desire that prompted his blog's generation of provenance—succeeds only if a copy is propagated. It is the song, the track, the sound recording, that matters most. For a song to be heard, it has to be played, so the blogger offers up a digital copy of a sound recording to an imagined audience of like-minded listeners as a past, a present, and a future. Their use, their access, their copy makes music "happen" (Hennion 2001: 10). It is the users' faith in the work that animates it, that moves the MP3 by reproducing it: an event that, in turn, makes a new musical moment possible (and all from the same, unchanged song).

Provenance aids navigation, providing a way to wade through masses of networked information with attention as the guide. (This is the same guiding principle behind many popular social networking sites: Dig it. Like it. Pin it. Make sense of the chaos. Feed the algorithm. It's the rise of the "affection economy" rather than the attention economy, suggests Crystal Abidin [2016].) The blogger's actions, their seeming faith in a song's transcendence, multiply not only the number of copies, but increase the number of possible intermediaries—that is, new sites of listening and, hence, reproduction. The production of provenance may help us find the needle in the haystack, but it is ultimately the generation of copies that increases the chances for "music to move" (Jones 2002) and to "happen" (Hennion 2001). Networked expression cannot be untangled from questions of networked distribution or digital reproduction; they are constitutive. If we want to understand how digital and network technologies have changed music culture, we would do well to consider the secret social and cultural histories of the MP3s that have accumulated on our hard drives, and to ask how these object-oriented tales of circulation have altered our own ways of knowing.

5.5 Rethinking participation and the folk aesthetic

The word *participatory* is often invoked as a synonym for user-generated content in the digital sphere, and is often closely related to claims about new forms of cultural agency and the "democratization" of cultural production. Viewed through a participatory lens, MP3 blogs can be seen as a new folk culture, one that grabs songs from the commercial world and turns them into folk artifacts, or as new digital mutations of the grass-roots fan practices that sprung up with mass culture but that previously circulated in small numbers (e.g., mixed tapes, zines, etc.). Many scholars argue that participatory practices predate the mass adoption of broadband technologies (cf. Deuze 2006: 64; Jenkins 2006a) and see the Web as accelerating and amplifying participation, as well as making it more visible. Yet, to say that a culture's key characteristic is "participatory" is to suggest its "other": There must exist another cultural sphere in which passive consumption reigns. A participatory culture, Henry Jenkins (2006a: 3) argues, "contrasts with older notions of passive media spectatorship." Jenkins (2004: 93) suggests that convergence is not a technological change, but a cultural one, and that cultural convergence creates "a new participatory folk culture by giving average people the tools to archive, annotate, appropriate and recirculate content." For Jenkins, "consumption has become a collective process" (2006a: 4) and, in an era of media convergence, this cultural shift is thus closely related to the circulation of media (2006a: 3).

In much the same way that Lessig saw remix as a return to Jeffersonian ideals of direct democratic discourse, Jenkins argues that convergence culture is a return to the folk culture that was displaced by the mass culture of the twentieth century.[7] Jenkins (2006a: 135) claims that, in nineteenth century folk tradition,

> Cultural production occurred mostly on the grassroots level; creative skills and tradition were passed down [from] mother to daughter, father to son. Stories and songs circulated broadly, well beyond their point of origin, with little or no expectation of economic compensation; many of the best ballads or folktales come to us today with no clear marks of individual authorship.

There was no pure boundary between the emergent commercial culture and the residual folk culture: "the commercial culture raided folk culture and folk culture raided commercial culture" (Jenkins 2006a: 135). Jenkins argues that the rise of twentieth-century mass culture pushed folk culture underground and saw the rise of new "grassroots fan communities" around mass media. These alternative cultural economies were not a threat to the culture industries: They took place mostly "behind closed doors and its products circulated only among a small circle of friends and neighbors" (2006a: 136). In a convergence culture, new technologies enable a revival of these grassroots models of creativity and cultural circulation. What makes network technologies so important to models of participatory media is that they facilitate *distribution*: It makes it possible to share what you create. "Once you have a reliable system of distribution, folk culture begins to flourish again overnight" (2006a: 136).

Jenkins is not alone in drawing comparisons between networked discourse and folk culture; like remix, folk is a common trope in discussions about networked culture. In Benkler's groundbreaking book on

---

[7]The parallel is not accidental: Lessig (2008) cites Jenkins' work as the key source for his understanding of the matter.

nonmarket production, we see the emergence of this idea that the new folk culture can stand in opposition to the mass-media culture of the twentieth century (though not necessarily in opposition to small-scale commerce), that power can rest in the hands of the people, rather than in corporations, and that participation transforms those who participate. It liberates the individual at the same time that it binds the individual to community. Closely related to the idea of a folk revival is the notion that the Internet can be seen as more democratic than other forms of mass media are. Such claims have attracted debate and critique. Graeme Turner (2009), for instance, argues that the increasing visibility of ordinary people in the media is better described as a "demotic turn" than as a democratic one. Evgeny Morozov (2011) is skeptical about absolute democratic claims, pointing out that the same technologies that make everyday discourse visible are also surveillance technologies that can be used against citizens. Rather than chronicle and rehearse these debates, however, I want to ask why we think of networked discourse as a folk revival. Why do we invoke folk culture, and what do we mean when we do so? It is here that scholarship about popular music is instructive. Many scholars of popular music will point out that "folk" is not merely descriptive: It is an ideological construction. Frith (1981b) argues that this construction of what counts as folk music and folk ideals has mutated over time to meet the needs of those who have invoked its name.[8] Folk is not a kind of music as much as it is a way of using music. Frith argues that scholarship on popular music needs to ask why we create the myths we do. Similarly, I join many other scholars (Flichy 2007; Friedman 2005) in believing that how we imagine the Internet and how we talk about it is an essential step towards understanding its culture and the changes associated with it. To begin to answer these questions, I draw some parallels between the emergence of ideas about participatory culture and about folk ideology in order to show that romantic ideals persists in our understanding of online discourse, despite claims to the contrary.

A "participatory" culture is thought to be a more authentic culture. They are perceived to "stress the personal and individual" (Marshall 2005: 61) and, insofar as participation is constructed as mass culture's "other," they are considered anticommercial, (ironically even when they are founded upon a commercial platform such as Facebook or Soundcloud). Underpinning this folk ideology are romantic ideals about authenticity as that which is genuine, sincere, and noncommercial. Folk participation, as a bottom-up form of culture production, when juxtaposed with commercial models of production, distribution, and consumption, is seen to be more authentic, as well as more communal. As discussed, a more

---

[8]For an exploration of how it was invoked, see also Barker and Taylor (2007).

accurate description of participatory music cultures might have them as anticorporate or antimainstream, rather than anticommercial. Yet, their oppositional posture is enough to secure their status as folk production and to secure this key element of authenticity. Neither Jenkins nor Benkler take a specifically anticommercial stance. Benkler is interested in accounting for the increasingly important role of nonmarket production in a networked information economy, and Jenkins argues that smart companies embrace convergence and new circulation practices as good business decisions—but he still posits an oppositional stance between so-called mass and folk cultures. Benkler notes that this new folk participation was "largely suppressed in the industrial era of cultural production," while Jenkins portrays the recent past as a time in which folk production went underground. Throughout Jenkins's potted history, folk music is presented as culture that can stand in opposition to commerce—it is either noncommercial or of little economic consequence. He even foregrounds the idea that nineteenth-century folk culture was developed with "little or no expectation of economic compensation," a claim disputed by Hugh Barker and Yuval Taylor (2007) in *Faking It: The Quest for Authenticity in Popular Music*. Acknowledging the morphing of folk as a category throughout the twentieth century, Barker and Taylor trace this idea that "free" is an important element in "folk" music to the collector Alan Lomax and in his manifesto, "Music in Your own Backyard" (1940). Barker and Taylor (2007: 63) write,

> Lomax abandons the traditional view—and that of his father too. No longer must folk song be specific to a homogeneous group. Now it can be shared by an entire nation. And beneath this gentle and seemingly all encompassing picture, Lomax is laying out a new, if hidden, criterion for what makes a song "folk": It is sung without expectation of remuneration.

Although it is not my aim to trace the fascinating history of folk as a changing signifier (particularly in American music), recognizing it as such is key to identifying the contradictions raised by romantic assumptions of authorship and ideals of authenticity. "Folk" was not always seen as noncommercial, yet the lack of remuneration seems key to our rankings of authentic discourse online. Bloggers were seen as trusted sources because they were not professionals (or, at the very least, they were off-the-clock professionals). They were perceived as doing what they did for love, not for money. They were being true to themselves. Many of the bloggers I spoke with had strong opinions about whether or not advertising on their blog would be ethical. One blogger ran what he called "useful" ads—links to retailers that made it easier to find the recordings you were interested in buying—while another, whose site, though costing him money to run, was attracting thousands of people every month,[9] said he would never have advertising there. He said,

> It's very unethical to make money off other people's copyright without compensating them and I think it would open me up to [a] very bad lawsuit. Some other pretty popular sites—they all do that. They all make a lot of money and they post a lot of leaks and no one has ever sued them. It would be really hard to defend them in a court but they're more ballsy than I am. At a certain point around February 2006 I had a job and it was a terrible job. I was really broke and I thought, "OK. I have this situation where I could conceivably make a lot of money. If I had advertising right now I would probably make double what I make now." It's very tempting. But I don't think it's worth it and I think it's better to hold on to the purity of what it is. This is my thing. I do it by myself. (Telephone interview, June 25, 2007)

To keep his blog "pure," to secure the space in which he can be true to himself and his experience, this blogger has to stay clear of monetary reward for his labor. This is not to say he is against being paid for his creative labor—in other situations, he writes about music for money—but his blog was a space outside of those material concerns, a space where he need not be concerned about anyone other than himself. (It is also an example of how what Frith [1981b] calls an "art ideology," that is an active disinterest in audience and money, can overlap with folk discourses.)

The ideology of participation also carries with it a kind of nostalgia that is typical of romantic thinking. In the romantic movement of the eighteenth century (Ong 1991), it was a concern for the "distant past" and "folk culture," that sparked the collection of oral folklore in that era. Similarly, contemporary ideas about participation and remix invoke a return to a preindustrial past as a way to explain new kinds of digital discourse. When academics such as Jenkins invoke "folk" today, they insert networked discourse into past discursive traditions. When we are speaking about cultural practices that transgress regulatory frameworks—as Jenkins does with online fan practices and as Lessig does with remix practices—one aim is to normalize or *naturalize* these activities by contrasting them with an artificial commercial culture.

If to call a music a folk music is to make a claim about how the music is used, rather than what it is made from (Frith 1981a), then to call a culture participatory is to project ideals about the value of authentic individual expression, while at the same time making a communal experience possible.

---

[9]This was an unusually large number among the bloggers I spoke with and in other reports. In 2004, music-journalist Adam Pasick reported that only the most popular blogs received "a few thousand visitors per day."

Jenkins' claims that consumption is becoming collective, then phenomena such as MP3 blogs begins to hint at how we can enact communal experience while we remain apart, separated by space and time. Frith (1981a) argues that we use myths about popular music to make sense of contradiction in everyday life. When we bring these romantic ideals of expression into the digital sphere, how do they help us conjure communal experience and intimacy while we are alone in the bedroom, commuting on the train, or bored at work? Frith applied this logic to recordings and how they were used, and I now argue that we have brought our romantic relationship with artifacts, along with the pleasure we find in these relationships, into the digital sphere, made up as it is of nothing but copies (in multiple senses of the word). Here, the two notions of authenticity bump up against one another and as such, the folk discourse compounds and mutates, grabbing whatever is needed from commerce and its "other" along the way. Buying a recording that represents the antimainstream was the quandary that Frith and Marshall's work addressed—but how do notions of authenticity come to be produced on platforms owned by multinational companies and when the items circulated were often made within a commercial context? As noted in the previous section, in the secondary art, antiques and antiquities markets, an object's provenance can be used to assess its authenticity—its story of ownership and circulation answers the question, is it real? This is the strong sense of authenticity, meaning that it is of "of undisputed origin or authorship" (Varga and Guignon 2016). One way of assessing this is by tracing its history of custodianship. Digital objects, being so stubbornly opaque and produced on demand, need to be contextualized to be used. The generation of provenance serves to animate copies—literally, to move them—and thereby making an argument about how to use them. It turns a rationalized electronic process into an individual argument for its perpetuation. Listen to this. But, most romantic of all—and making it a truly modern technology—the copy, once perpetuated, need not carry along that tradition, that provenance, that history. It can start over, remaining true to itself and obscuring its history.

5.6 Countercultures and anticommercialism

Marginal or niche cultural practices tend to be less specialized than their mainstream counterparts, and the lines demarking commerce, community, and leisure tend to be fuzzier. Such music scenes often conceived of themselves as grassroots, an alternative to, or even opposing, mainstream mass culture and the corporate music industry. Hence, the opening up of new channels of distribution and discovery, at a time when the RIAA was filing lawsuits against file sharers, and trying to curb the use of copyrighted material with digital rights management and the like, made the success and taste of independent bloggers—with nothing more than a connection and a collection—exciting and invigorating. Their oppositional stance was now visible, searchable and discoverable. As I will discuss, this pedigree—the idea that MP3 blogs were heirs to fanzines independence and countercultural cachet (Wolk 2002), and that they were on the right side of the divide between art and commerce—guaranteed their status as *authentic* listeners and, as Antoinne Hennion (2001) would have it, true lovers of music.

The bloggers I spoke to in 2006 through 2008 were exemplary of this tendency away from the mainstream and towards specialization in niche or marginal music scenes. They were all committed collectors of recordings: that is, active and regular consumers of recordings—and some even earned a living in jobs related to the music industry. (In some cases, the bloggers entered their music industry-related professions because the success of their blogs.) At the height of their popularity, some bloggers were even courted by both small and major labels (Schiffman 2007) and they were often cited as being instrumental in the rise of now well-known bands (Ganz 2005; Pasick 2004; *Rolling Stone* 2006). Many bloggers I interviewed said they were pleased their blogs could help contribute to a performer's success, and, like most fans, they were happy to favor and flatter their favorite artists. Despite an apparent tolerance of MP3 blogs by the recording industry, anxieties and risks remained. One New York-based blogger (now a professional journalist who at one time also ran an authorized MP3 blog for a news service) told me,

> If you go back in time—even 2004–2005—I think the feeling among a lot of people was, "This is nice for now but any day now the music industry is going to crack down on it." But it didn't. In fact, it's almost like the opposite—they embraced it. A lot of major labels definitely send things out [but] they can't give you permission for things. (Telephone interview, June 26, 2007)

In response to these risks, many blogs posted a disclaimer explaining that the MP3s were for "sampling purposes only," that they posted "out of love," that, if you liked what you heard, you should buy the recording yourself, and that, if you were the artist and wanted your work taken down, the blogger would be happy to oblige. These disclaimers suggest that bloggers did consider the ethical and commercial ramifications of their practice but they also highlight a tension that persists in popular music: a need for music to eschew commercial concerns and to represent a subcultural community; to abide by the folk ideology that underpins a great deal of popular-music discourse and its use in constructing authenticity and creating community (Frith 1981a).

Anticommercialism is an important element of romantic notions of authenticity and community, but, as Lee Marshall (2005: 156) explains,

"Romanticism is at once a challenge to the commodification of cultural goods and its ideological support." Frith (1981b: 177) has argued that rock fanzines in the 1960s and 1970s assumed an oppositional stance to mainstream taste: "They claim their music to be better than what most people like and they want to change people's ideas of how music should work." The importance of these fanzines, Frith suggests, was ideological rather than commercial, as they were "the source of arguments about what rock means, arguments not only about art and commerce, but also about art and audience." Blogs can be read in a similar light, regardless of their musical genre or focus. MP3 blogs were an anticommercial gesture: A recording is networked, and thus made available to be copied, with no money changing hands when a copy is generated. They do not, however, exist outside of the economic system as Jonathan Sterne (2012: 208–26) shows in his cultural history of the MP3; these free exchanges remain dependent on commercial platforms and technologies and many of the recordings themselves were made within the commercial recording industry. Ironically, they free the music from its industry shackles through a deep celebration of authorial expression (both the artists' and their own). Simultaneously, they illustrate an existing tendency in popular music that is not so much antimarket as it is anticorporate: They valorize the little guy over the corporate giant. Music journalist Simon Reynolds (2009) observed that the ethos of participation characteristic of so many micro-genres has proved compatible with a kind of micro-capitalism: participants are now interested in an "aesthetic underground" rather than a political one. Reynolds believes that this, in turn, could create a "sense of a hierarchy in terms of the medium via which you discovered music." Blogs might make the underground visible, but their relative obscurity, their mom and pop shop-ness, and their commitment to direct encounters with music and personal ways of knowing, made them a more suitable source of argument about what their particular niche might mean for those who participate in it.

So, while the tendency in digital-culture scholarship has been to use "participatory" as a term to describe new modes of user-generated content, expressive practices, etc., it might be more accurate to speak of ideologies of participation and then to ask if participation as an ideal has a romantic component, one that is overlooked when collaboration and nonmarket production are held up in opposition and as virtuous. There was an existing suspicion and resentment of the corporate music industry within niche music scenes (McLeod 2005b; Novak 2011) that lends the practice of inserting oneself into distribution a posture of rebellion, of thumbing your nose at the powers that be (even if you also link to the rest of the album on iTunes). This "whiff of rock rebellion," along with a notion that true art is above the market, even as it circulates as a commodity within it (Marshall 2005: 76) and that for music to be considered authentic, it must come from the people (2005: 60), are all part of what Marshall saw as the romantic underpinnings of rock music culture and the place of bootlegs within that culture. If sites of access and distribution can imbue a song with authenticity, that is if we can place value on where a recording comes from, then perhaps blogs as digital bodies (boyd 2006) were considered authentic precisely because they made the cultural intermediary visible;[10] they didn't cut out the "middle man," instead they multiplied the intermediary and humanized this figure of distribution and circulation.

In Marshall's (2005: 125) work, he argued that the bootlegging of rock records was a romantic gesture, in part because the bootleggers prioritized "aesthetic impulses for production over economic ones," but also because of their rebel stance. MP3 blogs are considered part of a "folk" culture because they are perceived to assume an oppositional stance toward the music industry, toward mainstream tastes, and toward the professional gatekeepers of such tastes—mainstream music journalists, for instance (cf. Frith 1981b: 177). This tension comes to a head in discussions about the ethics of networking copyrighted material. Yet, the same romantic conception of authorship that underpins copyright is also at play in the folk ideology that fuels networked participation (including its disregard for copyright) and the aesthetics of new forms of discourse. The tension is this: a suspicion or a devaluing of corporate commercialism, and a preoccupation with authenticity, subjectivity, and community, can prop up copyright regimes at the same time as they offer a justification for their rejection or refusal. This tension crops up because different notions of copy are at play in the functioning of digital technologies and in the discourse of popular music. The question, then, is: what can this tension illuminate about networked culture, digital discourse, and the role that romantic gestures and ideals continue to play within them?

5.7 Networking authenticity

Authenticity is considered a central concept in the study of popular music[11] and these debates and discussions offer many lessons for scholars of media. Claims about authenticity, Marshall (2005: 56) argues, are rooted in romanticism and span all genres of pop. Although different music cultures might not agree about what counts as authentic, they tend to use similar criteria to evaluate whether a musical work, performance, or use is considered authentic. Generally, these are perceptions that equate

---

[10] Following Shuker's reading, Bourdieu (1986) might see bloggers as a cultural intermediary made visible (2002: 84–5).

[11] See Barker and Taylor (2007), Frith (1981a, 1981b, 1998), Thornton (1995), Marshall (2005: 56–68), and Shuker (2002: 20–1).

authenticity with that which is genuine, sincere, and noncommercial. These romantic ideals about authenticity continue to play an important role in our perceptions of MP3 blogs and in defense of them. Upon scrutiny, these ideals appear to be closely related to the valorization of online participation (e.g., user-generated content and peer production) and to claims that blogs and similar forms of networked discourse represent a kind of folk revival. To interrogate these claims, I look to Frith's (1981a, 1981b) claim that popular music is underpinned by a folk ideology, Sarah Thornton's (1995) argument that new technologies make new concepts of authenticity possible and David Novak's (2011) suggestion that new authenticities are forming around redistribution while simultaneously drawing upon and remediating countercultural values of the 1980s and 1990s. According to Frith, popular music is underpinned by ideological assumptions that help users make sense of the contradictions they experience in everyday life (Frith 1981b: 168). Rock music adopts a folk ideology when it emphasizes its role in creating communal experiences, even when it does so through the circulation of recordings and the production of stars. To call a music folk, Frith argues, is to make a claim about how the music is *used*, rather than what it is *made from*. The notion of what constitutes a "folk" music has a history that, Frith (1981a: 160) posits, is rooted "not [in] existing musical practices but [in] a nostalgia for how they might have been."[12] Successive folk revivals throughout the twentieth century compound this nostalgia, projecting fantasies about preindustrial musical experiences and community life onto new material realities and cultural contradictions. Yet, each revival was also closely related to the creation of recordings—copies—that could circulate the particular variation of the myth at play. "Folk" becomes less descriptive of a music than it is aspirational. As Graham Smith (1997: 130, in Shuker 2002: 134) put it, "Folk is a shifting signifier which constantly mutates in meaning." Frith suggests that "folk," as a malleable concept, becomes a way for popular-music cultures—commodified mass culture—to be seen as representing a communal experience at the same time that it adheres to ideals about individual expression as a kind of truth to self and experience. It becomes a way to produce a myth about a music culture that can make sense of its contradictions. By adhering to a folk ideology, rock music could separate the musical work from its commodity form (as a recording); it could elevate the artist (and ignore the bureaucratic and technical apparatus) and emphasize individual expression, direct communication, instinct, and emotion as a reaction against a world that is commercial, rational, and mechanized (Marshall 2005: 65). The music would not have to represent the community: the recordings could be the communal

---

[12] This nostalgia for what might have been, parallels Friedman's observation that technological determinism creates a space for utopian thinking. These are both imaginaries that create new possibilities.

experience—you could buy into anticommercial culture. As I will show, these ideals of authenticity can also be found at play in current descriptions of online participation as a folk revival.

In Sarah Thornton's (1995) study of U.K. club culture, she parses the new senses of authenticity that recordings attract in disc cultures (disco, club cultures, etc.), as opposed to the "live" culture of rock.[13] While Frith has argued that in rock culture technology was often seen as fakery, a thing that distances the performer from the audience, Thornton showed that new technologies, once enculturated, make new concepts of authenticity possible. Thus, as records become essential to a popular culture, they come to have their own authenticities.

Thornton distinguishes between two notions of authenticity, both of which are at play in all popular-music cultures. The first is authenticity as it relates to ideas about originality and aura (or as it pertains to culture as works of art); the second is the idea of authenticity as *natural*, or organic, to the community (or, as it pertains to culture, as a way of life). Both live and "disc" authenticities value the genuine and the sincere and stand in opposition to commerce and hype; however, in a popular culture that values "live performance," these notions of authenticity, Thornton (1995: 30) argues, collide in authorship: "Artistic authenticity is anchored by the performing author in so far as s/he is assumed to be the unique origin of the sound, while subcultural authenticity is grounded in the performer in so far as s/he represents the community." By contrast, in a "disc" culture, such as that of contemporary dance music, recordings are understood as an authentic source of origin, and "the crowd makes it a 'living' culture" (1995: 30). Thornton (1995: 27–8) argues that these notions of authenticity have material foundations:

> In the process of becoming originals, records accrued their own authenticities. Recording technologies did not, therefore, corrode or demystify "aura" as much as disperse and re-locate it. Degrees of aura came to be attributed to *new, exclusive* and *rare* records. In becoming the source of sounds, records underwent the mystification usually reserved for *unique* art objects. Under these conditions, it would seem that the mass-produced cultural commodity is not necessarily imitative or artificial, but plausibly archetypal and authentic.

In both live and "disc" cultures, Thornton (1995: 26) argues that authenticity is a cure for alienation and dissimulation, that it "is valued as a

---

[13] In the rock culture of the 1970s, for example, rock stars like Bruce Springsteen even seemed to condone the bootlegging phenomenon. Recounts Clinton Heylin, "During a July broadcast from the Roxy, [Springsteen said] 'Bootleggers, roll your tapes this is gonna be a hot one!'" (He would later change his tune) (Heylin 2003: 104).

balm for media fatigue and as an antidote to commercial hype." Many of the bloggers I spoke with talked about the grassroots character of their practices and experiences and emphasized how they saw their practice as a celebration of discovery and encounter with the strange, the spectacular, and even the sublime. Consider that MP3 blogging came to prominence in an era of information abundance and accessibility—in a sea of data, to which artifacts should you give your attention? MP3 blogs came to be seen by users as an embodiment of authenticity, a genuine and sincere expression of taste, and, as such, they stand in opposition to the commercial hype that characterizes mass culture. The MP3 blog can stand as that "balm for media fatigue and as an antidote to hype" (ironically, at the same time that it appropriates hype and participates in it). This relief is rife with paradox: MP3 blogs are a form of *individual* expression that hinges on the use of recordings to produce a *communal* experience, admittedly, one that is mediated, its participants remaining isolated from one another; MP3 blogs value the intentionality of the user's actions and their participation in the network in the face of digital automation, atomization, and surveillance; MP3 blogs elevate the emotional, the instinctive, and the subjective as ways to navigate rational, distributed networks; MP3 blogs seem to be the work of autonomous and independent listeners, yet they are also entirely dependent upon the recordings they network for their very existence.

Novak (2011: 615) argues that new ideals of authenticity are building up around redistribution, as listeners attempt to create for themselves the conditions for "an authentically remediated experience." To do so they aim for "a blind encounter with mystery" (2011: 614), eschew authority and "official modes of explanation" (2011: 615). This suspicion of interpretation was particularly evident in MP3 blogs that comprised of a list of songs with no explanatory texts. When I asked one such blogger why he didn't write anything to accompany his daily sound file, he responded,

> I'm not an expert ... I think what it does is that it forces people to make connections between what's being posted ... The whole idea was to keep the mystery about everything. It was a way to keep people who are into it coming back. I didn't want to explain it away. (Telephone interview, June 19, 2007)

This statement suggests that the blogger values a direct connection between song and listener, unmediated by contextual information, and yet augmented by the magic of discovery.[14] This user's explanation also suggests that the experience of finding music and hearing it for the first

---

[14]Novak's (2011: 615) bloggers similarly aim for what he calls "authentic remediation."

time—a point of origin—is considered a valuable experience, and one he wants to re-engineer in the digital domain. "Mystery" might seem a strange value for someone who posts his or her favorite underground songs in public, yet, for this blogger, an encounter with mystery was a part of the experience of discovery. MP3 blogging, for this music user, was an attempt to author serendipity, rooted in his own past experiences with musical discovery, media, and discourse. He told me that even the structure of the site, was inspired by his own experience of "crate digging" as a mode of discovery. He said,

> One of the reasons I like to keep the site simple is that I grew up going to op shops, looking at vinyl and you just buy stuff because you have no way to listen to it. You buy it because of the cover or you buy it because it's cheap and looks interesting—that was always the most satisfying way to find music. It was the music that you weren't looking for or that you brought home and it was like "holy shit, these guys are blazing on this!" It cost you 50 cents, it was completely rejected by everyone and you just own this great thing. I kind of wanted [people] to get that feeling. It was like you don't know where it's from, you don't know the history of the stuff and you're going to click on the link and hear something insane. (Telephone interview, June 19, 2007)

It is a stance that is almost suspicious of any provenance that one has not created for oneself. Listening is the only test of taste, he implies. It is as if recorded music is capable of transcending any of its particular histories. They embody romantic expression but cannot control it.

5.8 Analog antecedents: Harry Smith's mystical collection

All collections are unique assemblages of knowledge and expression but not all are accessible or influential. Access is the much celebrated potential of networked collections, but the collection practices of gathering, archiving and connecting have always generated meanings distinct from the sum of its parts. How and why collections create meaning are more difficult questions to answer. In the early 1930s, while unpacking his books, Walter Benjamin wrote a short essay that considered the puzzling relationship between collectors and collections. He wrote, "For a collector, ownership is the most intimate relationship that one can have to objects. Not that they come alive in him; it is he who lives in them" (Benjamin 2007c: 67). In this, Benjamin, a Marxist, trades commodity fetishism for a kind of object-oriented historical mysticism; for Benjamin, objects in collections become a kind of "magic encyclopedia"[15] store housing memories, safe guarding truths, and granting access to secret histories and ways of knowing.

In this era of digital networks we are all collectors of sorts, fashioning digital selves from assemblages of digital artifacts, creating what Henry Jenkins (2006a: 3–4) calls our "personal mythologies." It is we who live in our digital collections. This archival vitalism is what that MP3 blogger taps into and why this practice of social distribution was understood as a creative one (see the discussion of archival vitalism and social authorship in 5.4). Benjamin suggests that this imperative is inherent to all practices of collection and it also produces for the collector an obligation of preservation and transmissiblity. "A collector's attitude toward his possessions stems from an owner's feeling of responsibility toward his property. Thus it is, in the highest sense, the attitude of an heir, and the most distinguished trait of a collection will always be transmissibility" (Benjamin 2007c: 66). In this section I consider Harry Smith's *Anthology of American Folk Music* as an analog antecedent to MP3 blogs and other online practices of collection and social distribution. My aim is to probe the *Anthology*'s status as a "magic encyclopedia," one that can shed light on the collector's imperative and how it lends meaning to circulation as a cultural practice.

An enabling anthology

American artist and eccentric Harry Everett Smith collected many things— paper airplanes, cats cradles, Ukrainian Easter Eggs, Seminole dresses—and many of his collections found their way into major cultural institutions such as the Smithsonian and the New York Public Library because of their great cultural significance. Smith is still best remembered for his *Anthology of American Folk Music*, a collection of eighty-four American folk songs, all recorded between 1927 and 1932, and re-released by Smith in 1952 on Moses Asch's Folkways label. The three volume boxed set of LPs was selected by Smith from his collection of over 20,000 recordings—most were out-of-circulation 78s, reproduced without permission, making the *Anthology* a "dubiously legal bootleg" (Marcus 1997: 87) as the critic Greil Marcus put it. In addition to the vinyl LPs, the boxed set also contained a booklet that Smith wrote and designed; A dedicated amateur ethnographer, Smith considered this text as an integral part of the *Anthology*. In this treatise, Smith is part musicologist, part provocateur, and part mystic, including information on the songs and recordings, a mysterious but intentional system of ordering and sequencing, and publishing a short but pithy

---

[15] "The period, the region, the craftsmanship, the former ownership—for a true collector the whole background of an item adds up to the magic encyclopedia whose quintessence is the fate of his object" (Benjamin 2007c: 60).

essay from Asch that contains a number of implied and pointed jabs directed at the recording industry for allowing great songs and important recordings to languish in obscurity. Writes Asch in the liner notes, "It does not 'PAY' to re-press this type of music (produced to sell only to a limited audience)."

Harry Smith's *Anthology* was celebrated during his lifetime and it continues to be considered an important achievement: In 1991, almost forty years after its release and shortly before his death, Smith was awarded a Grammy for his contribution to popular music, and still today the Smithsonian considers the *Anthology* as "one of the most influential releases in the history of recorded sound". I contend that we can also use the *Anthology* to better understand the MP3 blogs of the 2000s as Smith's collection was a kind of analog antecedent to these networked practices: both were examples of artifacts that highlight the transformative potential of collection, curation, and copying as cultural practices and both participate in that long, alternative history of piracy. I draw parallels between these artifacts as forms of expression to excavate patterns of use and highlight the possibilities that are related to the social, material, and rhetorical dimensions of media formats and their status as copies. Ideas about curation, remediation, distribution, and unauthorized use are important to understanding both practices, as is an understanding of the romantic tensions that crop up around practices that are considered piratical. In Smith's mysticism about collection and seriality, we can glimpse a prehistory of network affordances; in Smith's preoccupation with the odd and exotic there are parallels with the ideals of authenticity, serendipity, and redistribution found among MP3 bloggers. These possibilities and parallels, in turn, illuminate how the interaction and intersection of copies as identity and copies as instance can produce new meaning while being just the same.

Freak folk: **The Anthology** *and ways of knowing*

Robert Cantwell (1991) called *The Anthology of American Folk Music* an "enabling document," the "Musical constitution" of the folk revival of the 1950s and 1960s, an inspiration and guide to artists and performers like Pete Seeger, Joan Baez, and Bob Dylan. Cantwell took particular interest in how media technologies and formats shaped Smith's project,[16] its cultural context and its reception. Long before MP3 bloggers aimed to remediate their musical experiences of discovery and serendipity, Harry Smith had similar intentions when he released his own eccentric outlook and influential series of re-recordings on vinyl LPs. By the late 1940s, Smith had

---

[16] This is not a surprise as Cantwell's analysis of the *Anthology* was influenced by his reading of Marshall McLuhan. See Cantwell (1991: 370).

amassed more than 20,000 recordings of what were known as "commercial race and hillbilly recordings." (Smith disapproved of the segregation of records by race and he said as much in the liner notes, calling the terms "unpleasant.") Initially, Smith tried to sell the collection to Folkways, but the label's owner Moses Asch instead invited him to curate a selection of recordings and assemble them into what would become the *Folkways Anthology of American Folk Music*. All of the recordings in Smith's collection were commercial releases rather than his own field recordings, and most were by this time rare, produced in small numbers and circulated in niche markets. The shift in format, from 78s to the LP, recontextualized this music; in McLuhan's framework it was a material shift that amplified reach and offered rhetorical affordances. Microgroove technology enabled longer recordings than 78s, a physical affordance that allowed for more songs on a single disc, making anthologizing a possibility. At the time, LPs were also perceived as high status, as they were primarily associated with classical music and other high art forms. Taking dusty, discarded 78s and turning them into a vinyl long-playing record was alchemy of sorts; or, as Cantwell (1991: 365) argues, Smith turned forgotten regional, minority, and working class music into avant garde art. He writes, "[The] Folkways Anthology implicitly legitimized its material, investing it with the cultural authority both of its advanced technology and its rarefied sociopolitical connections" (1991: 364–5). Format shift served a rhetorical purpose; and this shift in meaning was enabled by the disposition of copy as a property.

Smith's collection may have followed on the heels of literary anthologies of songs—lyric books for sing-alongs were common at the time—but the *Anthology* was about aural knowledge and the recordings themselves as containers of knowledge. Cantwell (1991: 365) wrote, "the Folkways Anthology brought forward what could only be preserved aurally, the sound of the folk performance itself." The *Anthology* became a resource not only for repertoire, but also for style and sound. Cantwell notes that the styles documented on the *Anthology* were consciously imitated and reproduced by revivalists such as Pete Seeger, and also reignited the careers of long-retired musicians as a new generation of listeners sought more of the same.

Cantwell reminds us that at the time the *Anthology* was released, most of the recorded folk music that circulated could be traced back to the efforts of John and Alan Lomax, who traveled the country recording music chosen on overtly ideological grounds. John Lomax' conservatism was at odds with his son's radicalism; Cantwell points out that Alan Lomax had a distinct ideology and he "was in the business of constructing to the movement an idea of folk music consistent with its sublimated Leninist program and idealized Populist Outlook" (1991: 364). Although the *Anthology* played into a mythology of folk as authentic if it was noncommercial, amateur, and regional—Cantwell examines the overt romance with the New Deal and the WPA era that the packaging signaled—the *Anthology* was different precisely because it was made up of commercial recordings, many of which were recordings of professional regional musicians. These were not recordings chosen on traditional musicological grounds, or along ideological lines, instead they were selected along the decidedly eccentric and personal criteria of Harry Smith. Hugh Barker and Yuval Taylor (2007: 79) remind us about how radical Smith's conception of folk music would have been at the time: "Smith deliberately included songs that most folklorists would have excluded out of hand—songs composed by professional musicians and songs about the politics of the time. Instead he simply presented a fascinating mélange of disparate styles and an acoustic manifesto that implicitly equated 'folk', 'pop' and 'classical'." This point of difference—the "oddness" of the *Anthology*—is what aficionados and scholars celebrate as the collection's strength as a folk document.

Mystery and weirdness were for Smith, much like the bloggers in the 2000s, desirable traits. According to Smith, "'Songs were selected because they were odd'; 'I was looking for exotic records'" (Barker and Taylor 2007: 75). The past can indeed be a foreign country and, as Barker noted, "there was very little mystery in the popular songs of the 1950s and 1960s; by contrast the commercial cultural products of the South a generation or two earlier already sounded as weird to them as traditional Bulgarian, Mongolian, or Central African Music might have" (2007: 76). Smith thought it was imperative that these sounds be revived and recirculated. In the *Anthology*'s handbook he wrote, "Only through recordings is it possible to learn of those developments that have been so characteristic of American Music, but which are unknowable through written transcriptions alone. Then too, records of the type found in the present set played a large part in stimulating these historic changes by making easily available to each other the rhythmically and verbally specialized musics of groups living in mutual social and cultural isolation." Recordings don't only document and preserve, they enable.

There was an overtly mystical dimension to Smith's approach. When prompted to explain his selections in a 1969 interview, he described them as being "picked out from an epistemological, musicological selection of reasons" (Cohen 1969, in Singh 2010: 30). Marcus (1997) called the *Anthology* "an occult document disguised as an academic treatise on stylistic shifts within an archaic musicology." Or, as Cantwell (1991: 365) puts it: "The *Folkways Anthology* may be called, perhaps, a curriculum in mystical ethnography. It converts a commercial music fashioned in the 1920s out of various cultural emplacements and historical displacements into the 'folk' music of the folk revival." For Smith, seriality, the nature of the *Anthology* as an ordered list, as well as it's generation of a topology or map, are key elements of the *Anthology's* functionality; that is, they are the concepts that Smith thought might explain how it is that his tactics of collection, reproduction, remediation, and bricolage produced new ways of understanding the world. Smith was explicit: "The whole purpose is to have some kind of series of things." Collection, he believed, was a technology for "programming the mind." It was also a practice that was highly visual— Smith was also an accomplished experimental filmmaker and painter—and for Smith, this visual dimension was integral to the *Anthology* not only in terms of the design and contents of the handbook that served as a companion to the records, but also to collections in general. In a 1969 interview in *Sing Out!* he said:

> The type of thinking that I applied to records I still apply to other things like Seminole patchwork, or to Ukranian Easter Eggs. The whole purpose is to have some kind of series of things. Information as drawing and graphic design can be located more quickly than it can in books. The fact that I have all the Seminole designs permits anything that falls into the canon of that technological procedure to be found there, It's like flipping quickly through, its a way of programming the mind … as it goes through the vision, it is more immediately assimilated. (Cohen 1969, in Cantwell 1991: 373)

In Smith's archive fever we find a precursor to the networked drive to make the invisible visible (or at least more searchable or in Smith's case, findable). Cantwell recounts how Smith and his *Anthology* drew inspiration from the seventeenth-century occult philosopher Robert Fludd, who designed what was called a "Memory theater" or mnemonic library, based on a classical oration technique, *ars memoria,* in which concepts were matched with images as a way to remember them and then these images were arranged in sequence and embedded in the architecture of a familiar space to aid recall. Fludd adapted this technique to offer a way to organize human knowledge and understanding. "[It's] aim was to organize and present the entire cosmos of knowledge in the form of alchemical, astrological, and Cabalistic symbols … which a scholar could enter and study, discovering drawers or cabinets beneath each emblem" (Cantwell 1991: 373). Smith's first pressing of the *Anthology* (as well as the 1997 CD reissue) featured Fludd's drawing of the Celestial Monochord on the cover. Smith's debt to Fludd should not be underestimated and Cantwell offers an argument for understanding Smith's *Anthology* as a memory theater in which Smith uses a variety of media in sequence as a technology for recall and recirculation.

Descriptions of Smith's room at the Chelsea Hotel in New York City, with artifacts covering every possible surface including the bed, make it sound as if Smith lived in a curiosity cabinet of sorts. His memory theater, however, also shares a number of approaches and desires with one of his contemporary's speculation about what computing might be. That is, Smith's memory theater can be considered alongside Vannevar Bush's *memex*, a hypothetical device that, as Lisa Gitelman (2006: 99) pointed out, "imagined hypertext before the term hypertext was coined and any of the relevant digital technology existed." Bush wrote about his hypothetical device in an article "As We May Think" in the *Atlantic Monthly* in 1945, offering it as a solution to the problem of "information overload." In mid-century America, it seems, there was just too much knowledge and information—too many books—how could we possibly sort and search for it, asked Bush. His solution was that rather than rely on bureaucratic filing systems, that is on strict classification and order, we should devise a machine that was modeled on the flexibility and agility of human consciousness. Writes Gitelman (2006: 99), "He suggests that document might best be organized not by 'artificial' indexing systems with their rigid 'paths' and cumbersome rules, but by a more natural form of 'associative indexing.' Working in the manner of the 'intricate web of trails' that connects related thoughts in the brain." I have not encountered any evidence that suggests that Smith read Bush's article—although it is clear that he read widely—but I want to draw attention to the fact that a diverse range of artists and intellectuals were grappling with similar problems and offering solutions in parallel. Harnessing and harvesting highly personal ways of knowing, they thought, would afford new ways of understanding. The genius of Moses Asch was to release Harry Smith's eccentric world view into the world rather than simply buy his collection when Smith offered it to him.

Although Smith's intention was for the *Anthology* to be understood as a multimedia whole, it is after all the recordings themselves for which it is best remembered. Smith's decidedly anticanonical approach produced a new repertoire of songs and styles for the folk revival. Cantwell describes how both the *Anthology* itself and his larger collection became a resource for the revivalist of the period—they sang its songs, they studied and imitated the styles they heard and also sought out the original recording artists themselves for fresh rounds of concerts and recordings.[17] The *Anthology* became a template for future performances; the repeated play of these recordings prompted and then produced a new genre culture—folk. The folk revival may have valued the live and noncommercial, but if the *Anthology* is important as a founding document, then we should consider at least the irony of the recording at its heart. (It seems that the folk revival was electric long before Bob Dylan plugged in his guitar.) Folk imagines a new tomorrow, through a reappraisal and interpretation of the past. Or as I noted in the previous section, folk revivals project fantasies about preindustrial musical experiences and community life onto new material realities and cultural contradictions. This romantic impulse is a tactic that

---

[17] A similar phenomenon has arisen in our own networked era and MP3 blogs were among the forms and sites that contributed to what Simon Reynolds (2011) calls *Retromania*.

helps to make sense of larger contradictions. This is one of the transformative affordances of the copy.

There is also another mediated cultural backdrop to the *Anthology* that Cantwell (1991) highlights: that is that the *Anthology* offers an alternate view of the counterculture during the advent of TV. Both Smith and Asch were transfixed by audio technology and thought it could be instrumental in progressive cultural change. "I'm glad to say that my dreams came true—I saw America changed through music," were Smith's words when he was awarded a Grammy in 1991. The *Anthology*, in other words, was the counter-offer, an alternate way of perceiving and representing America's past, present, and future. The revival doesn't look back as much as it does listen to what's around. In D. A. Pennebaker's documentary *Don't Look Back*, we see Bob Dylan hiss at a disgruntled antielectric British audience: "It's not British Music, It's American Music!" Dylan was well aware of the debt American folk music owed to English oral traditions and the transatlantic trajectories of many folk songs. Instead, in Dylan's provocation "America" becomes a kind of floating signifier, an idea of folk not as a preservation of tradition but as a disruptor of time and space, and a technology for self-determination. So too, Smith's *Anthology* was a model for this new idea of folk—folk as mystery, folk as remediation, folk as a memory theater where artifacts that are just the same can be arranged and ordered to bring about new meanings.

David Novak adopted Christopher Kelty's (2008: 7, in Novak 2011: 625–6) notion of a recursive public—"[a public] concerned with the ability to build, control, modify, and maintain the infrastructure that allows [it] to come into being in the first place"—to describe and explain how the devotees of "World Music 2.0" remediated their underground values and analog aesthetics in the networked context. In Novak's research "World Music 2.0" is the social imaginary that formed around the project of redistribution in network culture, a culture that is defined by circulation rather than as a step between production and consumption or at a point between cultures.[18] In Novak's work on World Music 2.0 he highlights a number of characteristics about this contemporary music subculture in which there are parallels with Cantwell's reading of Smith's project and its influence and my study of MP3 blogs as process and product in the 2000s: Novak (2011) documents a subcultural practice that is centered on the project of redistribution but is ethically ambivalent about preservation and purity, values sensory displacement and mystery over explanation, and seems to be committed to an "ethic of openness" at the same time it is interested in technological limitation. Like many tales of bootleggers throughout the twentieth century, Novak points out that the groups he studied viewed

---

[18] This is Novak's definition of circulation as culture-making in *Japanoise* (Novak 2013: 17).

unauthorized copying (i.e., piracy) not as a transgression but as part of a participatory ethic, a noble freedom that trumps ownership and control. The romantic ethos of liberation is what the copy as a relational property affords; it would be criminal not to listen.

Projects of redistribution are projects of circulation and Novak (2013: 17) asserts that circulation was always already culture-making, that it "constitutes culture." The *Anthology* offers a good example of this claim in the context of analog technologies and an earlier era; MP3 blogging offers one of many networked examples from our own time. A focus on copies and copying recenters the discussion away from production and towards circulation and use. So, when we assert that new technologies make new concepts of authenticity possible as Thornton (1995) does, we should also consider the story of the microgroove LP, alongside the MP3, as *circulation* technologies. Both formats have histories that, when closely examined, demonstrate how the meaning of format and how it circulates can influence the meaning of the sounds that they helped to circulate; in this case both the *Anthology* and the MP3 blog, in their own ways, served to transform commercial recordings into a seemingly more authentic artifact of the *avant garde*. The material, social, and rhetorical dimensions of media intermingle making new possibilities from a ground that is just the same. Ideals of authenticity, serendipity, and redistribution that are not unfamiliar to the MP3 blogger or the underground subculture lurk in Smith's memory theater, conjured by the dance between the generation of copy and provenance, identity and instance, in piracy's long history.

5.9 Copies, networks, and a poetics of encounter

Just as DJs can be said to perform records, MP3 bloggers can be seen to play the network, and in doing so they make visible their collections and their ways of knowing. The affordances of the MP3—to replicate, to exchange, and to accumulate—provide them with a rhetorical tool in their effort to "get people to listen the right way" (Frith 1998: 8) but network visibility will also have effects on what is listened to and enable new possibilities. By this, I mean that it will alter what is available to us, and that this availability and exposure to multiple ways of knowing and interpretation will no doubt change the kinds of music made in future and influence what we do with it. Phonographic orality (Toynbee 2000) posits that recordings are a resource and that the availability and possibilities of recording alters and influences that which is recorded, a recursive proposition that suggests how and why recordings *qua* copies are possible source of renewal (just as Walter Benjamin [2007b] predicted). Harry Smith's *Anthology* as an enabling document is exemplary of this possibility. Digital networks can't help but compound these possibilities by making new networks possible.

That said, some of the romantic ideals about music and expression that kick-started blogging as a practice—the desire to replicate first listening, a faith in the transcendence of a work, a belief that art is above the market (and the belief that markets are not able to recognize greatness)—are also transformed by their own success and by other forms of networked musical discourse (e.g., Spotify, Apple Music, SoundCloud, YouTube). As these new technologies and platforms for listening arise, we see the emergence of competing discourses of authenticity. Most (though not all) of the bloggers I spoke with now post less frequently, or not at all. Some, such as the middle-aged bloggers I spoke with who were revisiting their collections of vinyl records, came to "a natural end," as one blogger in the U.K. put it. Others have gone on to write or to DJ professionally, and therefore do not have the time or inclination to blog anymore. One blogger started pressing small runs of vinyl records in the late 2000s—bootlegs of rare recordings and edits. Just as contemporary edit makers play with biases of the vinyl in tandem with the biases of the network as discussed in the previous chapter (see also Borschke 2011a), there is a renewed interest in analog formats and in the handmade (e.g., Crawford and Healy 2010; Luckman 2013; Reynolds 2009; Bartmanksi and Woodward 2015) as the "proper" place for the new, the exclusive, and the rare. The rebel status of the MP3 blog has dimmed, but its spirit has not disappeared as is evident in the private torrenting clubs that operate like secret societies with ritualistic rules of engagement and membership and the resurgence of boutique bootleg vinyl labels (Jarnow 2015). Yet, by shining a light on the romantic ideals that persists in musical discourse and culture about copying and recirculation, I hope we can begin to think about the pleasure listeners find in ideals of authenticity, authorship, and participation and how they use them rather than dismiss them as fantasies. In his critique of mid-twentieth century auteur theory in film, John Caughie (1981: 15) advised that "the attempt to move beyond auteurism has to recognize the place which auteurism occupies ... . It also has to recognize the figure of the auteur, and the way he is used in the cinephile's pleasure." We need to ask similar questions about the pleasure we derive from romantic ideals of authorship and art objects, as listeners, as producers and curators. MP3 bloggers fashioned themselves as archival auteurs—active listeners who attempt to create coherence from the activity of accumulation and to order the chaos inherent in that practice. This is what collectors do, says Benjamin (2007b: 59), "For what else is a collection but a disorder to which habit has accommodated itself to such an extent that it can appear as order?" From virtual hoarding to streaming, we must make sense of the pleasure we find in having data at our fingertips.

Consumption practices that foreground the agency of listeners in music culture do not preclude romantic articles of faith such as the transcendence of the work, the notion that the song exists apart from its instantiations, that it embodies meaning and can speak for itself. Nor does a disregard for copyright mean that users do not value self-expression or truth to self; indeed, the blogger's disregard for commerciality and legal strictures lends the activity a certain cachet in a world dominated by corporate behemoths. (Anticommercialism tends to be one of the guarantors of authenticity in popular music; a similar sentiment runs through network discourse where, as the saying goes, information wants to be free.) These "little guys" were seen in opposition to the corporate music business, as everyday music lovers reaching out to find others with similar interests and to distribute their own tastes, for love, not money. Or, so the story goes. The MP3 bloggers' status as authentic tastemakers in the 2000s was aligned with an ideology of participation, a folk ideology that renders music authentic if it emerges from the people (Marshall 2005: 60). Taking a longer view of copying practices, we see that participants brought these values with them to the network, rather than a possibility that the network produced them all on its own.

The chief lesson in my reading of MP3 blogs as a form is not actually about the form itself, but about how we might begin to think about the partial narratives of encounter that are offered to us online, and how we might begin to use them to understand media use, circulation, and its histories. Digital technologies make music audible by first making it visible, and this networked visibility creates biases or affordances that can be manipulated and played with. These new networked forms can change how we listen, as much as it changes what is available to us, and it requires an aesthetic of availability or a poetics of encounter to make sense of both. Yet, as Kate Crawford (2005: 34) has observed:

> [E]ncrypted networks can go beyond masking, and become a form of effacement, leaving no memories of the user and their activities. Akin to Susan Orlean's description of plants, the ideal encrypted network has no memory, and simply moves on to whatever is next.

Provenance can create identity and offer up arguments about taste, but in digital networks, it can also generate a copy that can move through, and even off, the network without any trace. This paradoxical liberation from the past seems to be the promise of the networked collection, just as it is the promise of many kinds of collecting. According to Walter Benjamin (2007a: 67), "Only in extinction is the collector comprehended." The generation of a copy might shake free of its history, but as Lisa Gitelman (2006: 147) reminds us, "Each lacuna in provenance (the discomfort of not knowing where a digital object comes from) can't help but put provenance on the table."

The possibility of a secret history is as much a part of archival vitality as the stories that are known. Writes Simon Frith (1998: 278),

Memories dance with the music too ... . This is what I mean, I think, by music both taking us out of ourselves and putting us in place, by music as both a fantasy of community and an enactment of it, by music dissolving difference even as it expresses it. The sounds on that Leamington dance floor, like the sounds now in this Berlin hotel room, are at the same time rootless, cut free from any originating time and place, and rooted, in the needs, movement, and imagination of the listener.

Your song can also be our song, and the song can remain the same.

CHAPTER SIX

Copies and the aesthetics
of circulation

As I write this chapter, Kim Dotcom's extradition trial is streaming live on the Internet. The contrast between the drama of his 2012 arrest, and the tedium of these important legal hearings is notable. Dotcom fought for this historic first in the name of transparency, but I can't help but think about how this live stream mirrors a shift in the culture of the Internet away from the downloading, archiving, and virtual hoarding of the 2000s, towards what we might call this decade's Internet pastoral:[1] the stream, the cloud, and the sharing economy. But in this constellation of metaphors, the culture-making power of circulation (Novak 2013) and their histories are obscured, the power and persistence of copying overlooked and the influence of media's material history ignored. The networked media landscape is only seemingly immaterial and, although streaming music companies claim to have solved the problem of piracy, they are to some extent built upon these verboten listening practices and remain dependent on copies and copying as are all digital technologies. To understand the new cultural possibilities that streaming might produce I argue that we need to excavate the copy from the stream, consider the forms that it remediates and examine the history of the practices that shaped it. We must ask: Why streaming now?

Throughout this book I've asked several related questions: Why copies now? Why remix now? Why vinyl now? Why projects of redistribution now? For me, these questions intersect in a consideration of technologies of distribution and questions related to circulation as a cultural practice. To study culture from the perspective of circulation is not only to study networks and how ideas and objects move around, but it is also to study how our material histories interact with everyday lived experience and the

---

[1] I nod here to Michael Pollan's ruminations on the supermarket pastoral of organic foods in the *New York Times Magazine* on May 13, 2001, which he later expanded upon in his 2006 book, *The Omnivoire's Dilemma*.

matter that constitutes it; to ponder how they shape rather than determine our present and future possibilities. Like Heraclitus, we continue to try to understand the ways in which "We step and do not step into the same rivers; we are and are not" (Heraclitus 49a, in Robinson 1987: 35).

To begin to understand the aesthetics of networked circulation and new ideals of authenticity that seem to spring from network culture, I've selected moments in the history of popular music that participate in piracy's long history, to consider what copies and copying can teach media studies about media and cultural change. To think through the material, historical, formal, and rhetorical dimensions of media culture, I have focused on media artifacts as copies and copying as a cultural practice. I have shown that people interact with media artifacts on various levels—they can use their material, rhetorical, and social dispositions.[2] In doing so, they can also alter the meaning of each. This interdependence and contingency presents a challenge for cultural research. Yet, as I hope this meditation on select moments in music culture has shown, by producing narratives of encounter and material histories, and by analyzing the rhetorical contours of media artifacts and their use, tackling this complexity offers rewards and dividends.

Copy as a concept is essential to the functioning of digital technologies and networks and yet we continue to treat the idea with either derision or naive celebration. This is the context in which remix comes to the defense of copying practices, but in doing so this metaphor may overshadow remix's own history and the people, recording formats, and events that forged new forms and experiences out of that which was just the same. My analysis of the rhetoric of remix recovered material histories—stories about magnetic tape, acetate, and vinyl—and highlighted the agency of media users, challenging accounts of cultural change that are either wholly socially or technologically determined. By emphasizing the long history of piracy, my aim has been to de-emphasize transformative use, to put the spotlight back onto exact copies, and the character and affordances of fixity and stability in the production of new meaning. Gilles Deleuze saw repetition as generating difference. However, my study shares more of an affinity with Benjamin's notion that modernity is a state of heightened historicity and copies, things that are just the same, but also distinct from one another, are a source of renewal within that state.

I also bring a transhistorical idea of copy to the table, and by doing so I have shown that a study of copies that takes an interest in distinctions between similarity and identity can highlight material, historical, and rhetorical differences among media artifacts. By staying alert to the differences between copies as instances (a particular copy of Plato's

---

[2]I am indebted to James Bucknell for many enlightening discussions on the subject of dispositions and powers as potential properties of objects. See also Bucknell (2015).

Republic) and copies as identity (the content shared by all the copies of Plato's *Republic*), and, by thinking about how and why these properties are interrelated, and how they are independent, our attention is drawn to overlooked materialities and material practices in media culture. My dualistic approach to copies helps to reconcile a tension that Grant Bollmer (2015) has identified as characterizing the material turn in media studies. Bollmer (2015: 95) writes, "One of the most notable challenges to emerge from the materialist turn in media studies is the rejection of the 'active audience' paradigm of British Cultural Studies." Bollmer contends that it is only if we sideline the materiality of technology that we can emphasize human agency. I disagree and believe that this work shows that we need not choose between materiality and reception; that a study of reception necessitates a study of materiality and vice versa. Debates in philosophy have shown that a material account of the world is compatible with and can account for human agency and free will (Hobbes 1997; Hume 1978, in McKenna et al. 2015). If human consciousness can be reduced to matter without abandoning agency, then surely we can offer a theory of culture and technology that is at once material and social.

Music culture is at once material and social, and it begs the question of how listening to recordings has changed that which is recorded. In this book, I have offered a selection of historical narratives and identified cultural tropes that contribute to a better understanding of this symbiosis among artifacts, users, and networks of circulation. I have shown that remix as a musical form and technique has a history that does not entirely jibe with the values sometimes ascribed to it (e.g., openness, participation, youthfulness, newness, etc.) or account for its material history. My critical reading of disco edits showed that issues of form and aesthetics were contingent upon the materiality of analog formats as well as the uses to which historically situated listeners put them. Dancers created dance music as much as DJs or producers did. The recent resurgence of vinyl was shaped by both these histories and its material affordances. Vinyl today is as much a networked artifact as it is an analog one. As a format, vinyl was once thought to be relatively cheap, long lasting, and mobile; yet in the context of on-demand digital distribution the same material becomes expensive, fragile, and hard to move. Its particular rhetorical qualities in our networked culture stem from these material affordances and people continue to value the format for a variety of social, cultural, economic, and aesthetic reasons—its sound, its ability to fly under the copyright radar, one's desire to perpetuate a tradition and ritual, etc. The network lends vinyl new affordances, both material and social. These qualities stem from the format's material dispositions, its intersection with the affordances of network technologies and the histories of each. If we foreground the materiality of media, we can begin to account for the new authenticities, styles, and forms of expression that build around discovery, circulation, and use in our culture.

Materiality is also a key theme in my arguments about the aesthetics of digital circulation and its antecedent practices. MP3 blogs, a form that was "born digital," were premised upon the materiality of MP3s and the affordances of digital networks as technologies for circulation. MP3 blogs were forms of expression that were also distribution technologies; a generative form that generates both copy and provenance. By reducing MP3 blogs to these constitutive parts (regardless of the intention of the producer), I was able to account for both the independence of media objects and how their partial histories of use and movement—their provenance—could generate new pathways of discovery and distribution. Although the influence of the MP3 blog was brief, my theorization of how the form produced new meanings suggests that by acknowledging the poetics of practices of redistribution we can begin to glimpse how it is that new authenticities build around networked expression and how the meaning of networked forms of expression, formats, practices, and artifacts can change overtime.

How ideals of authenticity become aligned with copies (rather than originals) and the longevity of romantic ideas of creativity and expression are important themes in my research. The persistence of romantic ideals of authorship and authenticity suggests that they are useful social imaginaries (cf. Anderson 1983; Taylor 1989). By raising awareness to the rhetorical dimensions of our understanding of new media practices, I want to understand why it is that romantic notions of expression and the value of cultural works are such a source of pleasure for users. Why do narratives of authenticity continue to have such currency, even when users acknowledge other nonromantic ideals of creativity and thumb their nose at copyright laws that share some of the same ideals? Lee Marshall (2005) offers a political economic response: Romantic ideals allow us to make peace with the contradictions of capitalism. They are a kind of spiritual survival mechanism. I would like to offer a more modest theory about the persistence of romantic ideals surrounding authorship and cultural works, in networked discourse, and in forms that seem to resist or deny such assumptions—like remix, unauthorized disco edits, and MP3 blogs. That is, romantic ideals about participation in networked discourse, with their continued valorization of production over use, help us to enact communal experiences even while we are alone in the bedroom, commuting on the train, or bored at the office—we are the ghost in the machine. Thus, it is unsurprising that ideas and ideals about folk music are invoked and recounted in the shaping of these narratives. As such, the folk discourse (if it is authentic, it is from the people) compounds and mutates, grabbing whatever is needed from commerce and its "other" along the way. In digital networks, where all cultural artifacts are materially the same, our romantic ideals about their production and meaning may become more important, rather than less so. Thus, we have brought our romantic quasi-mystical relationships with artifacts, along with the pleasures we find in them and their contradictions, into the digital sphere, made up as it is of nothing but copies (in multiple senses of that word). Just as new authenticities formed around recordings in dance music (Thornton 1995), new authenticities form around (the seemingly immaterial) digital copies, as well as our interpretation of metadata about them. In doing so, we have romanticized the copy and brought some of the qualities that were once only associated with the original to bear on them. Romantic rhetoric about remix and participation contextualizes a world that seems immaterial: It connects us to our humanity, while letting us retain our individuality and access to the modern promise of self-invention.

But copies as material instances are also independent of our rhetorical understandings of them and the social and cultural uses we put them to. This is true of the record on the shelf and the networked MP3. Both are said to be copies, and this property—copy—lends them certain affordances; their particular materiality, in turn, gives them another set of affordances. The networked copy is a source of cultural renewal, simply because it can be encountered, and that encounter can produce a double. This is the network's disposition—a disposition one may want to either exploit or avoid. The hybrid media use I presented in my work on disco edits sketched some of the ways contemporary users were using vinyl as a digital strategy. Analog media can be used rhetorically in digital networks through its documentation.[3] Digital networks alter the rhetorical contours of media by making everyday media practices—including social uses, identity formation, and creative expression—visible. The challenge for scholars of culture is to be alert to the changes that visibility and access bring to our understandings of the past, present, and future: They necessitate the uncovering and revival of less-known material and formal histories to illuminate their historical meanings and uncover their influence on contemporary practice. As my work on disco edits showed, the material disposition of vinyl, together with the use of vinyl in a social and cultural context, gave rise to a new form—which, in turn, facilitated new aesthetic experiences and cultures. And this cultural history has come to influence the contemporary use of technologies, format, and the form itself. The networked cultural history of the form also alters the meaning of the material format and lends it new rhetorical uses. Repeat cycle. This is a challenge, but also an opportunity to bring a far greater range of material collections and cultural understandings to bear on our cultural histories.

---

[3] I don't mean to say that all users *will* use analog media rhetorically, only that it is a possibility at hand. Digital and network technologies can reawaken old forms and formats through the repetition and availability of such histories.

Significance of study

This book contributes to the study of material culture by showing how copies can be used as a conceptual lens through which to explore the mutuality of matter and meaning. It has brought aesthetic questions about copies—in particular, questions about the relationship between form and format—into discussions about cultural change in media and cultural studies. It offers a critique of one of the dominant tropes, or metaphors, in the study of digital culture—that of remix—and sought to dig beneath the rhetoric, not to undermine its arguments about copyright, but to recover recent material histories and sets of cultural practices. These recent narratives of encounter, use, reuse, and innovation risk being rewritten in the service of political arguments if we do not repeat them and analyse what they can help us understand about the present, as well as the past. I have sought to renew a sense of history to discussions about change. Everything is not remix. Why would it be? History exists in the present, but it should aim to grapple with the differences between the past and the present, as well strike notes of commonality.

One such commonality is the persistence of romantic notions of creativity, authenticity, and cultural works in networked culture and underlying our seemingly endless celebration of participatory media. Rather than undermine ideas about collaboration, openness, and participation, my research suggests that the romanticization of copies and their quasi-mystical status, seems to underpin many of these ideas in networked culture.

I have suggested that a study of form offers a vantage point from which to observe and understand material, cultural, and social histories, and my critique of form suggests that form is not in and of itself ideological. A form can be put to different uses and can take on different political meanings. Remix can indicate mass-market industrial production (as the glut of cynically produced disco records in the late 1970s attests to [Shepherd 1986]), but it can also be used, as Lessig (2008) shows us, to speak of cultural critique, or, as Schütze (2003) does, as a resistance to the powers that be. Edits today can be a vanity project, and they can also make a dance floor go wild. The form carries material traces and cultural histories, each of which also have social, political, and economic histories—but I posit that form in and of itself is not politically charged. I would like to suggest that formal analysis offers some advantages to scholars when trying to understand an artifact's complicated and interdefined histories because it offers not so much a neutral point from which to perform cultural criticism, as one that can handle a variety of competing claims and the messiness of human affairs. By using edits as a form, for example, I was able to acknowledge the contributions of dancers to the form (as I simultaneously critiqued heroic narratives about the DJ's role and the valorization of production) and the commercial aspirations of some DJs versus the countercultural leanings of others, while thinking about the material affordances of technologies and considering the new meanings that analog formats can have in networked discourse. The form has many more lessons to offer, but my point is that a focus on form is productive since it allows competing narratives and political claims to bump up against each other in potentially enlightening ways. These simultaneous histories of materiality, reception, and use clarify questions of form and rhetoric and the differences between them. It begins to generate a cultural poetics of copies and networks that I think we need to make sense of digital culture.

I have also made a strong argument for recovering and using histories of reception to illuminate questions about the roles played by media technologies, artifacts, and users in cultural change. Technologies need not be deterministic, nor should they be seen as naturally progressive, but their existence matters, and they do have affordances and possibilities (both intentional and unintentional) that people can exploit or avoid. Media is also shaped by its use, and, hence, narratives of encounter, and reception clarify the complexity of media histories, while at the same time complicating them by participating in them. In my research, these histories have also offered challenges to certain rhetorical claims about networks and digital technologies, and the tensions they foreground offer lessons about the persistence of romantic ideals and notions about authenticity. One of the chief lessons my critical readings of these histories offer is that old media is not simply translated into a new media environment: Its formats can be put to new rhetorical uses in a digital networked environment, and, culture scholars and media historians must be alert to these rhetorical tendencies. This opens up the need for more research that traces the cultural histories of copies and networks—the way they interrelate, and how a consideration of form can help us access the reflexive relations among matter, meaning, and use.

The shift from analog to digital technologies, a shift that took place within living memory (and that, indeed, is not an all-or-none situation), has thrown the meaning of cultural artifacts into confusion. Convergence confuses the ontological status of media—not by rendering all media immaterial, but, instead, by rendering all media materially similar. Does this prompt a crisis of meaning? One answer is that the digital media's catholic nature means that we must pay more attention to the micromateriality of media—"towards the informational and infinitesimally small layer of materials that make up digital culture" (Morris 2010). Certainly the growing field of software studies (Fuller 2008), media archaeology (Parikka 2012), and other new materialist perspectives suggests that this will be an important avenue of cultural research in the years to come.

The focus on material properties in this book also offers lessons about encounter. Both the copy of Blondie's "Dreaming Is Free" on the Internet and the one at the thrift shop offer themselves up as a source of renewal—but their materiality also shapes their availability and possibility of encounter. One of the great advantages of networked artifacts is that they can potentially be discovered by anyone with access to the Internet. But you either have to go looking for them, or someone else must point you in the right direction. One of the advantages of the pile of records down at the thrift shop is also the quality that narrows its reach. Its physicality narrows the number of possible encounters, but it also means that, if I am in such a shop, I might literally trip over them. Both forms have their affordances and opportunities for encounter. How you come to discover something is also part of its story (and, as we have seen, new authenticities can build around different kinds of online encounter). One of the effects of networking of collections of music via MP3 blogs or streaming services is that the possibility that you might encounter something that was relatively rare, or produced in small numbers, increases. With the MP3 blog this marks the discovery with human passion, insistence, and authenticity. This, in turn, can radically change the history of a song since it puts it back into cultural circulation (or, in the case of new music, puts it into circulation for the first time). Whether recommendation algorithims can achieve the same is a multi-billion dollar question; predicting taste is the killer app of our time. Data analysts are standing by, ready to mine your trails of enthusiasm, your lines of desire (Williams 2014). Just as recording changes that which is recorded, networking will alter that which is networked in ways we might not imagine. We will play the network. We will flood it with data. We will withhold information from it. We will lie to it. We will whisper sweet nothings. Just as we always have done. Documentation and representation are always already just data. It is up to us how we use it. Same as it ever was.

ACKNOWLEDGMENTS

I would like to thank Catharine Lumby, for her encouragement to pursue this project and for her intellectual and professional guidance along the way. Thanks to Nicole Anderson and Macquarie University for helping me to carve out the time and space needed to complete this monograph. Thanks to my editor Leah Babb-Rosenfeld, and everyone at Bloomsbury Academic; I'm also very grateful to Ally-Jane Grossan and Kirstin Corcoran for their guidance and support in the early stages of this project. I would also like to thank everyone who read drafts of this book: in particular, thanks to Marcus Boon, Kate Crawford, Peter Doyle, Charles Fairchild, Gerard Goggin, and Gil Rodman. Many thanks to the DJs, producers, MP3 bloggers, dancers, and record collectors who took time to talk with me about their listening practices. Special thanks to the Paradise Lost crew in Sydney and to my resident DJ and philosopher, James Bucknell for many enlightening and challenging conversations about music and philosophy as well as for his love and support. Finally, thanks to my parents and family for cheering me on along the long road from PhD to monograph. Love is the message.

BIBLIOGRAPHY

Abidin, Crystal (2016), "A few shifts in the influencer industry," *Wishcrys*, August 3. Available online: https://wishcrys.com/2016/08/03/a-few-shifts-in-the-influencer-industry/ (accessed March 14, 2017).

Acland, Charles (2007), "Residual Media," in *Residual Media*, xiii–xxvii. Minneapolis: University of Minnesota Press.

Adorno, Theodor (1990), "On Popular Music," in S. Frith and A. Goodwin (eds), *On Record: Rock, Pop and the Written Word*, 301–14. New York Pantheon Books.

Allen-Robertson, James (2015), "The Materiality of Digital Media: The Hard Disk Drive, Phonograph, Magnetic Tape and Optical Media in Technical Close-up." *New Media & Society*: doi: 1461444815606368.

Anderson, Benedict (2006), *Imagined Communities*. London and New York: Verso.

Angeloro, Dan (2006), "Thoughtware: Contemporary Online Remix Culture," in M. Titmarch (ed.), *SynCity*, 18–25. Sydney: dLux Media Arts.

Armstrong, David. M. (1989), *Universals: An Opinionated Introduction*. Boulder: Westview Press.

Asmis, Elizabeth (1992), "Plato on Poetic Creativity," in R. Kraut (ed.), *The Cambridge Companion to Plato*, 338–64. Cambridge: Cambridge University Press.

Attali, Jacques (1985), *Noise: The Political Economy of Music*, trans. B. Massumi. Minneapolis: University of Minnesota Press.

Austin, Alec, H. Jenkins, I. Askwith, and S. Ford (2011), *How to Turn Pirates into Loyalists: The Moral Economy and an Alternative Response to File Sharing*. Edited by Convergence Culture Consortium. Boston: MIT Press.

Barker, Hugh and Y. Taylor (2007), *Faking It: The Quest for Authenticity in Popular Music*. New York: W. W. Norton.

Barthes, Roland (1977), *Image, Music, Text*, trans. S. Heath. New York: Hill and Wang.

Bartmanski, Dominik and Ian Woodward (2015), *Vinyl*. London and New York: Bloomsbury Academic.

Baudrillard, Jean (1994), *Simulacra and Simulation*, in *The Body in Theory*, trans. Sheila Faria Glaser. Ann Arbor: University of Michigan Press.

Benjamin, Walter (2007a), "The Storyteller," in H. Arendt (ed.), *Illuminations*, 83–110. New York: Schocken Books.

Benjamin, Walter (2007b), "The Work of Art in the Age of Mechanical Reproduction," in H. Arendt (ed.), *Illuminations*, 217–52. New York: Schocken Books.

Benjamin, Walter (2007c), "Unpacking My Library: A Talk about Book Collecting," in H. Arendt (ed.), *Illuminations*, 59–68. New York: Schocken Books.

Benkler, Yochai (2006), *The Wealth of Networks: How Social Production Transforms Markets and Freedom*. New Haven: Yale University Press.

Berry, David M. (2008), *Copy, Rip, Burn: The Politics of Copyleft and Open Source*. London: Pluto.

Berry, David M. and G. Moss (2008), *Libre Culture: Meditations on Free Culture*. Winnipeg: Pygmalion Books.

Beta, Andy (2008), "Disco Inferno 2.0: A Slightly Less Hedonistic Comeback." *Village Voice*, November 19. Available online: http://www.villagevoice.com/2008-11-19/music/disco-inferno-2-0-a-slightly-less-hedonistic-comeback (accessed November 29, 2008).

Blanchette, Jean-Francois (2011), "A Material History of Bits." *Journal of the American Society for Information Science and Technology* 62 (6): 1042–57.

Bollmer, Grant (2015), "Technological Materiality and Assumptions about 'Active' Human Agency." *Digital Culture and Society* 1 (1): 95–110

Boon, Marcus (2010), *In Praise of Copying*. Cambridge, MA: Harvard University Press.

Born, Georgina (2005), "On Musical Mediation: Ontology, Technology and Creativity." *Twentieth-Century Music* 2 (1): 7–36.

Bourdieu, Pierre (1986), "The Forms of Capital," in J. G. Richardson (ed.), *Handbook for Theory and Research for the Sociology of Education*, 241–58. New York: Greenwood.

Borschke, Margie (2010), "Hiding in Plain Sight: Regionalism and the Underground." *Artlink* 30 (2): 32–3.

Borschke, Margie (2011a), "Disco Edits and their Discontents: The Persistence of the Analog in a Digital Era." *New Media & Society* 13 (6): 929–44.

Borschke, Margie (2011b), "Rethinking the Rhetoric of Remix." *Media International Australia* 141 (November): 17–25

Borschke, Margie (2012), "Ad Hoc Archivists: MP3 Blogs and Digital Provenance." *Continuum: Journal of Media & Cultural Studies* 26 (1): 1–10.

Borschke, Margie (2012a), "Rethinking the rhetoric of remix: Copies and material culture in digital networks," Ph.D. dissertation, University of New South Wales, Sydney.

Borschke, Margie (2014), "The New Romantics: Authenticity, Participation and the Aesthetics of Piracy." *First Monday* 19 (10). Available online: http://firstmonday.org/ojs/index.php/fm/article/view/5549 (accessed March 14, 2017).

Borschke, Margie (2015), "Extended Remix: Rhetoric and History," in Eduardo Navas, Owen Gallagher, and xtine burrough (eds), *The Routledge Companion to Remix Studies*, 102–15. New York: Routledge.

Bourriaud, Nicolas (2000), *Postproduction: Culture as Screenplay: How Art Reprograms the World*, trans. C. Schneider and J. Herman. New York: Lukas & Sternberg.

boyd, danah (2006), "A Blogger's Blog: Exploring the Definition of a Medium." *Reconstruction* 6 (4).

boyd, danah (2007), "None of This Is Real," in Joe Karaganis (ed.), *Structures of Participation*, 132–57. New York: Social Science Research Council.

boyd, danah (2008), "Taken Out of Context: American Teen Sociality in Networked Publics." PhD diss., University of California, Berkeley.

Brewster, Bill (2009), "1000 Songs Everyone Must Hear: Part 7: Party: The History of the Remix." *Guardian*, March 20. Available online: http://www. guardian.co.uk/music/table/2009/mar/20/party-1000-songs-everyone-must-hear (accessed March 30, 2009).

Brown, J. (1985), "All-Star Record Takes Off." *Washington Post*, March 8.

Brown, J. (1989a), "The Divas with the Die-Hard Fans: The Latest from Diana Ross, Patti LaBelle, Stephanie Mills, Natalie Cole and Chaka Khan." *Washington Post*, August 13.

Brown, J. (1989b), "Lightning Flashes on Thunder Album." *Washington Post*, October 13.

Brown, J. (1989c), "Three Flavors of Miami Spice." *Washington Post*, August 2.

Bruns, Axel (2007), "Produsage: A Working Definition. (blog post)." Available online: http://produsage.org/node/9 (accessed February 15, 2012).

Bruns, Axel (2008), *Blogs, Wikipedia, Second Life, and Beyond: From Production to Produsage*. New York: Peter Lang.

Bucknell, James (2015), "Dispositions." PhD diss., University of New South Wales.

Burgess, Jean (2006), "Vernacular Creativity, Cultural Participation and New Media Literacy: Photography and the flickr Network." Paper presented at Internet Research 7.0: Internet Convergences (AoIR), Brisbane, September 28–30.

Burgess, Jean (2007), "Vernacular Creativity and the New Media." PhD diss., Queensland University of Technology.

Burgess, Jean and Joshua Green (2009), *YouTube: Online Video and Participatory Culture*. Cambridge: Polity Press.

Campbell, M. (1988), "Jellybean Jumps Up Charts by Remixing Batches of Tunes." *Chicago Sun-Times*, March 1.

Cantwell, Robert (1991), "Smith's Memory Theater: *The Folkways Anthology of American Folk Music*." *New England Review* 13 (3/4): 364–97.

Carter, M. (1997), "Several Nations Under One Groove." *Independent*, November 25.

Caughie, John (1981), "Introduction," in J. Caughie (ed.), *Theories of Authorship*, 1–16. New York: Routledge.

Chanan, Michael (1995), *Repeated Takes: A Short History of Recording and Its Effects on Music*. London: Verso.

Chang, J. (2005), *Can't Stop Won't Stop*. New York: St. Martins Press.

Cheliotis, G. and J. Yew (2009), "An Analysis of the Social Structure of Remix Culture." *Proceedings of the Fourth International Conference on Communities and Technologies*. ACM, New York, NY: 165–74.

Chin, Brian (1986), "Studio Remixers: From Club DJs to Innovators." *Billboard*, July 19, D-5.

Coombe, Rosemary (1998), *The Cultural Life of Intellectual Properties: Authorship, Appropriation, and the Law, Post-contemporary Interventions*. Durham: Duke University Press.

Corbett, Philip B. (2010), "The 'Tweet' Debate." *New York Times*, June 15.
Available online: http://topics.blogs.nytimes.com/2010/06/15/the-tweet-debate/

Coslovich, G. (2011), "Replica Faces Famous Design Names in Furniture
Showdown." *Sydney Morning Herald*, September 26.

Cramb, A. (1989), "Yo, Bro, New Age of Rap Has Huge Sound." *Sydney
Morning Herald*, September 14.

Crawford, Kate (2005), "Adaptation: Tracking the Ecologies of Music and
Peer-to-Peer Networks." *Media International Australia* 114: 30–9.

Crawford, Kate and Mark Healy (2010), "Typesetting broadband: Old media
futures in new network spaces," paper presented at *Cultural Studies
Association of Australasia (CSAA): A Scholarly Affair* (7–9 December).

Davis, A., S. Webb, D. Lackey, and D. N. DeVoss (2010), "Remix, Play, and
Remediation: Undertheorized Composing Practices," in H. Urbanski (ed.),
Writing and the Digital Generation: Essays on New Media Rhetoric, 186–97.
Jefferson, NC: McFarland & Company.

De Certeau, Michel (1984), *The Practice of Everyday Life*, trans. S Rendell.
Berkeley: University of California Press.

Dee, J. (2006). "The Guide: Preview: Internet: Apropos Comics." *Guardian*,
August 26.

Deleuze, Gilles (1983), "Plato and the Simulacrum," trans. Rosalind E. Krauss.
October 27: 45–56.

Demers, Joanna (2006), *Steal This Music: How Intellectual Property Law Affects
Musical Creativity*. Athens: University of Georgia Press.

DeNora, Tia (2000), *Music in Everyday Life*. Cambridge: Cambridge University
Press.

Deuze, Mark (2006), "Participation, Remediation, Bricolage: Considering Principal
Components of a Digital Culture." *Information Society* 22 (2): 63–75.

Diakopoulos, N., K. Luther, Y. E. Medynskiy, and I. Essa (2007), "The Evolution
of Authorship in a Remix Society." *Proceedings of the Eighteenth Conference
on Hypertext and Hypermedia*. Manchester: 133–6.

Drever, A. (2009), "Norwegian God." *Age*, February 6.

Duncan, V. (1969), *Guitar Guitar with Laura Weber*. USA.

Eagleton, Terry (2008), *Literary Theory: An Introduction*. London: Blackwell.

Edwards, R. and C. Tryon (2009), "Political Video Mashups as Allegories of
Citizen Empowerment." *First Monday* 14 (10). Available online: http://
firstmonday.org/htbin/cgiwrap/bin/ojs/index.php/fm/article/view/2617/2305
(accessed March 14, 2017).

Eisenberg, Evan (2005), *The Recording Angel: Music, Records and Culture from
Aristotle to Zappa*, 2nd edn. New Haven: Yale University Press.

Eisenstein, Elizabeth (2005), *The Printing Revolution in Early Modern Europe*,
2nd edn. Cambridge: Cambridge University Press.

Faber, Sebastin (2004), "Trope as Trap." *Culture Theory & Critique* 45 (2):
133–59.

Fagerjord, A. (2010), "After Convergence: *You Tube* and Remix Culture," in
J. Hunsinger, M. Allen, and L. Klastrup (eds), *The International Handbook of
Internet Research*, 187–200. New York: Springer.

Fairchild, Charles (2014), *Danger Mouse's The Grey Album*. New York and
London: Bloomsbury Academic.

Fennessey, S. (2011), "The GQ&A: Diplo". *GQ*, October. Available online: http://www.gq.com/style/wear-it-now/201110/diplo-interview-gq-october-2011 (accessed December 15, 2011).

Ferguson, K. (2010), "Everything is a Remix". Available online: http://www.everythingisaremix.info/ (accessed March 14, 2017).

"First Hype, Then Kill." (2006). *Rolling Stone*, October 19.

Fitzgerald, Brian and Damien S. O'Brien (2005), "Digital Sampling and Culture Jamming in a Remix World: What does the Law Allow?" *Media and Arts Law Review* 10 (4): 279–98.

Flichy, Patrice (2007), *The Internet Imaginaire*. Cambridge, MA: MIT Press.

Foucault, Michel (1977), "What is an author?" *Language, Counter-Memory, Practice: Selected Essays and Interviews*. Ed. Donald F. Bouchard. Ithaca, NY: Cornell University Press, 1977. 113–38.

Foucault, Michel (2010), *The Order of Things*. New York: Routledge.

Freeman-Greene, S. (2009), "Amateur Hour." *Age*, August 8.

Friedman, Ted (1999), "Electric Dreams: Computer Culture and the Utopian Sphere." PhD diss., Duke University.

Friedman, Ted (2005), *Electric Dreams: Computers in American Culture*. New York: New York University Press.

Frith, Simon (1981a), "'The Magic That Can Set You Free': The Ideology of Folk and the Myth of the Rock Community." *Popular Music* 1: 159–68.

Frith, Simon (1981b), *Sound Effects: Youth, Leisure, and the Politics of Rock'n'Roll*. New York: Pantheon Books.

Frith, Simon (1998), *Performing Rites: Evaluating Popular Music*. Oxford: Oxford University Press.

Frith, Simon (2003), "Music and Everyday Life," in M. Clayton, T. Herbert, and R. Middleton (eds), *The Cultural Study of Music*, 92–101. New York: Routledge.

Frith, Simon and Lee Marshall (2004), *Music and Copyright*, 2nd edn. New York: Routledge.

Fry, J. (2008), "Real Time: This is the Modding World." *Wall Street Journal*, February 25.

Fuller, Matthew (ed.) (2008), *Software Studies: A Lexicon*. Cambridge, MA: MIT Press.

Ganz, J. (2005), "To Generate Buzz, Clap Your Hands on the 'Net!" *NPR Music*. November 29. Available online: http://www.npr.org/templates/story/story.php?storyId=5023133 (accessed May 9, 2007).

Gary, Sullivan (2012), "Guilty Until Proven Innocent." *Bodega Pop* (blog), January 27. Available online: http://bodegapop.blogspot.com.au/2012/01/guilty-until-proven-innocent.html (accessed March 14, 2017).

Gibson, William (2005), "God's Little Toys—Confessions of a Cut & Paste Artist." *WIRED*, July. Available online: http://www.wired.com/wired/archive/13.07/gibson.html (accessed February 2, 2009).

Gilbert, Jeremy and Ewan Pearson (1999), *Discographies: Dance Music, Culture and the Politics of Sound*. London: Routledge.

Gitelman, Lisa (2006), *Always Already New: Media, History, and the Data of Culture*. Cambridge, MA: MIT Press.

Gitelman, Lisa (2014), *Paper Knowledge: Toward a Media History of Documents*. Durham, NC: Duke University Press.

Gliatto, T. (1989), "Lifeline." *USA Today*, October 4.

Goodwin, Andrew and Simon Frith (1990), *On Record: Rock, Pop and the Written Word*. New York: Pantehon.

Greenblatt, Stephen (1987), "Towards a Poetics of Culture" *Southern Review (Australia)* 20: 3–15

Greenblatt, Stephen (2011), *The Swerve: How the World Became Modern*. New York: W. W. Norton.

Gundersen, E. (1997), "U2's Snap, Crackle and 'Pop' Album Puts Intelligent Songwriting to an Infectious Beat." *USA Today*, March 4.

Hagen, Anja Nylund (2016). "The metaphors we stream by: Making sense of music streaming." *First Monday*, March. Available online: http://ojphi.org/ojs/index.php/fm/article/view/6005 (accessed August 30, 2016).

Harkin, Eamon (2008), "Greg Wilson: Interview, Exclusive Mix & Prime Time Appearance." *Eamon Harkin Blog*. Posted October 19. Available online: http://www2.eamonharkin.com/2008/10/greg-wilson-interview-exclusive-mix.html (accessed July 15, 2010).

Harrington, R. (1989), "Dave Marsh's Right Numbers." *Washington Post*, November 22.

Harrison, Nate (2007), "Can I Get an Amen?" *Nate Harrison* 8. Available online: http://nkhstudio.com/pages/amen_mp4.html (accessed January 12, 2012).

Heffernan, Virginia (2008), "The Hitler Meme." *New York Times Magazine*, October 24. Available online: http://www.nytimes.com/2008/10/26/magazine/26wwln-medium-t.html (accessed March 14, 2017).

Hennion, Antoine (2001), "Music Lovers: Taste as Performance." *Theory Culture and Society* 18 (5): 1–22.

Hennion, Antoine (2008), "Listen!" *Music and Arts in Action* 1 (1): 36–45.

Herman, Bill D. (2008), "Breaking and Entering My Own Computer: The Contest of Copyright Metaphors." *Communication Law & Policy* 13 (2): 231–74.

Hetcher, Steven A. (2009), "Using Social Norms to Regulate Fan Fiction and Remix Culture." *U. Pa. L. Rev.* 157: 1869.

Heylin, Clinton (2003), *Bootleg! The Rise and Fall of the Secret Recording Industry*. London: Omnibus.

Horyn, C. (1991), "Fashion; In Paris, Sheer Kicks; From French Designers, a Mix to Match the Mood" *Washington Post*, March 13.

Hyde, Lewis (2007), *The Gift: Creativity and the Artist in the Modern World*. New York: Vintage.

Ihlein, Lucas, Nick Keys, and Astride Lorange (2009), "Push and Pull Redfern". Available online: http://www.pushandpull.com.au (accessed March 14, 2017).

Innis, Harold (1949), "The Bias of Communication." *Canadian Journal of Economics and Political Science* 15 (4): 457–76.

Innis, Harold (1995), *The Bias of Communication*. Toronto: University of Toronto Press.

International Foundation for Art Research. "Provenance Guide." Available online: https://www.ifar.org/provenance_guide.php (accessed August 29, 2016).

Jarnow, J. (2015), "The New Explosion of Bootleg Vinyl" *Pitchfork*, October 19. Available online: http://pitchfork.com/thepitch/932-the-new-explosion-of-bootleg-vinyl/ (accessed March 14, 2017).

Jenkins, Henry (1992), *Textual Poachers: Television Fans & Participatory Culture*. New York: Routledge.

Jenkins, Henry (2004), "The Cultural Logic of Media Convergence." *International Journal of Cultural Studies* 7 (1): 33–43.

Jenkins, Henry (2006a), *Convergence Culture: Where Old and New Media Collide*. New York: New York University Press.

Jenkins, Henry (2006b), *Fans, Blogger, and Gamers: Exploring Participatory Culture*. New York: New York University Press.

Jenkins, Henry (2009), *Confronting the Challenges of Participatory Culture: Media Education for the 21st Century*. Cambridge, MA: MIT Press.

Jenkins, M. (1989), "Industrial-Strength Dance Tracks." *Washington Post*, October 20.

Johns, Adrian (2002), "Pop Music Pirate Hunters." *Dædalus* 131 (2): 67–77.

Johns, Adrian (2010), *Piracy: The Intellectual Property Wars from Gutenberg to Gates*. University of Chicago Press.

Jones IV, J. T. (1989), "Songs Find New Life in the Remix." *USA Today*, June 15.

Jones, Steve (2002), "Music That Moves: Popular Music, Distribution and Network Technologies." *Cultural Studies* 16 (2): 213–32.

Keil, Charles. M. H. (1966), "Motion and Feeling through Music." *Journal of Aesthetics and Art Criticism* 24 (3): 337–49.

Kennedy, R. (2005), "With Irreverence and an iPod, Recreating the Museum Tour." *New York Times*, May 28.

Kent, A. (2010), *Vintage 1970s Edits & Mixes*. Available online: http://mddaudio. com/pajweb/pajdiscomix.html (accessed November 11, 2011).

Kirschenbaum, Matthew, E. Farr, K. Kraus, N. Nelson, C. Peters, and G. Redwine (2009), "Digital Materiality: Preserving Access to Computers as Complete Environments." Paper presented at iPRES, Mission Bay Conference Center, San Francisco, October 5–6.

Krauss, Rosalind E. (1985), *The Originality of the Avant-garde and Other Modernist Myths*. Cambridge, MA: MIT Press.

Kripke, Saul (1980), *Naming and Necessity*. Rev. and enlarged edn. Library of Philosophy and Logic. Oxford: Blackwell.

"Labels Mix Records for Club Scene." (1974), *Billboard*, November 2.

Labato, Ramon (2014), "The paradoxes of piracy," in Lars Eckstein and Anja Schwarz (eds), *Postcolonial Piracy: Media Distribution and Cultural Production in the Global South*, 121–33. New York and London: Bloomsbury Academic.

Lakoff, George and Mark Johnson (1980), *Metaphors We Live By*. Chicago: University of Chicago Press.

Lawrence, Tim (2003), *Love Saves the Day: A History of American Dance Music Culture, 1970–1979*. Durham: Duke University Press.

Lawrence, Tim (2008), "Disco Madness: Walter Gibbons and the Legacy of Turntablism and Remixology." *Journal of Popular Music Studies* 20 (3): 276–329.

Lawrence, Tim (2009), *Hold On to Your Dreams: Arthur Russell and the Downtown Music Scene, 1973–1992*. Durham: Duke University Press.

Lech, V., V. Tajan, and P. Zandrowicz (2008), *Nu Disco: Re-edit Yourself*. (Online video). France. Available online: http://www.dailymotion.com/video/x4tjx1_ the-art-pack-nudisco-re-edit-yourse_music (accessed March 14, 2017).

Lee, E. (2008), "Warming Up to User-Generated Content." *Illinois Law Review* 1459: 1544–5.

Leibovitch, E. (1977), "Search for Perfection: Direct-discs Sound Great, but They May Not Be What You Want to Hear." *Globe and Mail*, December 28.

Lejeune, Patrick (2007), *Disco Patrick's Disco and Funk Page*. Available online: http://www.discopatrick.com/ (accessed March 14, 2017).

Lessig, Lawrence (2002), *The Future of Ideas: The Fate of the Commons in a Connected World*. New York: Vintage.

Lessig, Lawrence (2004), *Free Culture: How Big Media Uses Technology and the Law to Lock Down Culture and Control Creativity*. New York: Penguin.

Lessig, Lawrence (2005), "The People Own Ideas." *Technology Review*. June 2005. Available online: http://www.technologyreview.com/ communications/14505/ (accessed March 14, 2017).

Lessig, Lawrence (2007), "Larry Lessig on Laws that Choke Creativity." *TED*. Available online: http://www.ted.com/talks/larry_lessig_says_the_law_is_ strangling_creativity.html (accessed March 14, 2017).

Lessig, Lawrence (2008), *Remix: Making Art and Commerce Thrive in the Hybrid Economy*. London: Bloomsbury.

Le Tan, A. (2008), "Greg Wilson discusses Re-Editing." *Cosmic Boogie Blog*, April 4. Available online: http://www.cosmicboogie.co.uk/2008/04/07/ greg-wilson-re-editing (accessed May 10, 2008).

Levitin, Daniel (2007), *This Is Your Brain on Music: Understanding a Human Obsession*. London: Atlantic.

Lin, T. (2008), "Disco As Operating System, Part One." *Criticism* 50 (1): 83–100.

Litman, J. (2001), *Digital Copyright*. New York: Prometheus Books.

Loughlan, Patricia. L. (2006), "Pirates, Parasites, Reapers, Sowers, Fruits, Foxes. The Metaphors of Intellectual Property." *Sydney Law Review* 28 (2): 211–26.

Loughlan, Patricia. L. (2007), "'You Wouldn't Steal a Car': Intellectual Property and the Language of Theft." *European Intellectual Property Review* 29 (10): 401–5.

Luckman, Susan H. (2013), "The Aura of the Analogue in a Digital Age: Women's Crafts, Creative Markets and Home-Based Labour after Etsy." *Cultural Studies Review* 19 (1): 249–70.

Lumb, J. (1999), "This Is Remix." *Electronic Musician* 15 (7): 46.

Lynskey, D. (2004), "Change the Record." *Guardian*, October 15.

MacInnis, Craig (1989), "Tracy Spins Wheels in Her Much-Awaited Crossroads Album." *Toronto Star*, October 10.

Mackenzie, Scott (2007), "The Horror, Piglet, the Horror: Found Footage, Mash-ups, AMVs, the Avant-Garde, and the Strange Case of Apocalypse Pooh." *Cineaction* 72.

Manovich, Lev (2001), *The Language of New Media*, R. F. Malina (ed.). Cambridge, MA: MIT Press.

Manovich, Lev (2005), "Remixability and Modularity." Available online: http://manovich.net/index.php/projects/remixability-and-modularity (accessed March 14, 2017).

Manovich, Lev (2007a), "Understating Hybrid Media," in B. Hertz (ed.), *Animated Painting*, 36–45. San Diego: San Diego Museum of Art.

Manovich, Lev (2007b), "What Comes After Remix." Available online:http://manovich.net/index.php/projects/what-comes-after-remix (accessed March 14, 2017).

Marcus, Greil (1997), "The Old, Weird America," in *A Booklet of Essays, Appreciations, and Annotations Pertaining to the Anthology of American Folk Music*, 5–25. Washington, DC: Smithsonian Folkways Recordings.

Markham, Annette N. (2013), "Remix Culture, Remix Methods: Reframing Qualitative Inquiry for Social Media Contexts," in Justin. N. Denzin and M. Giardina (eds), *Global Dimensions of Qualitative Inquiry*. 63–81. Walnut Creek, CA: Left Coast Press.

Marshall, Lee (2004), "Infringers," in L. Marshall and S. Frith (eds), *Music & Copyright*, 189–207. New York: Routledge.

Marshall, Lee (2005), *Bootlegging: Romanticism and Copyright in the Music Industry*. London: Sage.

Maslin, J. (1984), "A Bushman and the Clash of Cultures." *New York Times*, July 6.

Mason, M. (2008), *The Pirate's Dilemma: How Youth Culture Is Reinventing Capitalism*. New York: Free Press.

Marx, Karl (1978), "The Grundrisse," in R. C. Trucker (ed.), *The Marx-Engels Reader*, 221–93. New York: W. W. Norton.

McClellan, J. (1996), "This Is the Future." *Observer*, June 23.

McLeod, Kembrew (2001), "Genres, Subgenres, Sub-Subgenres and More: Musical and Social Differentiation within Electronic/Dance Music Communities." *Journal of Popular Music Studies* 13 (1): 59–75.

McLeod, Kembrew (2004), "How Copyright Law Changed Hip Hop: An Interview with Public Enemy's Chuck D and Hank Shocklee." *Stay Free* 20: 22–5.

McLeod, Kembrew (2005), "MP3s Are Killing Home Taping: The Rise of Internet Distribution and Its Challenge to the Major Label Music Monopoly." *Popular Music and Society* 28 (4): 521–31.

McLeod, Kembrew (2007), *Freedom of Expression®: Resistance and Repression in the Age of Intellectual Property*. Minneapolis: University of Minnesota Press.

McLeod, Kembrew and Peter DiCola (2011), *Creative License: The Law and Culture of Digital Sampling*. Durham: Duke University Press.

McLuhan, Marshall (2006), *Understanding Media*. London: Routledge.

McMillian, N. (2002), "Cut Up or Shut Up." *Disco Patrick*. Available online: http://www.discopatrick.com/1-History%20Of%20Mixing.html (accessed March 14, 2017).

Middleton, R. (1999), "Form," in B. Horner and T. Swiss (eds), *Key Terms in Popular Music and Culture*, 141–55. Oxford: Blackwell.

Miller, Paul (2004), *Rythym Science*. Cambridge, MA: MIT Press.

Milner, Greg (2009), *Perfecting Sound Forever: An Aural History of Recorded Music*. London: Granta.

Mirapaul, M. (2001), "Why Just Listen to Pop When You Can Mix It On Your Own?" *New York Times*, August 20.

Morozov, Evgeny (2011), *The Net Delusion: The Dark Side of Internet Freedom*. New York: PublicAffairs.

Morris, J. W. (2010), "Understanding the Digital Music Commodity." PhD diss., McGill University.

Morris, Meaghan (1988), "Banality in Cultural Studies." *Discourse* 10 (2): 3–29.

Munster, Anna (2006), *Materializing New Media: Embodiment in Information Aesthetics*. Dartmouth, NH: Dartmouth College Press.

Murray, Laura J. (2009), "Review: RiP!: A Remix Manifesto (2009) dir. by Brett Gaylor." *Culture Machine*, June. Available online: http://ssrn.com/abstract=1865230 (accessed March 14, 2017).

Navas, Eduardo (2009), *Remix: A Critical Analysis of Allegory, Intertexuality, and Sampling in Art, Music, and Media*. San Diego: University of California and San Diego State University.

Navas, Eduardo (2010), "Regressive and Reflexive Mashups in Sampling Culture," in S. Sonvilla-Weiss (ed.), *Mashup Cultures*, 157–77. New York: Springer Wien.

Navas, Eduardo, Owen Gallagher, and xtine burrough (2015), *The Routledge Companion to Remix Studies*. New York: Routledge

Negus, Keith (1996), *Popular Music in Theory*. Cambridge: Polity Press.

Nobles, Barr (1989), "Bowie Project Starts Out Big." *San Francisco Chronicle*, September 23.

Noonan, Harold (2009), "Identity," in E. N. Zalta (ed.), *The Stanford Encyclopedia of Philosophy*. Stanford: Stanford University Press.

Novak, David (2011), "The Sublime Frequencies of New Old Media," *Public Culture* 23 (3): 603–34.

Novak, David (2013), *Japanoise: Music at the Edge of Circulation*. Durham NC: Duke University Press.

Nuttall, C. (2008), "Electronic Arts Banks on Slow Evolution." *Financial Times*, September 8.

O'Donnell, P. (2006), "The Users and Marketing Efficacy of MP3 Music Blogs." PhD diss., Florida State University.

Ong, Walter (1991), *Orality and Literacy: The Technologizing of the Word, New Accents*. London: Routledge.

Palmer, R. (1980), "The Pop Life." *New York Times*, November 28.

Palmer, R. (1984), "The Year's Best: 1984 in Review: Pop Music Made a Comeback and Video Helped It Out." *New York Times*, December 30.

Pareles, J. (1985), "Bruce Springsteen: Rock's Popular Populist." *New York Times*, August 18.

Pareles, J. (1989), "Pop View: Meaning Is in the Ears of the Beholder." *New York Times*, January 15.

Parikka, Jussi (2008), "Copy," in M. Fuller (ed.), *Software Studies: A Lexicon*, 70–8. Cambridge, MA: MIT Press

Parikka, Jussi (2012), *What is Media Archaeology*. Cambridge: Polity.

Pasick, A. (2004), "New UK Copyright to Enable 'Remix Culture'." *Reuters*, October 5.

Paskin, Norman (2003), "On Making and Identifying a 'Copy'." *D-Lib Magazine* 9 (1). Available online: http://www.dlib.org/dlib/january03/paskin/01paskin.html (accessed March 14, 2017).

Pearce-Moses, Richard (2005), *A Glossary of Archival and Records Terminology*. Chicago: Society of American Archivists.

Pinker, Steven (2007), *The Stuff of Thought: Language as a Window into Human Nature*. New York: Viking.

Plato (1941), *The Republic of Plato*, trans. and ed. F. M. Cornford. Oxford: Clarendon Press.

Plato (1973), *Phaedrus, and, The Seventh And Eighth Letters*, ed. W. Hamilton. Penguin Classics. Harmondsworth: Penguin.

Potter, M. (1989), "Sometimes the Kool One Raps his Knuckles." *Toronto Star*, December 1.

Porcello, T. (1991), "The Ethics of Digital Audio Sampling" *Popular Music* 10: 69–84.

Rapoport, Carla. (1984), "Britain's Pop Music Industry: So Can Frankie Go to Hollywood?" *Financial Times*, August 11.

Reynolds, Simon (2001), "Disco Doubletake: New York Parties Like It's 1975." *Village Voice*, July 10. Available online: http://www.villagevoice.com/2001-07-10/news/disco-double-take/ (accessed March 14, 2017).

Reynolds, Simon (2009), "Notes on the Noughties: The Changing Sound of the Underground." *Guardian*, December 21. Available online: http://www.guardian.co.uk/music/musicblog/2009/dec/21/changing-sound-underground (accessed March 14, 2017).

Reynolds, Simon (2011), *Retromania*. London: Faber & Faber.

Rietveld, Hillegonda (2007), "Vinyl Junkies and the Soul Sonic Force of the 12-Inch Dance Single," in C. Acland (ed.), *Residual Media*, 97–114. Minneapolis: University of Minnesota Press.

Robinson, T. M. (1987), *Heraclitus Fragments: A Text and Translation*. Toronto: University of Toronto Press.

Rodgers, Tara (2004), "On the Process and Aesthetics of Sampling in Electronic Music Production." *Organised Sound* 8 (3): 313–20.

Rose, Tricia (1994), *Black Noise: Rap Music and Black Culture in Contemporary America*. Middletown, CT: Wesleyan University Press.

Rosen, Jay (2006), "The People Formerly Known as the Audience." *Press Think* (blog). Posted June 27. Available online: http://archive.pressthink. org/2006/06/27/ppl_frmr.html (accessed March 14, 2017).

Rowlands, M. (2008), "Are Re-Edits the Real Revenge of Disco?" *Guardian*, May 5. Available online: http://www.guardian.co.uk/music/musicblog/2008/may/05/arereeditstherealrevengeo (accessed March 14, 2017).

Ruffin, M. (1989), "Withers Is Still No-Frills." *Chicago Sun-Times*, December 17.

Saunders, M. (1993), "Getting Hip to Pop." *Boston Globe*, May 9.

Schiffman, B. (2007), "Mp3 Blogs Offer File Sharing Even the RIAA Could Love." *Wired*, December 4.

Schloss, Joseph G. (2004). *Making Beats: The Art of Sample-Based Hip-Hop*. Middletown, CT: Wesleyan University Press.

Schulz, D. P. (2002), "The Rhetorical Contours of Technological Determinism." PhD diss., Pennsylvania State University, University Park, PA.

Schütze, Bernard (2003), "Samples from the Heap: Notes on Recycling the Detritus of a Remixed Culture." *Horizon Zero* 8. Available onliine: http://www.horizonzero.ca/textsite/remix.php?is=8&file=5&tlang=0 (accessed March 14, 2017).

Seneviratne, Oshani and Andrés Monroy-Hernandez (2010), "Remix Culture on the Web: A Survey of Content Reuse on Different User-Generated Content Websites." In *Proceedings of the WebSci10: Extending the Frontiers of Society On-Line*, April 26–27. Raleigh, NC: USA.

Shepherd, S. (1986), "Labels Plot Year in Inches—12-inch Singles." *Billboard* 98 (29): d-2.

Shuker, Roy (2002), *Popular Music: The Key Concepts*. Routledge Key Guides. London: Routledge.

Sigal, Jason (2012), "Music Blogs React to Megaupload Seizure & Cyberlocker Lockdowns", WFMU's Beware of the Blog, January 26. Available online: http://blog.wfmu.org/freeform/2012/01/music-blogs-react-to-megaupload-seizure-cyberlocker-fileserve.html (accessed March 14, 2017).

Sinclair, D. (1988), "Gloss and Floss." *Times*, October 15.

Sinclair, D. (1989a), "Body and Soul." *Times*, July 1.

Sinclair, D. (1989b), "Dancing at the Bleach Party." *Times*, January 7.

Singh, Rani (2010), "Harry Smith, an Ethnographic Modernist in America," in Andrew Perchuk and Rani Singh (eds), *Harry Smith: The Avant-Garde in the American Vernacular*, 15–61. Los Angeles: Getty Research Institute.

Snoman, R. (2004), *The Dance Music Manual: Tools, Toys and Techniques*. Oxford: Focal Press.

Spencer, N. (1998), "Pop Cds." *Observer*, December 6.

Spice, A. (2013), "Cars, condoms and credit cards: The use and abuse of vinyl in advertising." *The Vinyl Factory*, September 11. Available online: http://thevinylfactory.com/features/cars-condoms-and-credit-cards-the-use-and-abuse-of-vinyl-in-advertising/ (accessed March 14, 2017).

Spieker, Sven (2008), *The Big Archive: Art from Bureaucracy*. Cambridge, MA: MIT Press.

Sterne, Jonathan (2003), *The Audible Past: Cultural Origins of Sound Reproduction*. Durham: Duke University Press.

Sterne, Jonathan (2006), "The Mp3 as Cultural Artifact." *New Media & Society* 8 (5): 825.

Sterne, Jonathan (2012), *Mp3: The Meaning of a Format*. Durham NC: Duke University Press

Stibal, M. E. (1977), "Disco: Birth of a New Marketing System." *Journal of Marketing* (October): 82–8.

Straw, William (1993), "The Booth, The Floor And The Wall: Dance Music And the Fear Of Falling." *Public* 8: 169–82.

Straw, William (2000), "Exhausted Commodities: The Material Culture of Music." *Canadian Journal of Communication* 25 (1). Available online: http://www.cjc-online.ca/index.php/journal/article/viewArticle/1148/1067 (accessed March 14, 2017).

Straw, William (2002), "Value and Velocity: The 12-Inch Single as Medium and Artifact," in K. Negus and D. Hesmondhalgh (eds), *Popular Music Studies*, 164–77. London: Edward Arnold.

Streeter, Thomas (2011), *The Net Effect: Romanticism, Capitalism, and the Internet*. New York: New York University Press.

Tannenbaum, Rob (1992), "Remix, Rematch, Reprofit. Then Dance." *New York Times*, August 30.

Taylor, Charles (1989), *Sources of the Self: The Making of the Modern Identity*. Cambridge, MA: Harvard University Press.

Théberge, Paul (1997), *Any Sound You Can Imagine: Making Music/Consuming Technology, Music/Culture*. Hanover, NH: Wesleyan University Press.

Théberge, Paul (2003), "'Ethnic Sounds': The Economy and Discourse of World Music Sampling," in R. Lysloff and L. Gay (eds), *Music and Technoculture*, 93–108. Middletown, CT: Wesleyan University Press.

Thornton, Sarah (1995), *Club Cultures*. Cambridge: Polity Press.

Thornton, Sarah and K. Gelder (1997), *The Subcultures Reader*. London: Routledge.

Tinari, Philip (2007), "Original Copies: The Dafen Oil Painting Village." *Artforum* (October).

Titmarsh, Mark (2006), *SynCity*. Sydney: dLux Media Arts.

Toop, David (1995), *Ocean of Sound: Aether Talk, Ambient Sound and Imaginary Worlds*. London: Serpent's Tail.

Toynbee, Jason (2000), *Making Popular Music: Musicians, Creativity and Institutions*. London: Arnold.

Toynbee, Jason (2001), *Creating Problems: Social Authorship, Copyright and the Production Of Culture*. Milton Keynes: Pavis Centre for Social and Cultural Research.

Toynbee, Jason (2004), "Musicians," in L. Marshall and S. Frith (eds), *Music & Copyright*, 123–38. New York: Routledge.

Turner, Graeme (2009), *Ordinary People and the Media: The Demotic Turn*. London: Sage.

Tushnet, Rebecca (2004), "Copy This Essay: How Fair Use Doctrine Harms Free Speech and How Copying Serves It." *Yale Law Journal* 114 (3): 535–92.

Tregoning, Jack (2010), "The Art of DJing, by François K." Inthemix.com.au, December 22. Available online: http://inthemix.junkee.com/the-art-of-djing-by-fran%C3%A3%C2%A7ois-k/14377/2 (accessed March 14, 2017).

"12-inch 45 r.p.m. Disco Disks A&M Experiment." (1976). *Billboard*, October 23.

Vaughan, W. "Romanticism." *Grove Art Online. Oxford Art Online*. Oxford University Press, accessed March 14, 2017, http://www.oxfordartonline.com/subscriber/article/grove/art/T073207 (accessed March 14, 2017).

Vaidhyanathan, Siva (2003), *Copyrights and Copywrongs: The Rise of Intellectual Property and How It Threatens Creativity*. New York: New York University Press.

Vautour, Bart (2006), "Remix Culture," in S. R. Steinberg, P. Parmar, and B. Richard (eds), *Contemporary Youth Culture: An International Encyclopedia*, 306–10. Westport, CT: Greenwood Press.

Varga, Somogy and Charles Guignon (2016), "Authenticity," in Edward N. Zalta (ed.), *The Stanford Encyclopedia of Philosophy* (Summer Edition). Available online: http://plato.stanford.edu/archives/sum2016/entries/authenticity/ (accessed March 14, 2017).

Von Hahn, K. (2007), "The New Icons: Opposites Attract." *Globe and Mail*, March 3.

Wark, Mackenzie (2004), *A Hacker Manifesto*. Cambridge, MA: Harvard University Press.

Wharton, Mary (2009), "Joan Baez: How Sweet The Sound," in *American Masters*. PBS. October 14.

Wikstrom, Patrik (2009), *The Music Industry: Music in the Cloud*. Cambridge: Polity Press.

Williams, A. (2009), "On the Tip of Creative Tongues." *New York Times*, October 4.

Williams, Kathleen (2012), "Fake and Fan Film Trailers and Incarnations of Audience Anticipation and Desire." *Transformative Works and Cultures* (9). doi: 10.3983/twc.2012.0360

Williams, Kathleen (2014), "The Recut Film Trailer as Networked Object: Anticipation and Nostalgia in the YouTube Era." PhD diss., University of New South Wales.

Williams, R. (1998), "Fixing It in the Mix." *Guardian*, January 23.

Williams, Robert (2004), *Art Theory: An Historical Introduction*. Malden, MA: Blackwell.

Wolk, Douglas (2002), "Mp3 Blogs Become the New Zines." *Spin*, December 21.

Zalta, Edward N. (2015), "Compatibilism," *The Stanford Encyclopedia of Philosophy* (Summer Edition). Available online: http://plato.stanford.edu/archives/sum2015/entries/compatibilism/ (accessed March 14, 2017).

INDEX

CPSIA information can be obtained
at www.ICGtesting.com
Printed in the USA
LVOW10*1627220218
567557LV00011B/192/P